Films and Feminism

Films and Feminism

Essays in Indian Cinema

SECOND EDITION

Edited by
JASBIR JAIN
SUDHA RAI

Institute for Research in Interdisciplinary Studies, Jaipur

RAWAT PUBLICATIONS
Jaipur • New Delhi • Bangalore • Hyderabad • Guwahati • Kolkata

ISBN 978-81-316-0712-1

First Edition, 2002
Second Edition, 2015

Published by
Prem Rawat for **Rawat Publications**
Satyam Apts, Sector 3, Jawahar Nagar, Jaipur 302 004 (India)
Phone: 0141 265 1748 / 7006 Fax: 0141 265 1748
E-mail: info@rawatbooks.com
Website: www.rawatbooks.com

New Delhi Office
4858/24, Ansari Road, Daryaganj, New Delhi 110 002
Phone: 011 2326 3290

Also at *Bangalore, Hyderabad, Guwahati* and *Kolkata*

Typeset by Rawat Computers, Jaipur
Printed at Chaman Enterprises, New Delhi

to the creative use of reality

Contents

Introduction 1

Introduction to the Second Edition:
The Intervening Years and the Present Scenario 8

1 Rituparno Ghosh: The 'Woman's Director' of Bangla Cinema 17
- Somdatta Mandal

2 Saffronizing the Silver Screen: The Right-Winged Nineties Film 39
- Gita Viswanath

3 Female Bodies and the Male Gaze: Laura Mulvey and Hindi Cinema 52
- Bindu Nair

4 Courting: Hindi Film Ishtyle 59
- Malati Mathur

5 Women in Indian Cinema: Fictional Constructs 65
- Vrinda Mathur

6 Bollywood Portrayals of Women With Disabilities 72
- Meenu Bhambhani

7 Muslim Women's Identity: On the Margins of the Nation 86
- Supriya Agarwal

8 Towards the Radicalization of the Indian Family 94
- Veena Singh

9 Crossing the Boundaries: Woman in Search of Self 106
- Anshoo Sharma

10 Body as Text: Women Transgressors and Hindi Cinema 119
- Jasbir Jain

11 The Working Woman in Three Bengali Films: A Retrospect 140
- Dipendu Chakrabarti

12 Comedy and Gender: A Study of *Katha* and *Chashme Baddoor* 147
- Jyoti Bhatia

13 Questioning the Confines of Marriage: *Khushboo* and *Arth* 163
- Bandana Chakrabarty

14 Symbolism and Space in Aparna Sen's *Paroma* and Deepa Mehta's *Fire* 170
- Mini Nanda

15 Breaking the Silence: Gender, Caste and Transgression in *Phaniyamma* and *Bandh Jharokhe* 179
- Sudha Rai

16 Journey into the Mind of a Woman: From *Rajni* to *Mashaal* 195
- Tripti Jain

17 Maternal Enthrallment in Satyajit Ray's *Aparajito* and *Devi* 208
- Madhuri Chatterjee

18 The Mythical Text of Woman's Re-Presentation in Cinema: The Image-Icon Interface in *Devi* 214
- Anu Celly

19 *Tamanna*: Desiring the Undesired 225
• Santosh Gupta

20 From Victimhood to Potential Threat: Rape and Patriarchy in *Damini* 236
• Renuka Pamecha

21 *Mirch Masala*: Film with a Purpose 242
• Krishna Rathore

22 Spatial Contours in *Zubeida* 249
• Veena Jain

23 Battling for Being: Manjrekar's *Astitva* 257
• Ranju Mehta

24 Locating Perception and Paradoxes Within an Image: Manjrekar's *Astitva* 266
• Rakesh Thakur

25 En Route to Freedom and Self Discovery: *The Lunchbox* and *Bhaji on the Beach* 271
• S. Asha

26 Strengthening Identity and Choosing Freedom: *Queen* and *Hasee Toh Phasee* 282
• Manasvini Rai

27 *The Road Not Taken*: The Emergence of Women Wanderers in Hindi Cinema 296
• Avinash Jodha

28 Female Picaro and the Fairytale Structure: *The Dirty Picture* and *Kahaani* 316
• Vijaya Singh

Contributors 335
Index 339

Introduction

Films as an art form embrace both elitist and popular concepts of art and work closely with literary aesthetics. The two art forms – verbal and visual – are not merely parallel but interactive, reciprocative and interdependent. Yet the two mediums are very different and the reader/viewer relationship is very complex. One can demarcate areas and raise issues which could highlight the disparities between the two and at the same time go on to emphasize areas of similarities. But at an ideological level what does feminism imply in the context of films?

The visual medium offers choices which the written narrative may not. There is a greater freedom in the choice of perspective; the agencies are multiple – camera eye, narrator, lights, use of space, the spoken dialogue, body language, facial expression as well as the silences. There is also the strategic projection of stereotypes. Against such a background, deviations immediately send out signals. They raise questions and problematize issues.

To look for meaning in mainstream cinema is to critique an art form which often has loud, melodramatic tones and is more directly geared to entertainment than art cinema. The functioning of reality and fantasy acquire altogether different dimensions in the films which aim at mass audiences and pure entertainment. But, at times, even through these strategies they reveal the society's unconscious positioning of woman and the prejudices which work against her and her need for personal freedom. Stereotypes become a language of their own and the message awaits to be decoded.

Film criticism has a value for literary studies for it allows us to view them differently, to look for the unconscious reflection of social reality, the underlying power structures, the frames which melt into each other, the repetitive narrative patterns, the dialogues which use myth and history, the juxtapositions which take place and the simultaneity which the medium allows. There is no possible way that literature departments can hold themselves aloof from the cinematic medium, specially when the cinema has never shown any hesitation in appropriating literature for its purpose.

When we decided to look at Indian films from the point of view of gender, a number of questions cropped up. What does feminism mean? Do we mean the focus on women's issues? Or empathy with the feminist agenda? Women film directors, story writers, or lyric writers? Or does it mean the position of women vis-à-vis the nation and their search for the subject position. These and many allied issues are all encompassed by feminism.

For feminism itself, the written text and social activism are no longer enough in themselves. It needs to interact with all forms of media – newspapers, journalism, theatre and film. One can no longer afford to turn away from these mediums as they appropriate a much larger space in our lives than they did in the past. They project role models and sustain stereotypical ambitions while at the same time interrogating them or projecting them in an ambivalent manner. Even the focusing on female occupations and household chores can be done differently and subsequently perceived differently. Interpreting or 'reading' a film is as much a discipline as any other and meanings are often rooted in perspectives and positions.

The cinematic medium has its own limitations. In its search for a mass audience it tends to be rhetorical and melodramatic. The frames it chooses are different from those of the written narrative. And, if it links onetime viewing with appreciation, it has to plant its clues in a linear fashion as there is no possibility of the viewer referring back to check. The dialogue also tends to use symbols, myths and inferences which are easily recognizable and names carry a resonance within them. In Raj Kapoor's *Awara* the two girls were named Vidya and Maya and lovers often bear names such as Gopal and Radha. They immediately evoke memories of myths, traditions and facilitate a lot of bandying of words around the themes of eternal love, the image of *pativrata* or introduce the polarities between good and evil present in Hindu mythology. The sensitive director and the sensitive viewer, both have to work their relationship through and around these very visible symbols, in order to make a dent in the stereotypical presentations and interpretations.

* * *

The beginnings of the present volume can be said to have been made at least three years ago when we organized a film appreciation workshop. This was followed by several collective viewings of films followed by discussions and later by a full-fledged seminar on "Films and Feminism". Many of the papers included in this volume were first presented at that seminar. Later we invited some other papers and decided to bring them together in a volume. At no stage was there any desire to project any linear account of the gender question or trace a point to point history across different languages and film centres. The idea was to put together different responses and interpretations of the contemporary gender scene in the world of movies. In large measure the idea was to explore the projections of women both in what we normally refer to as mainstream (read commercial) cinema as well as in art movies (parallel cinema). Surprisingly, it became evident that art movies of the 70s also did not necessarily view the woman as a 'subject'; very often they only presented the oppression and exploration of women in a more sensitive manner framed within categories like caste or class. Whereas mainstream cinema did, at times, project powerful women characters. The boundaries between the two were extremely fluid.

The twenty-four papers in this volume cover a wide range – directorial approaches, male interventions, empathy and sensitivity, religious conservatism and tradition, the working of a novel into film, stereotyped constructs and images, the popular idea of romance and sexual aggression, the male gaze, women, religion and the nation, the transformation of the great Indian family, women with disability, the search for self definition, rape, the girl child, patriarchal domination and the rest. There are papers which look at intertextualities, project their analyses within comparative frameworks and those which focus an individual films like *Tamanna, Mirch Masala, Damini, Zubeida* and *Astitva.* Most of the films analysed belong to the period of the last thirty years though references and comparisons may take us further back.

Of the papers, four are in depth studies of directorial handlings. Dipendu Chakrabarti, Somdatta Mandal, Jyoti Bhatia and Sudha Rai explore this dimension. While Chakrabarti and Mandal focus on male directors. Bhatia and Rai take up women directors. Jyoti Bhatia additionally focuses on comedy, highlighting the significant contribution of Sai Paranjpe as she moves away from 'the woman as victim' image, Bindu Nair, herself a film person, focuses on the exploitation of the female body in this medium with the purpose of teasing in the male imagination, while Malati Mathur and Vrinda Mathur explore the viewer's perspective related to the aggressive eve-teasing and courtship patterns in the first and the sacrificing mother image in the second. Meenu Bhambhani focuses on a yet another important area – the projection of disabled women in a medium which is highly conscious of the desirability of the female body.

The 'self' is central to the construction of a selfhood and a subjecthood. Anshoo Sharma and Bandana Chakrabarty focus on the journey which women make towards the discovery of their identity. Chakrabarty questions the institution of marriage while Veena Singh deconstructs the great Indian family as it is reshaped by extra-marital relationships. Rakesh Thakur, Ranju Mehta, Veena Jain, all of them, work through single-film analysis to understand patriarchy and the feminine struggle against its impositions. Female solidarity as a means of change surfaces as a major theme and is reflected even in the rural situation in Krishna Rathore's paper on *Mirch Masala*.

The other end of woman as the object of male gaze, and as the desired possession, is rape - which is inflicted upon her both within marriage and outside marriage. The assault on a woman's body runs parallel to the assault on her emotions and attacks her last stay - her body - as she is thrown out of both her natal and marital families. Renuka Pamecha explores its social dimensions in her paper on *Damini* while Sudha Rai does the same in her study of *Bandh Jharoke*.

Chastity, virginity, female worship vis-à-vis male desire (and its sublimation) become the central discourse in the analysis of Satyajit Ray's *Devi*. Both Anu Celly and Madhuri Chatterjee explore this movie and focus on the director's interpretation. Female morality is a significant element in the ideology of patriarchy - a patriarchy which seeks to construct the nation accordingly. The projection of a 'devi' is only one dimension of it. Gita Viswanath works through the political agenda of the Hindu Right while Supriya Agarwal exposes its underside by focusing on the projection of Muslim women and the stereotypes and marginalization which frames this projection.

The issue of morality crops up again and again in paper after paper as the territorial limits of feminine identity are questioned. Self, freedom, equality, existence - all relate to it from beginning to end. When the laws of female morality are laid down, the hypocrisy of the male attitude is exposed. Santosh Gupta's perceptive paper on *Tamanna* juxtaposes male hypocrisy with female cowardice and connivance in upholding false values. The abandoned girl child who grows up to question this hypocrisy and rejects her father offers a strong comment on the male desire for a male child.

The interconnections between desire, sexuality, freedom and the right to body are major themes of Indian cinema today. These are debated in different ways. Self respect is another major component of the idea of self. Tripti Jain goes back to the film version of Bankim Chandra's novel *Rajni* to establish the ongoing concerns with these issues in the last hundred years. The paper allows us to see the oblique manner in which these questions are raised. the symbols which are employed, the lyrics which articulate the unstated and simultaneously enlarge the individual concerns. Midpoint in the century, the film looks both before and after; it is also an indicator of what we have lost in terms of poetry and subtlety in our desire for a more prominent voicing of sexuality.

The body remains central to the self. Marriage, adultery, rape, all work on it and through it. Several papers problematize the body. Mini Nanda works through her analysis of *Paroma* and *Fire* while Jasbir Jain frames it through the images of victim, rebel and transgressor, bringing in not merely morality or physicality but also the human will. One way to transcend the body, to learn to treat it as a medium and not a "self", is to bring it under the control of the will. The construction of femininity is controlled by patriarchy – by fathers who murder the girl child, by fathers-in-law who convert her into the image of a 'devi', by mothers who yield to male pressure, by husbands who bypass female desire, by men who take pride in male lineage and impose a code marked by chastity, submission and asceticism. When women question it, they are compelled to question all social constructs (and rituals) be they religious, political or romantic. Love, romance, marriage or singleness, motherhood or absence of it – all have to be deconstructed. To realize the self, the nature of desire needs to be questioned. What does this do to feudalistic structures? There is a strong suspicion in my mind that all pretensions to democracy are empty and hollow if patriarchal values are not reformed and re-formed.

Even though all the papers do not reflect film theory, they invariably work through dialogues and space. They reflect upon the images and the non-verbal articulations. And occasionally on the camera eye. They also reflect upon the nature of meaning and on interpretative strategies. And they establish the need to bring together literary approaches and the visual ones of the film medium.

* * *

During the course of bringing these papers together, I have incurred many debts. I would like to acknowledge the help given by friends and colleagues. Bindu Nair and Shammi Nanda helped us in the organization of the film appreciation workshop and viewed several films with us, Professor M.L. Raina who loaned us the video-cassette of *Devi*, and made it possible for us to discuss it in the seminar. My thanks are also due to Mr Ranbir Singh and Dr Ravi Chaturvedi – men of the theatre who added valuable comments on the dramatic medium. All those who responded to our requests – Somdatta Mandal, Gita Viswanath and Dipendu Chakravarti – we are grateful to them for their contribution. I would like to thank all the contributors to the present volume and hope that this will be an ongoing relationship. Finally, the pleasant task of thanking Sudha Rai both – for the loan of *Bandh Jharoke* for a collective viewing and for being the co-editor of this volume. She has been of immense help as we have worked through editing problems and used each other a sounding boards as we discussed and debated over our cups of tea. I hope we have more of these sessions.

At this point of time, there is the feeling that films need to be discussed more widely and more openly if we are not to be carried away by extravaganzas. By discussing them we seek to legitimize our role as viewers.

Introduction to the Second Edition

The Intervening Years and the Present Scenario

Films and Feminism first came out in 2002, at a time when academic interest in film studies was in its early phase. It was also a time when feminism as a discipline was struggling to build its legitimacy in more than only the economic questions of equal wages and economic independence. Now, more than a decade later, it is time to review the changes that have taken place in both: filmmaking and the feminist movement. Both are areas affected alike by socio-culture spaces and technological inventions. There is need not only for a re-assessment but also additions and supplements. Where are we located and in which direction are we heading? Is the representative filmic image reflective of real-life situations? Are films working also as agencies of social change? The editors in their Introduction to *Multiple Voices in Feminist Film Criticism* ask: Whether gender is a meaningful category for the purpose of organizing knowledge around women, is it a 'valid delineation of subject matter?'. And whether such an organisation of knowledge accomplishes something or does it leave out other issues (Carson et al.). The above queries are relevant everywhere, irrespective of cultural differences. Today gender alone is not enough, primarily because it is firmly grounded in socio-cultural backgrounds. This relationship is further complicated by the ideological issues involved, issues which neither filmmaking nor feminism can shake off.

Right from financing, censor boards to marketing and reception, films are subject to various kinds of controls. These controls have a direct relationship with almost everything that goes into a film. Hence if a note of dissent has to be introduced, it has to be subtle and muted, which at times misses the average viewership. It is against this background, one needs to look at the shifts since 2002 and to examine the interventions made by technology and market forces in the art of representation. Today, Indian films have captured a sizable foreign market changing the dimensions of viewership and the showcasing of Indian themes. Technology has immensely impacted the art of filmmaking and its organisation of space. It has also, subtly and indirectly, begun to control the human body with body building techniques. The six-ab fantasy seems to have possessed most male actors and the zero figure the women. Alternative or new wave cinema has quietly allowed itself to be submerged in the commercial cinema. Low budget films surface only now and then. Single producers are also on the way out with TV channels and corporate houses investing in the film industry. True, they have reduced the role of the mafia but they too, in turn, demand the heightening of the saleable images.The financing, the advertisements, the extended foreign market, the improved technology, the fast-moving cinematography have all changed the nature of filmmaking as have the multiplexes where movie runs are short and spread flat in a simultaneous multi-screening.

In some measure, films are different from the TV serials. While the latter are more family based, traditional with whole families crowding in the sitting space (see the families in *Balika Vadhu* and *Simar Ka Sasural* for instance), and the scheming and the manipulations emanating from there, movies spread out and use open spaces and urbanscapes. In ideology as well, most serials portray the obedient docile wife, heavily jeweled, expensively dressed and engaged in household work. Films are bolder, stepping out as they do in others spaces of business, sports, corporate houses and expanding horizons, with women more boldly dressed, showcasing the figure. While, even today, in most serials the boldly dressed woman is still stereotyped as an outrageous person who is a disruptive and a threat to traditional culture strongholds. Despite the daily viewing of serials and the more selective viewing of films, films are more effective in creating role models for the urban youth. They spell the world of fashion, action and romance. All these factors place a heavy responsibility on the film medium, which unfortunately, it does not always live up to.

Similarly, the issues which engage feminism have changed. The challenge is no longer the oppressive domestic space or political and economic rights; it has moved on to more comprehensive social issues and human rights. In recent years several women-centered films have been made, films which explore areas which on the face of it do not seem to be feminist, but a closer analyses at once reveals the woman's struggle, subjectivity and agency in constant negotiations with political and identity problems. The working and professional woman has surfaced in in *Rajneeti* (2010), where Katrina Kaif's role is powerful as she outsteps the directives given to her. There are several rebellions that mark her: her joining the left-wing, giving birth as an unwed mother and later marking her own space in politics, refusing to be a puppet in male hands. The film stands comparison with the 1975 *Aandhi*, a film semi-biographical, idealist and romantic. Similarly, Rani Mukherjee and Vidya Balan in *No One Killed Jessica* (2011), carry on a fight against a manipulative and corrupt society, in the interests of justice. The social indifference, the connivance of the authorities with the powerful, all are exposed through a long persistent struggle against money-power, insecurity and political control. This too highlights the strength of a woman's will and the compassion that sustains it.

Last year *Mardaani* (2014) has been screened. Once again it is about a social cause as was the earlier *Page 3* (2005), except that by equating the protagonist's determination with a male role, the issue of a woman's strength is hijacked. *Page 3*, on the other hand, depicts the woman's persistence not only for an equal place in her profession and her refusal to be sidelined and assigned soft beats, but also the strength with which she first pursues and then exposes the powerful and the mighty. *Mary Kom* (2014) despite being a biopic, also brings out the feminist resistance both at home and in the choice of profession, and later at a third level against the male authorities. It is hard for anyone to fight oppression, it is all the more difficult for a woman as the forces that seek to control her are many. The parents at home and the male world outside connive with each other to coerce the woman's freedom of choice. Another thing which one needs to recognize is the manner in which the compassionate and understanding men are portrayed. This brings home the wider perspective of a feminist world with its recognition that the world is not divided across gender lines but on the basis of values and attitudes. The understanding and honest police officer in *No One Killed Jessica*, the sympathetic and helpful colleague in *Page 3*, the boxing instructor and the husband, who gives up his own career, in *Mary Kom* are all men who extend a helping hand and reach out to them.

Defiance to authority is possible in several ways – by working gently at it and convincing the other or by determinately pursuing one's aim, no matter what the attitude. Perhaps there is a third way of outright defiance. In earlier films such as *Dilwale Dulhaniya Le Jayenge*, it is the first way. In some measure, even in *Queen*, it is the same way. But *Page 3* and *No One Killed Jessica*, demand more determined stands. Independent women, women with professions have another world to conquer and forces to resist in pursuit of private space. A film I would like to draw attention to is *Wake Up Sid* (2009). It is not a film which is woman-centred but one that focuses on the need of a young man to grow up and become emotionally mature. Sid's moving out of his parents' home and the role they wish to thrust on him, leads him to stay with a woman friend. As they share the space and the household chores, he gradually realizes that he cannot encroach on her private space. It is not sex, not romance, but understanding and communication that develop between them. *Wake Up Sid* successfully portrays the possibility of a man-woman friendship at a non-romantic level.

These films all have a social agenda, one which is woven into gender dimensions and place within collaborative lives. Their world is never singularly defined. It has multiple angles. Women don't live in isolation; they too inhabit an outside world; they do not only live or merely survive, they also need to find fulfillment. The idea of sisterhood is now replaced by a support structure which consists of both the genders. One of the few movies that still uses the concept of sisterhood and is located in a rural environ is *Gulaab Gang* (2014). It uses, as a base, social activism employed in the improvement and empowerment of rural women. This is a representative film as far as the social reality is concerned and intervenes in the prevalent discourse of single-cause and urban-based women's struggles.

To return to the queries that the editor of *Multiple Voices* have raised: whether gender is a meaningful category for the purposes of organizing knowledge and whether this organization of knowledge has a validity or not – the answer to both these is yes. Gender becomes a legitimate category for exploring the socio -political scenario, so intimately linked with cultural and ideological formations. When we use this as a positioning, it becomes possible to perceive where the oppression is and how power needs to be transformed in its very nature. In some of the films briefly referred to above, the vulnerability of the body is overcome; we see women who get married, have children and yet pursue their passions. We also see women who are capable of winning male support. They introduce the right degree of balance so much needed for a healthy society. To respond to the second query, partly addressed above, it needs to be pointed out that the revelatory aspect of such a perspective cannot be under assessed. Looking at the socio-cultural world, at the 'I' and the 'Other', at the essence of *being,* a gendered positioning acts like a mirror. We begin to see the *other side*, the one we had been oblivious to earlier.

A great deal has changed in the intervening year — between 2002 and the present — both in feminism and in filmmaking. Thus critiquing some of the recent films goes to mark these changes. The four essays that have been added to this edition cover this. S. Asha looks at the limited space which women have, no matter where located. She also brings out the need to dream and to grow up as also the need to defy. The domesticated wife breaks bounds; the middle-aged lonely woman learns to open her heart to a man of another race (*The Lunchbox* and *Bhaji on the Beach).* The contrast is there even in terms of space. The freedom in each - closed or open - has to come from the human mind and the human will.

Space, personal space, is also the question in *Queen* and *Hasee Toh Phasee*. Manasvini Rai in her essay explores their right to choose, no matter how they work towards it. Rani in *Queen* through the marriage rebuttal and her parents' support, while the young protagonist in *Hasee Toh Phasee*, is led by her determination to pursue her research, never mind if she has to steal from her parental home. It is the homecoming and the father's acceptance of her that is meaningful and logically sustains her position. She is the agent of change as she brings her family to realize the value of her step.

Avinash Jodha, perhaps the only male contributor to this volume, treats the woman as a powerful subject in her own external world, a person in her own right. He points out that spatial constructs do matter and women need to step out into the world, out of the veil and the *antahpura*, out of confined domestic spaces into a world full of dangers and challenges. The two important issues are the manner in which they cope with them and the means through which they motivate themselves.

Vijaya Singh's opening out of the two Vidya Balan films *Kahaani* and *The Dirty Picture* mock at the male exploitation of the female body. In both it is the body that is foregrounded, the pregnant body, the bearer of life on one hand and the voluptuous beauty on the other. *The Dirty Picture* is based on a real life experience of a Malayalee actor Silk Smitha, who was pushed to suicide in the world of exploitation which is ruthlessly indifferent to the individual. The film reflects the murkiness of film life and compels one to look at it as a mirror-image and stirs the conscience of men. The underlying strand is the whole issue of social respectability. *Kahaani* works with an imagined construct and is the projection of an intelligent mind overcoming the obstructive authorities through strategy.

These four essays reflect the shifts in both feminism and filmmaking. Yet, the validity and the relevance of the introduction to the earlier volume remain. These are additions not supersessions. Further, it also needs to be realized that all the above mentioned films have been directed by men. This points out towards the growing sensitivity of men on these issues and incidentally also, the decreasing number of women directors.

We would also like to thank our four new contributors for their analysis of the current films in the relationship to feminist concerns.

Reference

Carson, Diane, Linda Dittmar and Janice R. Welsch. eds. Introduction, *Multiple Voices in Feminist Film Criticism.* Minneapolis: University of Minnesota Press. 1994, 1–23.

Filmography

Aandhi. Dir. Gulzar, Pro. J. Om Prakash and Gulzar. Perf. Suchitra Sen, Sanjeev Kumar, Om Shivpuri, A.K. Hangal and C.S. Dubey. 1975.

Bhaji on the Beach. Dir. Gurinder Chadha, Pro. Nadine Marsh-Edward, Perf. Kim Vithana, Jimmi Harkishen, Zohra Sehgal, Sarita Khujaria. 1993.

The Dirty Picture. Dir. Milan Luthria, Pro. Dr Luke, Benny Bianco Frrazer T. Smith. Perf. Vidya Balan, Emraan Hashmi, Tusshar Kapoor, Naseerudin Shah, Anju Mahendru. 2011.

Gulaab Gang. Dir. Soumik Sen. Pro. Anubhav Sinha and others. Perf. Madhuri Dixit, Juhi Chawla, Priyanka Bose, Divya Jagdale, Tanunistha Chatterjee. 2014.

Hasee Toh Phasee. Dir. Vinil Mathew, Pro Karan Johar,Vikas Bahl, Avinash Kashyap and others, Perf. Parineeti Chopra, Sidharth Malhotra. Manoj Joshi, Sharat Saxena. 2014.

Kahaani. Dir. Sujoy Ghosh, Pro. Kushal Guha, Sujoy Ghosh. Perf. Vidya Balan, Parambrata Chatterjee, Nawazudin Siddiqui, Saswata Chatterjee, Indraneil Sengupta. 2012.

The Lunchbox. Dir. Ritesh Batra. Perf. Nimrat Kaur, Irfaan Khan, Nawazuddin. 2013.

Mardani. Dir. Pradeep Sarkar, Perf. Rani Mukherjee, Tahir Raj Bhasin, Jisshu Sengutpa. 2014.

Mary Kom. Dir. Omung Kumar, Producer Sanjay Leela Bhansali Perf. Priyanka Chopra, Darshan Kumar, Sunil Thapa. 2014.

No One Killed Jessica. Dir. Raj Kumar Gupta. Perf. Rani Mukherjee, Vidya Balan, Rajesh Sharma. 2011.

Page 3. Dir. Madhur bhandarkar, Pro. Bobby Pushkarna and Kavita Pushkarno. Perf. Konkana Sen Sharma, Atul Kulkarni, Boman Irani. 2005.

Rajneeti. Dir. Prakash Jha, Perf. Katrina Kaif, Ranbir Kapoor, Ajay Devgan, Arjun Rampal, Manoj Bajpayee. 2010.

Wake Up Sid. Dir. Ayon Mukherjee. Perf. Konkana Sen Sharma, Ranbir Kapoor, Anupam Kher, Supriya Pathak. 2009.

Queen. Dir. Vikas Behl. Producer Phanton Film. Perf. Kangana Ranaut, Lisa Haydon, Rajkummar Rao. 2014.

1 Rituparno Ghosh: The 'Woman's Director' of Bangla Cinema

Somdatta Mandal

He explores human relationships with a rare sensitivity. In all his films he handles human frailties with tenderness and understanding, humour and irony. It is this quality that won the young Bengali director Rituparno Ghosh, laurels for all the six films he's made till date. In less than a decade, he has acquired a reputation that takes him far beyond his immediate area of creative operation in West Bengal. A simple story line and superb acting make his movies special. As his films revolve around relationships, they are emotionally gripping and do not need the props of songs and dance. Moreover what gives Rituparno an edge over other directors is that he wins awards and draws crowds. His successful film career has already made him the bridge between good Bangla cinema and crowds – something that eluded other greats like Satyajit Ray, Ritwik Ghatak and Mrinal Sen. Born in 1961, Rituparno began his life in advertising and had no formal training in filmmaking but being the son of a documentary filmmaker, he grew up within the ambience of filmmaking. His films offer the Bengali film cognoscenti an enthralling time and prove once again that he is a specialist in 'human relationships' and in the 'female mind', particularly when in turmoil. Asked why he concentrated so much on relationships, he candidly admitted, "Relationships fascinate me. I was born in a middle class family, so naturally, relationships played a very important part in my life. Even today, relationships are essential to me. So it [exploring relationships] comes easily to me – it is not a concerted, laborious effort on my part."

Rituparno began his directorial venture in 1992 with *Hirer Angti,* a children's film that was never publicly released. As the traditional saying goes, "Behind the success of every man there is a woman." In his case, it was Shabana Azmi. "I used to interact with Shabana Azmi a lot. I wanted to do a film with her, but she couldn't. However, she heard the script, and she offered finance and assistance from the Children's Film Society of India, of which she was the chairman" says Rituparno and also adds, "Obviously she saw some potential in me." But from this point onwards most of his films started revolving around women, so much so that he has often been labelled as "the woman's director of Bangla cinema." Rituparno's explanation of course is simple: "It's just that I feel I understand the inner feelings of women, their passion, agony and suffering."

Unishe April (1995), the first feature film to be released, and actually the film with which Rituparno arrived, portrays the changing intimacies in a mother-daughter relationship. Though dubbed by many cinema pundits as having "nothing new," this film on a celebrity mother danseuse Sarojini, and doctor daughter Aditi, successfully exploited the middle class sentiment and basic family problems and became a super hit with its polished presentation. It also showed that the director was "comfortable with female psychology and their intricate relationship." The linear development of the plot is quite simple. On the 19th of April, Aditi lovingly remembers her father who died on this day when she was only eight years old. Aditi's love for her father leads her to follow in his footsteps by becoming a physician, while loathing her mother, a professional dancer, who was performing at the time her husband died. On this anniversary, her mother receives word that she is receiving the nation's highest artistic prize, which ultimately ends Aditi's engagement to her fiancé when his family discovers that her mother is the acclaimed dancer, Sarojini. Throughout the film there is a deep undercurrent of tension about Aditi's prevaricating boyfriend's commitment to their relationship. Through a series of flashbacks and a storm that rages both outside the family home and between mother and daughter, they both finally face the truth of their relationship. *Unishe April* makes a concession to the delicate Bengali sensibility and leaves out the explicit sex scenes unlike Aparna Sen's *Paroma* but it has one thing in common – both the films promise new beginnings to women who have been through fire. Though it is really quite irrelevant whether or not Rituparno had seen Ingmar Bergman's *Autumn Sonata* before he made this film as some critics feel, [he said that Bergman hasn't been a conscious influence] but nevertheless the two films can be compared as works of art. Debashree Roy, who plays the daughter's role in the film feels that Ghosh is "brilliant" in the handling of female emotions.

Rituparno's next venture, *Dahan* (*Crossfire*, 1997) is another award-winning film where the focal point is a well-reported rape attempt. The girl and her family are at the receiving end of society's disapproval. It portrays the plight of a woman, assaulted by a group of men and who succumbs to the pressures of her husband and in-laws by giving a false statement in court. The story line of this film is once again quite simple. On her way home one evening from teaching school, Jhinuk witnesses an assault on a young woman, Romita, and her husband. Through this fateful and transforming event, the lives of the two women from different social backgrounds intersect. After rushing to assist Romita, Jhinuk convinces the couple to file a complaint with the police. The event becomes headline news and Jhinuk is hailed as a heroine. But these moments of glory are fleeting, and any feelings of goodwill evaporate as the families of the two women bristle at Jhinuk's unwavering pursuit of justice. Such persistence becomes especially embarrassing for members of Romita's upper-class family, who must endure endless questions and criticism from friends, relatives and neighbours. Fearful of any deeper involvement or further attention, both families pressure Jhinuk and Romita not to appear as witnesses at the final hearing. Individual liberties and the pursuit of justice collide with middle and upper class sensibilities and lose the battle for survival. As the director, Rituparno unflinchingly challenges society's willingness to deny the rights of individuals when they threaten the comforts and conventions of the economically privileged. Women in Indian society are among those still enslaved by the restrictions and codes of behaviour born of society's hypocrisy and complacency – Jhinuk and Romita both have to contend with unspoken codes that coil around them with a silent but oppressive strength. Viewers feel intimidated at the way the two women are asked embarrassing questions and the five men try to get free with the help of corruption and male domination.

It will not be out of place to mention here an interesting controversy that is raging in Kolkata at present regarding *Dahan*. The film was screened in the third week of November in Kolkata as part of the international fortnight of violence against woman, organized by an NGO, *Sanlaap*. It was a platform where the 'reel' and 'real' life were starkly portrayed. On 27th November, the audience at Nandan got an insight into the situation of the couple harassed by four youths at the Tollygunje Metro station in 1992 and the woman who fought for the couple seeking justice. This formed the basis of the film. Present on the occasion were author Suchitra Bhattacharya and Ananya Chatterjee, the journalist who inspired the character Jhinuk in the film. Bhattacharya, who wrote *Dahan*, said, "My story was a little different from the original film. A lot of my readers asked me why I had portrayed Jhinuk, the sole witness to the assault of the couple, as a loser in the end. Because I wanted women to realize the pain and suffering; I wanted readers to act." Some in the audience said that though women were becoming more independent, it was up to the male members of society to react to such injustice and violence. But Ananya Chatterjee lambasted the film. In an act of unusual courage, she had come to the aid of a young couple when they were being roughed up by a bunch of hooligans. But when her story was adapted on celluloid, she found that it was flawed by male stereotyping. From the very beginning she had a problem with the film and felt that it had been majorly unfair to the male characters, especially the victim's husband. She reported:

> Though the film says that it is based on a true-life incident, I am surprised at the way the characters are portrayed. The woman's husband has been portrayed in a negative role whereas in real life both the woman and the man fought against social pressure and always appeared in court seeking justice. In real life, the couple, who were college students, had got married after the incident. The man stood firmly by his girlfriend, and had supported her against immense societal pressure. The couple married in UP and the case is still in court.

Firm in her belief that she will certainly get justice, Ananya said, "They had no right to portray the couple as they have done in the film." Emphasizing her firm belief that the actual cause of the trouble was that one cannot handle unwanted male attention, she also regretted that it had taken her such a long time to react to what happened at the metro station on the evening of June 24, 1992. Stating categorically that she never made any money out of the film, nor was in any way involved in its production process, she put the entire blame on Rituparno Ghosh for misrepresenting the actual story and taking recourse to male stereotypes:

> It would have made me greatly happy to see him (the victim's husband) portrayed as the man he actually was – the first one to protest (not me) at the scene of the incident, who dared to speak

up when everyone was looking away, who got beaten up badly because of this, who stood by the girl in the police station, at the identification parade, in the court, at home, amongst friends and relatives. He was a man who chose to marry the woman he loved despite everything - a man who was clearly not a stereotype. When stereotypes take over, real images make way for plastic ones. Real people often fall prey to such situations when they have to live out of these images, often under immense stress. The stereotype takes away the rational thought process and encourages popular views to ride over reality. It would be wrong to assume, however that stereotyping happens only with women. A man can become a victim to the same stereotyping as can a relationship.

This clearly happened in the case of *Dahan*. I can never understand how a novel or a film can be referred to as based on a real life story when none of the characters concerned were consulted on what really happened, on the day and thereafter. As a result what happens is a stereotyping of characters where both the men are shown as villains, patriarchs who are insensitive to their women. This is clearly the fruit of a vision which has chosen to follow the beaten track and attempt at hitting 'safe' targets: men. Just like some men in real life hit at what they consider to be safe and soft targets: women - regardless of age, race, class, caste and colour. If she is a child, she can be molested, if she is a teenager she wants to be molested, if she is single she is waiting to be molested, and if she is married, she must be unhappy and therefore.....

If this stereotype has to be broken, it has to be attacked from both sides. For it is not some men who need to be broken, it is this easy, shortcut method of stereotyping to justify one's actions and mind-set that needs to be addressed and broken down. When such stereotyping happens in a group or in a home it is dangerous enough. But when it happens in literature or in a film which leaves lasting impressions on people's minds it is likely to be catastrophic.....We are not yet ready to accept real men and real women.

The debate about the authenticity of representation of fiction into film is perhaps a century old, beginning right from the days of cinematographic history. Whether we can rely on the director's choice or deal with an adaptation as an interpretation is also a debatable point. But the kind of charges that Ananya Chatterjee has labelled upon the director of the film *Dahan* will need several thousands of storms over teacups to resolve the issue. Till date, Rituparno Ghosh, has not replied or reacted to this charge against him.

In his next feature film *Asookh* (*The Malaise*), 1998, Rituparno slightly shifts from his earlier stance but nevertheless sticks to his explorations of human relationships. "While *Unishe April* explored the mother-daughter relationship, *Asookh* is about the father-daughter relationship," says Ghosh. But the similarity ends there. While in the former film Debashree Roy plays the role of Aditi, the unglamorous daughter of a stunner, in the latter she is Rohini, the filmstar daughter of Sudhamoy, played by veteran actor Soumitra Chatterjee. Rohini, aged thirty-five, a well-known actress, is a foolish woman. Despite her years in the industry, she expects her boyfriend to keep his hands off nubile nymphets. But Annirudha, the intellectual with the generic beard and *jhola*, seems more committed to better cinema than Rohini. He starts a roaring affair with Rohini's own protégé, a sizzling starlet highly stocked on estrogen. Only Rohini does the honourable thing: she sinks into gloom. She takes to brooding with a passion. If her world does not collapse, it is because she alienates herself from it. The dark, closed, air-conditioned room where she sits becomes a giant reflection of the interior of her mind. And Rituparno proves once again that he is a specialist in the female mind, particularly when in turmoil.

What is interesting about Rohini in this film is that she is not up against another woman, but she drowns herself slowly into the treacherous private world of her own self, of sleeping pills and oblivion. In her claustrophobic room, where the thin light only exaggerates the haggardness of her features, Rohini looks longingly at a handful of sleeping pills before gulping them down all together. Obsessively attached to her lenses and her eyedrops, she watches the world through a film, as if naked sunlight will hurt her. *Asookh*, the disease of alienation, of being cut off from one's feelings and natural being, spreads like an infection throughout her. But to ask Rituparno why he is obsessed with women as the subject of his films is to get an insight into a director's relationship with his audience. Like his earlier two films, here he is again found portraying a vulnerable face. But vulnerability with him did not necessarily mean weakness. It meant sensitivity. Women afford him that. "It is not that men cannot be vulnerable or sensitive," says Rituparno, who himself is often seen in flamboyant *kurtas* not many of his sex would dare to sport. In fact, he believes that human qualities are androgynous, beyond sex really. "But to the Indian audience, a woman would be more acceptable as vulnerable than a man. Every medium has its set definitions, including definitions of masculinity and femininity. Every medium has its code," says the director. He knows his audience matters, so he does not shock them, as long as he has another story to tell. He only challenges their expectations, regarding gender, especially according to the demands of his story.

Some critics feel that delving too deeply in human relationships can have its flipside too. The sense of *déjà vu* and the overpowering sense of pain, grief and anxiety within the four walls can be claustrophobic too. In *Asookh*, Rohini has problems other than her boyfriend. But unlike Aditi, the embittered daughter in *Unishe April*, also ditched by her boyfriend, Rohini has a loving family. Her old parents, touchingly proud of their talented daughter, yet untouched in any way by tinsel glamour; are as attached to each other as to their only daughter. The father (played by veteran actor Soumitro Chatterjee), works late at night with a scrap-book for his own private collection of the pictures of his glamorous daughter. But sometimes such closeness suffocates Rohini. When her mother falls ill, her father becomes obsessed with her. In one scene, while father and daughter are having dinner, he starts talking about his wife's health. "She didn't pass stools this morning," he says. After some time, he mentions her urine trouble. Then he comes back to her constipation. While it is black comedy to the viewer, Rohini gets up, quite disgusted. She seems put off by such intimacy, yet it is the only center of stillness in the whirlpool of her emotions.

Then something terrible happens and a small doubt lurking inside Rohini's head looms into a huge suspicion. Her mother gets fever and is advised to have her blood tested for HIV. While her parents, ignorant about HIV and allied issues, are at peace with themselves, Rohini is petrified at the prospect of losing her mother. And because her father can be the only source of infection, she is racked with doubt and fear. The last frontiers of her defense against the world go down. Rohini finds herself alone – alone perhaps as only a woman can be to whom nothing matters more than her relations. But Rituparno knew how to pick up things and make them whole again. It takes a small medical report to do that. As she sees light, metaphorically and otherwise, with her father trying to light the candle as the lights go off, Rohini suddenly, in a flash, realizes she has been wrong, very wrong. Not only because she had suspected her father, but because she had created a hell of her own making, in her own mind. She is alone, because she has only been looking at herself. And even if a boyfriend strays, love does not cease, nor trust, not even for him. And it's good to have parents who care too much about each other.

Asookh scores in having a rich literary content. "My inspiration for this film was a poem by Tagore," said Ghosh. The poem *Chhotto amar meye,* (My Little Daughter), is from the *Hariye Jawa* anthology. In the film, Rohini is shown to be an avid fan of Rabindranath Tagore. A portrait of the poet looms large in her bedroom and the walls of the apartment have prints of his paintings. The poet plays an important role in the director's life as well. For Tagore, Rituparno feels, works on the same bewitching quality that leads the director to his subjects in the first place: vulnerability. Like Rohini feels at the end of the film, Rituparno thinks that one can be strong despite one's vulnerability. Her awakening is reassuring and different from the way mother and daughter came together in a stormy scene in *Unishe April*, which Rituparno himself feels is "a less mature work. That was a union of passion and happened somewhat despite themselves. But here Rohini makes the journey herself." Asked about what happens to the boyfriend who wants to come back to Rohini and whether she should have taken her back, Rituparno stated, "I don't know. I hope she is strong enough not to take him back." Like Kate Chopin's *The Awakening, Asookh,* is the story of a woman breaking the barriers of her own self.

Rituparno's favourite subject of the changing pattern of human relationships in the context of a now defunct joint family becomes the subject of his next film *Utsab* (*The Festival*, 2000). Exploring the grey areas of family bonds, and set in a crumbling mansion outside of Kolkata, it is a drama that is similar to the Dutch film *Celebration* that explores the dynamics and secrets of a family that meets each year for four days to participate in a Durga Puja and visit its matriarch, Bhagabati (played by Madhabi Mukherjee who has acted in the Satyajit Ray films *Charulata* and *Mahanagar*). Initially it seems as if the tensions that seep into the siblings' interactions are based on petty arguments, such as who was given the room with the better view, but on further inspection the friction runs much deeper. Amidst the rituals and hoopla of the puja, we slowly learn that Asit, the younger brother, is on the verge of losing his job while Keya, the youngest daughter, is experiencing serious marital difficulties. She has returned to the house after three long years, with her belligerent, alcoholic husband, Arun, whom no one seems to like. Parul, the eldest daughter, is an emotional mess who is harbouring a deep, dark secret from the family's past. After one of her moody outbursts, a sister-in-law advises her, "Don't brood over the past." From their subtle references and sly innuendoes, we infer that she was involved with a long lost cousin named Sisir, who was subsequently banished from the home. Years later, and now a successful businessman, he wants to buy the place. Meanwhile, her son Joy is filming the whole ordeal while shamelessly flirting with his lovely cousin, Shampa.

As the harbinger of an ensuing trauma, one of the characters vehemently declares, "Daughters of this house are great at making mistakes." Unfortunately, their learning curve isn't very high and they continue to commit the same blunders. Some critics feel that in this film Rituparno deals with such problems rather superficially. There are so many people to cover that their issues get only skimmed over rather than fully explored and it seems that in Rituparno's fictional world the entire Bengali family becomes dysfunctional. "My films are not about what should be, but what is," he asserts. Apart from the slow pace of the film, as in his last film, Ghosh infuses an element of self-critique into the plot. By having Joy record the gathering, he adds a discourse on film – to be continued in his next ventures as well.

Bariwali (*Lady of the House*, 2000), which won hearts at the Berlin Film Festival, once again, is an account of human relationships that often go wrong due to certain miscalculations. In this film, the lonely protagonist Banalata (played by Kiron Kher), is a middle-aged spinster who lives in a bucolic mansion outside Kolkata. Stately, but crumbling and neglected, the mansion serves as an efficient metaphor for Banalata's own state. At the heart of the film is the problem of an oppressive loneliness and it has been dealt with in different ways on the screen. Here it is set in a personal and social context and produces some inspiring insights. Extremely lonely, Banalata spends her days cloistered in a corner of the mansion with her two perpetually-quarreling servants. She is someone who has lost touch with the world and even detests the idea of television invading her world but cannot prevent her maid from revelling in that glossy world of make-believe. Her loneliness is reminiscent of Ray's *Charulata*, though Charu does not have to think about financial matters while wallowing in loneliness. Again, though the film does not have the passion or the intense sense of desolation of something like *The Lonely Passion of Judith Hearne*, Rituparno makes it an interesting foray into a theme that is rarely tackled in Indian cinema. Being the last of her dynasty, Banalata had given up all hopes of finding a husband after her prospective groom died of a snake bite before her wedding day. Impractical as she is in practical matters, the misplaced deed to her house leads to a sense of financial insecurity which in turn leads Banalata to consider the unthinkable – letting out her house for a film shooting. The unit is to shoot Tagore's *Chokher Bali* but Banalata is not at all interested in the world of glamour. Her only mission is to raise funds for the house tax which the municipal assessing officer could ask for.

When film director Dipankar first comes to her house the electricity has tripped in Banalata's upstairs quarters. Dipankar uses a screwdriver to fix the problem and the symbolism is instant – he has brought a spark of light into her dark existence. Once the shooting of the film begins in the mansion, the painfully shy Banalata slowly comes to idolize the director (even having full knowledge about his flaws). Adept at handling women to suit his purposes, he is extremely well-spoken with her and the moony-eyed. Unworldly Banalata just can't see him for what he is. Ironically he is a director of presumably sensitive art films. But, in a tight budget, he isn't above exploiting Banalata for his own ends – getting her to hand over her family heirlooms from paintings to silverware as free props for his shoot. Banalata doesn't mind as he has now become part of her romantic fantasies manifested only as dreams through her subconscious. Without committing himself in any way, Dipankar smoothly accepts her offer to waive the rent when he runs into financial difficulties and even persuades her into enacting a small scene in the film. In a *suhaagan's* saree and demeanour she speaks her lines looking directly into his eyes. The public knowledge of her devotion is not spelt-out, but is implicit. However, for Banalata, there is only one subtle humiliation around the corner. Once thc film unit leaves the mansion, there is no communication from Dipankar. She is unable to realize how ruthlessly exploitative the real world can be. She keeps on waiting for a line or two from Dipankar in reply to hers. She reads in a newspaper that the film is ready to be released. On the day she was just getting ready for attending the matinee show of the film, finally a missive does arrive, but it's only to send a belated cheque and to relate the news that Banalata's scene has been edited from the film - there is not even that tiny space for Banalata in Dipankar's film ... or his life. As the film inches towards its end, a shattered Banalata is faced with the electricity going off on her floor once again - completing the symbolism that had begun with Dipankar's entry into her life. But hopefully she is now better equipped to take control of her life.

But Rituparno makes his missive clear - it is always expectation that leads to exploitation. But this exploitation that is perpetrated by the members of the filmi clan is done a bit too subtly. For although one does understand Banalata's need to be accepted by this and in her life, thereby becoming a victim of her own desires, never once does Dipankar come across as the villain of the piece, if he was ever meant to be that way.

Throughout *Bariwali,* one is attracted by the nuances in Banalata's character, tracing her growth in what could be called one of the most tumultuous periods of her life and when she tries to reconstruct her past on the fragmented memories of those few shooting days. Outwardly the film has some similarity with Mrinal Sen's *Khandahar.* Rituparno, the master storyteller deftly paints the pangs, pains and loneliness of the spinster and deals with emotions like disappointment, sadness, loneliness and hurt. Though much of the script concentrates naturally on the central character, it also offers cameo performances of other characters who all contribute in some way or other to the total experience. For instance, the juxtaposed portrait of the over-ebullient maid Malati (played by Sudeepta Chakrabarty) and the scenes where she bosses over Banalata carry the charge of reality. Finally, the film is interesting because of its structure of a film within a film. Rituparno's primary interest is in people who are observed with their subtle shades mirroring a world in the grip of exploitative and amoral principles partly redeemed by the vestiges of innocence.

Abhinay (Acting), Rituparno Ghosh's first telefilm made this year (2001), with story, screenplay and dialogue by the multi-faceted director, is as starkly stunning in its insights into human nature as *Unishe April, Dahan* and *Bariwali*. And like his earlier films – *Asookh, Bariwali, Utsab* and the forthcoming *Titli* – this one too touches on a world he knows best – the world of cinema and the beautiful people who bring it to life on screen. This 70-minute film-within-a-film telefilm was made as one of the specials for Alpha Bangla channel's anniversary celebrations. *Abhinay* is a simple story, simply told, and yet stunning in its effect. Completed in just four-and-a-half-days, it was shot in a hotel in Bolpur (rechristened Kusumdanga to perhaps touch on Sujata's erudite wisdom that leaves her girl-Friday, Beethi wide-eyed and won over), it is a film that quite obviously revolves around an actress Sujata (played by Roopa Ganguly) – an *abhinetri* with the rest of the cast playing out their parts like pawns on a chessboard. She's a star, unreal and seemingly unreachable even when she's conventionally dressed like the simple, suburban housewife next-door and pleading with a "blessed" tree for the life of her ailing child. Perhaps it is because her tears are glycerine-induced and her world appears so far removed from such harsh realities. Naturally, her director is surprised when she points out to him that a mother whose son is dying wouldn't use so many words and certainly not so many clichés. "How would you know? How would any of us know considering that we have never lived through a similar situation and can only emulate standard, stereotyped responses?" he argues. Sujata, his striking, sophisticated, well-read heroine, isn't convinced. And to appease her the director promises to sit in with her after pack-up and re-work the dialogues.

That evening, he has to wait a while for Sujata to finish with her mysterious visitor from Kolkata. A visitor is the object of everyone's curiosity. The reasons for his closed-door visit with *didi* is speculated on endlessly by Sujata's hairdresser, Beethi, during her romantic rendezvous with the cameraman who's trying to seduce her on the dim stairway. It is the director who finally meets up with this "guest" when he is eventually summoned to Sujata's room. He finds her relaxing in the air-conditioned comfort of her room with a glass of Scotch, coldly dismissive of the bearded stranger who's still hanging around even after being summarily shown the door. Awkwardly the director sits around waiting for his star's visitor to leave and is a privy to what should have been a confidential conversation. Sujata's guest turns out to be her ex-husband Mihir who begs her for Rs. 15,000 that can help save the life of a child – her child! The revelation is shocking but what's even more shattering is Sujata's reaction. The director can only watch in horror as his heroine, so sensitive to every nuance in the script, remains completely unmoved by her husband's plea. Without so much of a flicker of emotion, he's told that he will have to wait till she returns to the big city for the money "since I don't carry so much cash with me when I'm on location."

Unwilling to be a mute spectator to the unfolding drama anymore, the director offers to advance a loan. But Sujata stops him and slipping off a gold *kangan* from her wrist, hands it to Mihir with the offhand suggestion that he can raise the money needed for their daughter's treatment by selling it. Mihir leaves with what the director knows is only an imitation bracelet and will not fetch him more than Rs.150. When he points out the "costly mistake" to her, Sujata drops her head into her hands and sighs, "Oh, I'm sorry I didn't think! The bangle's part of my get-up, right? Now there'll be continuity problems!" Her callous, almost inhuman disinterest in her little girl brings forth a torrent of angry accusations from the director who now refuses to change even a line in his script. "You can say the lines as they are, or you can walk out, I really don't care!" he spits out angrily. She looks at him, understands his anger and outrage at her behaviour, and tells him quietly that she does care. Or rather did care for the daughter who was born after two years of marriage and time enough to realize that the man she'd married was a wastrel. Ahana who came into her life with the first rays of the sun but couldn't keep her tied down to the man who had ironically been christened Mihir, meaning the Sun. Realizing that the only way out of the darkness of her marriage was to concentrate on her acting career, Sujata leaves Mihir, and also leaves her daughter Ahana with her mother-in-law, helping out occasionally with money.

She goes on to confide that she was in Mumbai, shooting a film, when she learnt from one of Mihir's friends that her daughter who was always a sickly child, was grievously ill. Sneaking into the hospital room, concealed behind a *burkha*, [a trope that remains unexplained for the audience], Sujata was with Ahana when she died. Watching silently, helplessly, as her daughter is wrenched away from her. "She died four years ago, but Mihir has yet to tell me that she's gone. He continues to come to me using the excuse of her illness to raise some money, little knowing that I know the truth," Sujata tells her director in a voice that's drained of all emotion. The director is stunned! "You know and you still give him the money?" he asks her incredulously. "Well, he needs the money and he has his self-respect," she rationalizes.

However, *Abhinay* despite being set in the celluloid world, doesn't offer much by way of glamour or technical wizardry. Rituparno's forte is the unravelling of dark secrets and he does it with a brevity of emotions and an overloading of mundane everyday details that makes the climax all the more unforgettable. Roopa Ganguly is the perfect choice for Sujata. There's a veneer of sophistication in Roopa that comes from being associated, however briefly, with Mumbai's film city. An air of hauteur and arrogance that cloaks every top-ranking star, sparking off awe and admiration amongst the commoners whose lives she touches, be it the owner of the shanty tea stall whose curds she's been sampling or the girl-Friday who is her constant companion. The male members of the unit are more clear-eyed and carnal in their character analysis, but even they don't grudge her the only air-conditioned room in the hotel that comes with the privileges of being a star. Even the director who's closer to her both intellectually and emotionally, keeps his distance and difference. Roopa makes the transition from a touch-me-not star to a human being touched by tragedy with ease and conviction, proving just why she's being sought out by sensitive directors like Aparna Sen or Rituparno Ghosh. Apart from her, the role of Sujata's hairdresser, sketchy and still-to-be-developed, it is interesting to see how Rituparno uses her flirtatious smiles and intense eyes to flesh out this cameo. However, her "affair" with the cameraman seems a wee bit contrived and forced into the script perhaps to hint on the transitory web of relationships that begin and end with every film.

Rituparno's latest production, *Titli* (*Butterfly*) is in its completion stage. The credit for the story and script of this film again goes to Ghosh himself. It is a rather unusual story that has Aparna Sen and her daughter Konkona Sen Sharma paired for the first time as mother and daughter in the film as well. The title of the film is after Konkona's character, named Titli. The last film in the trilogy focusing on mother-daughter relationships,

Rituparno tries to live up to his reputation as a "feminine ideologist". After *Asookh*, Ghosh once again toys with a film star within the narrative in the film. This time, it is Mithun Chakrabarty playing the struggling young man with dreams of making it big in filmdom. During his struggling days, he was encouraged by a very close female friend (played by Aparna Sen). He makes it big, the friend marries a tea planter and shifts to North Bengal. She has a daughter who, in time, evolves in a great fan of this mega-star. When they meet by accident in North Bengal during one of the location shoots for one of his films, Titli is shocked to discover that her mother and the actor were once very close. "What transpires between the mother and the daughter after this makes the rest of the film," stated Rituparno.

Rituparno's next venture is Rabindranath Tagore's *Chokher Bali.* In an interview he admitted, "*Chokher Bali* has been my dream project for a very long time. So when I made my director-protagonist in *Bariwali* make a film on that novel, I was vicariously fulfilling my dream. Today's Bengali cinema has moved away from literature towards Hindi cinema and South Indian films. But I am finally making *Chokher Bali.*" Aware of the industry superstition that it is a cursed subject and no one has been able to do it till date, Rituparno's first tryst with Tagore stars Nandita Das as the rebellious Binodini and Raima Sen as the homely Ashalata, the young widow caught between the Brahminical predominance of the 18th century Bengal and the influence of the West. A woman-centered story no doubt, how this young girl goes about her life and finds her identity forms the crux of the film. Maybe this is what attracted him towards this novel in the first place. Since it is a classic and a period piece, Rituparno says he has to be careful how the time frame of the novel is recreated in the film and that he will leave the job of art direction to his brother. The release of this film is eagerly awaited to see how the director contemporizes issues and treats the relationships that grow out of extramarital involvement – themes that seem quite close to his heart.

Rituparno Ghosh is perhaps the only Bangla director in whom good qualities of two outstanding filmmakers have assembled. His films, like those of Tapan Sinha, are narrative in style and emotional in approach. Moreover he makes films which do not follow the mainstream song-dance-action pattern. At the same time, like Aparna Sen, he excels in exploring inner recesses of the human mind right from his first feature film, *Unishe April.* His connection with, and influence of Aparna Sen has become too widely known to be called accidental. It is also not accidental that Aparna has starred in many of his films. Every viewer can trace similarities of situations, themes, and characters of Rituparno's films with Aparna's directorial ventures like *Paroma* (*The Ultimate Woman*, 1984), *36 Chowringhee Lane*, *Paromitar Ek Din* (*House of Memories*, 2000). For instance the similarities between the lonely Anglo-Indian teacher Miss Stoneham in Aparna Sen's film and Banalata, the middle-aged spinster in Ghosh's film cannot be overlooked as accidental. When asked whether *Bariwali* was inspired by *36 Chowringhee Lane,* Rituparno admitted, "There are some inherent similarities between the two films. The lonely spinster, yes. But then, loneliness runs through all my films." Actually, the influence of his 'godmother' Aparna Sen is evident from his very first film *Unishe April*. In this film he gets away with making a bold statement which is usually thought as too strong for the middle class milieu. Sarojini, the famous dancer (played by – who else? Aparna Sen) on the threshold of middle age, still very attractive, who is frankly contemptuous of the demands of her family, has chosen her career over it, doesn't mind having a boyfriend even with an angry grown-up daughter around and doesn't bother to be a 'good mother.' Yet the audience understands her – the same audience which was scandalized by Aparna Sen's own *Paroma*, which had shown a middle class married woman's search for identity leading her to a sexual relationship outside marriage. As Rituparno himself says "There would have been no *Unishe April* without *Paroma*. I have consciously avoided the explicit sex scenes following *Paroma's* example." Though Rituparno stated that "Aparna Sen has been an influence as a human being, not as a filmmaker" and that he has "been quite close to her and one reason for that is our affinity to the cinema of Satyajit Ray," many viewers and film critics have started mentioning Aparna Sen and Rituparno Ghosh in the same breath because they feel that their films are increasingly beginning to look alike. One sees the same faces, hears the same intonations, ponders similar poignancies, explores the same interiors and visits the same emporiums. The films even talk to one another with the same mutual admiration and familiarity as their makers do with each other on prime-time regional television. Moreover, both in their films like to stay within the cosier ambience of the *bhadralok* they know.

Rituparno's films are indeed inspired by Satyajit Ray and he has no qualms about being constantly compared to him. "It is a proud thing to follow your father's footsteps," he said. Ray is considered one of the world's best filmmakers of all time and it is difficult for anyone, including Rituparno Ghosh, to break out of such a shadow. Though all of his films are technically superb, what is still missing in him is that subtle touch that differentiates between a good and a great filmmaker. Maybe his post-forty productions will overcome the drawbacks found in some of his films. But when asked from whom he derived inspiration, he candidly admitted the name of the great master again: "Satyajit Ray. It was after seeing his films that I thought of filmmaking." Of course he also mentioned that unlike his mentor he was "quite non-musical" and used music only when it spoke for itself. Asked whether he feared the responsibility of being the neo-Ray who'll revive the Bengali film industry, Rituparno replied in the negative:

> If my films help the Bengali film industry in any way, I'll be extremely happy. I'm extremely flattered that I'm being compared with Satyajit Ray. But I feel I'm majorly overrated. I came into Bengali cinema at a time when intelligent urban films were going out of fashion. That's why I found a place quickly. I can't compare myself to the masters of the Bengali cinema.

Though the director admits that he was influenced by Ray, there is one subtle difference in his handling of women. Unlike Ritwik Ghatak's *Meghe Dhaka Tara,* Mrinal Sen's *Ekdin Pratidin*, and Satyajit Ray's *Mahanagar,* his films do not deal with the condition of women in Indian society. In other words, there is no concern in Rituparno's films with the working woman though career stands in the way of proper understanding of mother and daughter in *Unishe April.* Taking a step beyond the women protagonists of the earlier films mentioned, whose prime aim was to support their families, Rituparno's women have no other familial obligations. Actually Bengali films which did focus upon women did not take any interest as Rituparno does in exploring women to women relationships and simply remained confined to women pitted against a strong patriarchal society.

What are Rituparno Ghosh's dreams? He dreams of making films from the mythological stories of *Manasha-Mangal* – with Ma Manasha, the snake goddess, with Lakhinder and Behula (once again note the choice of familial relationships!). Though he wants to stick to family drama and to the classical narrative style, he has no penchant for working in other forms. But he would love to do real satire, good comedy, and black humour films too like Satyajit Ray's *Parash Pathar* he admitted.

In an interview given during the dubbing sessions of the forthcoming film *Titli,* Rituparno once again stressed on the androgynous nature of human character. Asked whether he thought that a male director was more capable of exploring a female psyche than a female director, he replied, "No, I don't. I don't believe in gender discrimination between artists. I believe in the art of androgyny which includes the male and female opinion." In fact, he feels that he understands the psyche of women better because he can offer a more objective approach. He specified that there is a difference between a woman's point of view and a woman character's point of view. To illustrate the point he mentioned the story of *Ramayana* and how it would be totally different if it would be told from Sita's point of view.

There would be several technical questions that would crop up then, he insisted. For instance, why did not Sita conceive any children though she lived for fourteen long years in the forest? But he regretted that such issues are never touched upon and instead a very simplistic narrative structure is opted for. Thus, Rituparno reiterated that the actual problem lies in the fact that we are not used to looking at things from the other's point of view. Therefore, it is not necessary to be a woman to understand gender related issues. Asked about his views on marriage and whether he had any plans to get bound in a familial bondage, the filmmaker, who is now literally labelled as a "feminist ideologist," replied in the negative and confessed that he was "yet to experience the need." When asked whether cohabitation or the concept of living together was better than so-called bondage – as marriage is often identified so, Rituparno replied, "Perhaps so. At least, it doesn't have any binding and it leaves a much-required space between two minds. It enables the two personalities to possess their individual identity."

A survey of various other interviews that Rituparno has given elsewhere shows that in all of them he admitted to a special affinity for women: "It's just that I feel that I understand the inner feelings of women, their passion, agony, and suffering" he reiterated in a rediff.com interview. At the felicitation of the Bimal Roy Memorial Committee for his contribution to Indian cinema, he even gave us a list of the women he likes and admires. "My all time favourite actresses are always those whom I work with. Besides them I have five more actresses whom I admire." These actresses are Jaya Bachchan, Sabitri Chatterjee, Tabu, Shabana Azmi and Waheeda Rehman. There is a rumour that Rituparno has also planned an untitled film with Amitabh Bachchan based on a story by the noted Bengali novelist, Shirshendu Mukhopadhyay and it will deal with a man in his mid-life crisis. Till this 2004 targeted film is released, it would not be over-emphasizing to conclude by stating that the *raison d'etre* for Rituparno Ghosh's films remains, "I understand women."

2 Saffronizing the Silver Screen: The Right-Winged Nineties Film*

Gita Viswanath

Introduction

Hindu nationalism enjoys a hegemonic status in present day India. Growing disillusionment with the inadequacies of the Nehruvian interventionist and tutelary state coupled with technological advances and economic imperatives forcing India to open its doors to Western market forces, and the resurgence of religion are some of the factors that helped foster the growth of Hindu nationalism. It impacts upon the cultural productions in significant ways and this will be dealt with in detail in this paper with specific reference to Hindi cinema of the nineties. Hindu nationalism is based on the construction of a homogeneous and assimilationist culture which equates Hindu culture with "Indian" culture. In my paper, I attempt to show the flawed nature of such a construction of culture and its inadequacy in imagining the nation. Further, it holds potential for a dangerously regressive formulation of ideas of womanhood. I also suggest that there is a clear paradigm shift in popular

* First presented at the annual workshop of the *Forum of Contemporary Theory*, Baroda, 1999.

Hindi cinema. Such an ideological shift seems to have a destabilizing effect for the liberal tenets of secular democracy on the one hand and for women's agenda on the other.

Cultural Nationalism

Some critics have expressed their intuitions about nation being supplanted by culture in the postnational world.[1] Far from smacking of postmodernist prescience, such a view would be woefully inadequate to understand and theorize the clash that seems to be increasingly evident in recent times, between nation and culture. Both these important categories are in the process of interrogating each other and the play seems most evident on the silver screen. Cultural nationalism believes in the notion of a shared culture. It is a culture commonly identifiable by all members of the nation-state. Culture then becomes a source of national identity, giving the crucial sense of belonging. Culture may be disseminated by various signs, which are recognisable and decodable by all. An important component of cultural nationalism is distinctiveness. In a multicultural setting, such as in India, if the culture of one religious/linguistic/regional/ cultural group is hegemonized as the national culture, then within a political/territorial unit itself, there can be claims of distinctiveness of one group over the other like for instance Hindutva's claims that Hindu culture is "Indian" culture and vice versa. Morality is one of the prime concerns of cultural nationalists. Dismissing moral relativism as one of the abhorrent features of modernity, cultural nationalists who base their very notion of nation on an admixture of culture and religion, turn to doctrinal and scriptural prescriptions on individual behavioural modes.

Rise of Hindutva

Broadly, Hindutva would mean Hinduness. It is the name given to Hindu nationalism. According to Christophe Jaffrelot, Hindu nationalism is best theorized within the conceptual framework of ethnic nationalism (Jaffrelot 1999). This explains the configuration of monoculturalist and racist premises in Hindutva. While it would be outside the scope of this paper to go into the circumstances that nurtured the growth of Hindutva forces, it would suffice to say that these forces consolidated themselves around the late eighties as a challenge to the secular credentials of the nation. It was around this time that the nation was desperately searching for a narrative, so to speak. Separatist movements were challenging the aphorisms such as "unity in diversity" that had been used to define the nation. Reeling under an economic crisis, the nation opened its doors to market forces from the West. This led to disproportionate fears of cultural invasion. The fears and anxieties began to be expressed in the sphere of cultural production The film industry, itself insecure with the advent and growing popularity of satellite television, responded wholeheartedly to the nativist definitions of "Indian" culture offered by proponents of Hindutva.

Hindutva and Cinema

The nineties films in popular Hindi cinema show a marked departure from the films that preceded them. The leftist films of Raj Kapoor in the 60s made way for the action-filled, angry young man films of Amitabh Bachchan in the seventies and eighties. Nevertheless, the hero usually belonged to the working class, still indicating the leftward swing of Hindi cinema. By contrast, the nineties films have swung to the other side of the spectrum, deleting from its frames, some of the most salient features of Hindi cinema. The nineties films with *Hum Aapke Hain Kaun* (*Who am I to You?*) is the pioneer culprit perhaps, having no working class characters in the lead. The stories revolve around mostly upper middle class people. I use the term, middle class not merely as a socio-economic category, but also as a cultural entity. A national culture begins to be constituted by a process of exclusion, not inclusion. In addition, the characters are all Hindus and if there are minority community characters, they are the enemies, as in action films, which mostly show terrorism aided by Pakistan. Since building a strong nation is important for the rightist ideology, militarization acquires a prominent place in the project of nation building and imagining. If there is a villain in the nineties films, it is either the West or Pakistan. Of course, the representation of minorities in the earlier films left much to be desired. Mired as they were in stereotypes, they had at least notionally some place, even if liminal, within the narrative. Thus while the earlier films' representation of minorities was characterized by a Manichean dichotomy, the nineties films have taken the othering process to its extreme form viz. elimination/erasure, on the one hand or totally demonizing on the other hand.

In the nineties, there have been two dominant genres in Hindi cinema, i.e. the action film and the family drama with the ubiquitous love story as its major component. These, I would suggest are only apparently antithetical. The ideological underpinnings of both remain the same. Both genres tackle an imagined enemy. Right wing ideology indulges in creating paranoia about threats to the nation, both territorial and cultural. The enemy in the action films is cross border terrorism with veiled references to Pakistan. The other genre tackles an insidious enemy, which appears in the form of cultural invasion. This is a threat to the idea of an essential India. While tackling the first enemy is the job of the patriotic Indian male, the second enemy is reserved for the Indian woman. Here, I find useful Partha Chatterjee's division of material domain and spiritual domain to stand in for the West and East. The "material domain" with its engagement in the public world of economy, labour, political struggle and the like remains the male world. The "spiritual domain" is the private world of family, rituals, home and tradition inhabited by and the responsibility of women (Chatterjee 1999). Conflict that occurs in each domain is split between the two genres of action films and family drama. The "back-to-roots" command of Hindutva simplifies conflict with its implicit belief that if only we are rooted in tradition, then there can be no conflict at all. In such a set up, the woman is assigned specific roles, which she is shown to accept willingly. A return to roots formula may be a counter strategy to the anarchic uncertainty, flux, ambivalence and in-betweeness of postmodernism. However, what is unsettling is that such a move leaves little option for women who are forced back into the strait jacketed roles of several decades ago. The "roots" in a so-called authentic past are themselves not unproblematic temporal and spatial zones to which one may return. Hence, such a strategy can at its best, be described as a form of romantic nativism.

Women and Hindutva in the 90s Film

The women are shown in subordinate roles, upholding traditional values. They represent the community and are seen as repositories of community values. Women authenticate a national/cultural identity. The body of the woman is the carrier of cultural signs. Symbols of marriage like the mangalsutra, sindoor etc. are fetishized. The traditional/modern dichotomy with reference to the women's question is located within another dichotomy of body/soul, outer/inner. In the film *Kuch Kuch Hota Hai*, (*Something Happens*), Tina a young college girl is dressed in a mini skirt but sings a bhajan ("*Om Jay Jagadeesh Hare*") to the utter amazement of the crowd gathered around her in a ragging scene in college. This is followed by her predictable dialogue about how even if she has lived and studied abroad, she has not forgotten her *Bharatiya Sanskriti.*

The family is a significant social unit in the rhetoric of the Hindu Right. The private domain of the family is the space within which the values of Hindu culture are inculcated. The socialization of men and women occurs here. This explains the focus on celebration of festivals and observance of rituals. All such family events reinforce the idea of a strong, stable family as microcosm of a strong, stable nation. The rigid hierarchy of a family structure calls upon the young members to live by its rules. In this structure, women have their demarcated spaces in which they fulfill their designated tasks. The woman's identity is constituted within and through the family. The central trope on which rests the Hindutva notion of woman is *matru shakti* (maternal power). Valorizing the good wife and mother follows from such a notion. The Hindu Right's construction of womanhood is not entirely based on tradition. It envisages the ideal Indian woman as one who is both modern and traditional. The primacy of a woman's traditional role as wife and mother is reiterated. The Hindutva discourse grants women the freedom to pursue educational and professional interests but only if they do not lose focus on approved feminine roles. To put it in the words of Lynda Nead, " 'woman' is offered as a unified and coherent category through the fulfillment of her domestic duties and mission." (Ussher 107). My analysis of three Hindi films that follows will I hope bring to light some of the issues raised so far.

Hum Dil De Chuke Sanam (1999) (*I Have Given Away My Heart*)

Sameer, son of an Italian father and Indian mother comes to India to learn music from an eminent musician.[2] He falls in love with his guru's daughter, Nandini. The father does not agree to their marriage. Instead, Nandini is married off to Vanraj, a lawyer. The marriage is not consummated. Vanraj discovers Nandini's relationship with Sameer and leaves for Italy along with Nandini to find Sameer. However, an accident later, Nandini changes her mind and remains with Vanraj. On finding Sameer, she tells him, "You taught me to fall in love, but my husband has taught me how to be steadfast in it."

Nandini in HDDCS, is already traditional. She is only temporarily led astray by an "outsider", during which time she does all the "wrong" things, like helping her cousin to run away with her lover, or daring to choose her own life partner. Her marriage to Vanraj is a process that helps recover her essential self, which embodies the female subjectivity as constructed by the Hindu Right. It is not so much a creation of new subjectivities for the woman, rather it is the recovery or resurrection of an idealized/essentialized subjectivity always already existing in a historical time-space.

Nandini's choice at the end of the film does not merely contribute to the conventional happy ending typical of popular Hindi cinema. From the ending, can be teased out a trajectory of concerns dear to the Hindu Right. The sanctity of marriage as a social institution is upheld. The outsider/alien/foreigner is expelled. The value of the family and by extension, the community is endorsed. In addition, Nandini's ultimate decision is made out to be of her own choice, although many scenes in the film reveal otherwise. The constant reminders from the elders of the sacredness of the *mangalsutra*, the husband applying the *sindoor* in a hospital scene to the accompaniment of Vedic chants, press upon a vacillating heroine as well as a curious audience The accident gives many opportunities to the husband to show his ability for caring, making it almost impossible for Nandini to choose otherwise. Ultimately, when she refuses to go back to Sameer, there is a sense of restoration of order without any disruptions in the domain of family and community, albeit at the cost of free will and individual choice, unimpaired by the quirks of fate or the oppressive weight of tradition. The Nandini-Vanraj relationship is devoid of sexuality. Taking sexual permissiveness to be the bane of Western culture, the heterosexual relationships in most nineties films are picturized as "clean" and safe to be viewed with the family. Eastern asceticism is valorized as against Western promiscuity. The film foregrounds the value of festivals and observance of rituals, which is part of the cultural revivalism of the Hindu Right. Colourful and fun-filled festival scenes, accompanied by riotous dancing and foot tapping music form a major part of the film.

Aa Ab Laut Chale (1998) (*Come, Lets Go Back*)

In AALC, Rohan unable to get a job in India decides to go the US. There he meets Pooja, who leaves her brother's house on learning that he has arranged her marriage with his boss. Both of them do a series of odd jobs to subsist. Along the way, they fall in love. But Rohan, keen on getting the coveted American citizenship woos Loveleen, an American girl of Indian origin. In the meanwhile, Pooja gets the job of a nurse to an elderly Indian called Balraj. In a highly implausible plot, Balraj turns out to be the father of Rohan, who was taken to be dead after his bus met with an accident, in which he was making a journey to the city for a better life, after an altercation with his father. Balraj, it turns out, survived the accident and ashamed to go back home due to the fight leaves for America and sets up a successful business. He marries an American and has a son, Karan. However, he pines for his family in India, and even tries contacting them, but fails. The American son is a Western stereotype, morally degenerate and lacking in values. Like a true Hindi film, it ends on a happy note. Rohan and a reformed Karan are happy to have found each other. The Indian wife weeps on the telephone while talking to her still-alive husband and coyly asks him to return home. Rohan returns to Pooja when he discovers Loveleen to be "un-Indian." They all say goodbye to America and return to India.

The long-suffering, Sita-like woman is a permanent fixture in Hindi cinema. She is invariably cast as a foil to the sensual, pleasure-seeking vamp, usually associated with Western culture through recognizable visual signifiers (mini skirts, short hair, heavy make up, cigarette in mouth and so on). AALC has two such pairs of women. The elder pair is the first and second wife of Balraj. The latter, though an absentee character is revealed through the other characters' dialogues as one who left her husband for another after two years of marriage. The morally degraded son's behaviour and his straying into a drug-peddling gang are traced to his improper (or rather lack of) upbringing. The second pair is that of Pooja and Loveleen. Their accouterments and behaviour conform to the East/West stereotype. Pooja is the archetypal good Indian woman who according to exponents of Hindutva is one who combines the attributes of tradition and modernity. She is independent enough to walk out of her brother's house to resist the marriage fixed up for her, yet patient and submissive enough to quietly wait for the return of Rohan, who is busy manipulating his way to Loveleen's heart. In the script of femininity, the suffering women get their rewards i.e. husbands. This is not exclusive to the Indian literary or other narrative traditions. It can be found in the Western literary tradition too, most decidedly in the genre of the fairy tale.

As much as the East is perceived by the West through stereotypes, the West too is set within a neat schematic arrangement of stereotypes. The East is always shown as morally superior when juxtaposed with the West, which is spiritually degraded and its inhabitants excessively materialistic. Such a divide is crucial to the Hindu Right in order to grant legitimation to its claims of cultural superiority.

Pardes (1997) (*Foreign Country*)

Ganga is the daughter of a rural couple. Ganga's father's friend, Kishen Lal who lives in the US visits the village, likes everything Indian, including Ganga whose hand he asks for his son, Rajiv. Ganga's father agrees. However, the friend sends Rajiv along with his foster son, Arjun to "see" Ganga. In an unusual move, Ganga is sent to the US before marriage. Here, she discovers that her fiance is a drunkard and a debauch. On a trip to Las Vegas, the fiancé, peeved that Ganga rejects his advances tries to molest her. She escapes from the hotel and decides to return to India. Arjun accompanies her back to India. An ashamed Kishen Lal follows and once more asks for Ganga's hand but this time for Arjun. Arjun had always loved Ganga and Ganga, prodded by her grandmother and posse of cousins accepts Arjun as her husband.

Arjun belongs to the current breed of non-resident Indians (NRIs) who are supportive of the Hindutva ideology. These are immigrants, who boast about having retained their "Indian" values even after years of living abroad. Madhu Jain uses the term "Scuppies" (saffron-clad yuppies) in an article in *India Today* to refer to this brand of immigrants. (cited in

Juergensmeyer: 190). Arjun has his values intact, unlike his foster brother who is portrayed as his foil. Ultimately, when Ganga marries Arjun, Indianness is endorsed and depicted as victorious. The foreign is rejected, just as in HDDCS.

Most of the 90s films have strong figures of authority, usually a father, grandfather or uncle. Such figures may be seen as embodiments of the Hindu Right's belief in the notion of centralized governance. Kishen Lal, in *Pardes* is a dominating father figure who takes it as his right to fix his sons' marriages to girls of his choice. By reclaiming the idea of the joint family system as essentially an Indian way of life, the film foregrounds the idea of domestic bliss, achievable through submission to a hierarchy. Young men are unbelievably obedient to the elders and the women are subordinate both to the men in the family and the older women, who in their turn exercise power over the younger women. As Ratna Kapur and Brenda Cossman in their essay "Communalising Gender Engendering Community", point out in the context of Hindutva elements in legal discourse, "these different roles of women and men, in the family and in society, are affirmed and celebrated as a harmonious synthesis" (Sarkar and Butalia:100).

The objectification of women is perpetrated by the Hindu Right with the help of scriptural sanction. Kumkum Roy in her essay, "Where women are worshipped, there the Gods rejoice," locates the Hindutva attempts at constructing an identity for the Hindu woman in *Manusmriti,* an ancient Indian text. In it, women were equated to material goods with men in command of them (ibid) In *Pardes,* the heroine is framed within the male gaze throughout the film beginning with the voyeuristic camera handled by the male director, the heroes who covet her, and the male audience who fantasize about her. In the film, a kabbadi match is played between two contending parties who wish to get their son married to Ganga. Ganga is the trophy the winner gets to carry home. One wonders how a scene of such crassness and insensitivity got past a Censor Board which created a huge fuss about the use of an archaism to refer to a part of the female anatomy in Shekhar Kapoor's *Elizabeth.* Hence, the reference to *Manusmriti* made above is not a mere proleptic leap but is made to show the danger of using texts like these as modular forms in identity formation.

By Way of Conclusion

The narratives of the films analyzed above are not didactic in a literal, distasteful way. On the contrary, these films are huge box office hits. Hit songs with elaborate dance sequences, foreign locales, designer clothes, superb photography and above all, gorgeous heroines who sometimes are achievers in their own right, before making their screen appearance. With the help of such rich visual tapestries, these films push forward norms/ prescriptions for the youth that form large segments of the audience. They continue to enthrall audiences everywhere, resulting perhaps, slowly and steadily in a transformation of the way we think and behave in our worlds. If such a change does indeed occur, the ideologues would have succeeded in entrenching their ideas that are majoritarian, patriarchal and non-egalitarian. It is this transformative potential of cinema that seems most threatening to a secular liberal democracy and to the feminist cause.

It is not that such films as analyzed above are new to Hindi cinema. In fact, we have had an excess of them. Then what is it that makes the 90s film specifically right wing? Firstly, the 90s have spawned exclusively, with rare exceptions, the kind of films described above. It is an offshoot of the genre called family drama, popular among audiences, especially women audiences. However, earlier these family dramas co-existed with other genres, while the 90s have produced these to the near extinction of others. Secondly, the 90s films have stretched the tradition/modernity dialectic to cover the immigrant theme as well. The Indian-Western interface has revealed the moral superiority of what is constructed as Indian culture. The Hindutva propagators have built a large constituency for themselves among the NRIs in UK and USA. These films cater to such a constituency, evoking nostalgia of a happy domesticity among the first generation immigrants. To the second generation foreign-born Indians, they are parables, preaching the values of "Indian" life, i.e. a non-materialistic, communitarian outlook on life, in contrast to the materialism and individualism of the West. Lastly, the 90s film narratives run parallel to the changing political and social environment in India, generated by the growth and consolidation of right wing parties. Political compulsions may have forced the ruling *Bharatiya Janta Party* (BJP) to put its hard-core issues on the backburner. However, its hidden agenda has been cleverly hijacked by Bollywood filmmakers of the 90s. It is for these reasons that the 90s films can at best be read as cinematic translations of the rhetoric of the Hindu Right. Vinay Lal in his essay, "The Impossibility of the Outsider in the Modern Hindi Film" comments, "As the idea of India as a nation-state takes precedence, the idea of India as a civilization will become imperilled, and the cultural pluralism and accommodation of that civilization will most likely become, as they have already to some degree, the first victims of that nefarious development." He concludes optimistically that the Hindi film continues to be loyal to the more generous tenets of the idea of India as a civilization and wonders if it too "will become a hostage to the nation-state" (Nandy:253). I have tried to show, hopefully with some degree of success, that the Hindi film has become one such hostage.

Notes

1. For a detailed study of interculturalism see Richard Schechner 'Interculturalism and the Culture of Choice' in *The Intercultural Performance Reader*, Routledge, London and New York, 1996.

2. Sameer's Italian connection is an uncanny reminder to the audience of the BJP's obsession with Sonia Gandhi's "foreign origin", which went on to become an electoral issue this year. Predictably, Sameer is the loser, driven out by Nandini's father.

References

Chakravarti, Sumita S. *National Identity and Indian Popular Cinema.* Delhi: Oxford University Press, 1998.

Chatterjee, Partha. *The Partha Chatterjee Omnibus*. Delhi: Oxford University Press.

Jaffrelot, Christophe. *The Hindu Nationalist Movement in India, 1925 to the 1990s*. New Delhi: Viking, 1999.

Juergensmeyer, Mark. *Religious Nationalism Confronts the Secular State*. Delhi: Oxford University Press, 1993.

Nandy Ashis. *The Secret Politics of Our Desire.* Delhi: Oxford University Press, 1998.

Sarkar, Tanika and Urvashi Butalia, eds. *Women and the Hindu Right,* New Delhi: Kali for Women, 1995.

Ussher, Jane M. *Fantasies of Femininity*. Harmondsworth: Penguin, 1997.

Filmography

1. *Hum Dil De Chuke Sanam* (1999)
   Director: Sanjay Leela Bhansali
   Cast: Aishwarya Rai, Salman Khan, Ajay Devgan
2. *Aa Ab Laut Chale* (1998)
   Director: Rishi Kapoor
   Cast: Aishwarya Rai, Suman Ranganathan, Akshay Khanna, Rajesh Khanna
3. *Pardes* (1997)
   Director: Subhash Ghai
   Cast: Mahima Chaudhury, Shah Rukh Khan, Apoorva Agnihotri, Amrish Puri, Alok Nath

3 Female Bodies and the Male Gaze: Laura Mulvey and Hindi Cinema

Bindu Nair

> "Men act, women appear. Men look at women, women watch themselves being looked at." (John Berger: *Ways of Seeing*)

The above quote suggests very succinctly the position of women in the realm of the 'look', including within the mainstream Indian Cinema. Consider the first part of the statement, "Men act, women appear". In Indian cinema, women have been relegated to the passive position in film after film, as "bearer, not the maker of meaning", merely an appendage to the man, the wielder of power (Mulvey 834). What Budd Boeticher says about the narrative cinema in the west also applies here: "What counts is what the heroine provokes, or rather what she represents. She is the one, or rather the love or fear she inspires in the hero, or else the concern he feels for her, who makes him act the way he does. In herself the woman has not the slightest importance" (quoted by Mulvey 837).

The stories played out on the screen are the men's – their conflicts, their dreams, their aspirations, their tragedies, their revenge, their desires and their heroism. The women exist only in relation to the men, as their mothers, their wives, and especially their lovers. It is hard to find even one story revolving around a single unattached woman. And of course there is the worship of youth and 'beauty'. We rarely ever see a woman act independently, make her own decisions, question authority or even be a working woman unless her mother is on her death bed, or the father crippled, and definitely never once she gets married! Traditionally, women have been reduced to being a mere spectacle in the movies, pretty faces commodified for their beauty, with hardly any dividing line between beauty contests and acting in films (Juhi Chawla, Aishwarya Rai, Sushmita Sen et al).

Women's specially constituted role as spectacle, as the subject of the Look, is especially evident in the song and dance numbers which are such an important part of the publicity and the selling of a film. In fact there is an entire genre of songs, called 'item numbers' in industry parlance, which generally have a showgirl or dancer performing, and a predominantly male audience watching, that are deliberately inserted into the film, often without any direct connection with the rest of the film, to attract audiences. Sometimes the one item song ends up making a film a hit, such as '*Chamma Chamma*' from the film *China Gate*.

In these songs, the styling in terms of make up and costumes, and the cinematic elements of lighting and shot taking, i.e. the way the body is arranged with respect to the camera and hence the eye of the audience, the movements of the body, all add up in turning the woman into a spectacle. The gaze is invited to certain parts of the body selectively considered sexual – the eyes, the lips, the breasts, the navel, the buttocks and the legs. Make-up techniques include brightly colored, glossy lips, cleavage rouged darker than the rest of the body, tattoos on the navel etc. The costumes are often dazzling with sequins or a metallic finish, brightly colored, and revealingly cut. The natural contours of the bodies of the actresses are frequently distorted with push-up bras, breast and/or buttock paddings. And to emphasize these unnaturally distended body proportions, the women are frequently shot either from a low angle, or from a high angle to show the cleavage. The actions of the women in the dance often mimic sexual movements with numerous shots of just body parts, like that of heaving breasts, of pelvic thrusts. All these add up in objectifying and sexualizing the body of the woman for the benefit of the (male) viewer.

As Laura Mulvey says in her seminal article, "Visual Pleasure and Narrative Cinema," "in their traditional exhibitionist role, women are simultaneously looked at and displayed, with their appearance coded for strong visual and erotic impact, so that they can be said to connote to-be-looked-at-ness" (837). The woman displayed has functioned on two levels: as erotic object for the characters within the story, and as erotic object for the spectator within the auditorium.

As in the songs, using the device of the show girl or dancer, the two looks are unified, so that the gaze of the audience and male characters in the film are combined neatly, providing both with a sense of control and possession. This also extends to most other visual representations of women with men, be it a photograph in an advertisement of a condom, or a love scene in a film, whether mainstream or pornographic, even if the woman is shown in an amorous pose with a man, the real display is for the spectator of the representation.

One can differentiate the kinds of gazes in the following ways:

(1) The gaze of the male character towards the female character and the gaze of the female character towards the male character within the narrative. The male gaze is always more predominant and importantly placed in the films. The moment the male first sees the woman is very well foregrounded through the use of action (removing the sunglasses and looking at the woman from head to toe or whistling) dialogue (*kya dikhti hai*), background music etc. For example, the moment of Rani Mukherjee's entry in

Kuch Kuch Hota Hai. Witness the way her body appears in slow motion, her walk, the clothes and even her challenging look, all signify to her as a sexual spectacle to be looked at, by the hordes of young men sitting around the campus, as opposed to Kajol's character in the beginning of the film. In fact Rani's look by and large has a somewhat different quality of challenge compared to the usual coy looks given by heroines to sundry heroes, but inscribed within that is merely a sexual challenge whose ultimate aim is in being overcome.

(2) The gaze of the audience towards the characters, the reverse, i.e. the gaze of the characters towards the audience rarely ever exists, since that would break the carefully constructed verisimilitude of the screen story as something taking place on its own volition, and not something especially arranged for the eye of the viewer.

But when one considers the gaze of the audience, it is definitely not homogenous, men and women have different responses to the stories of desire being played out on the screen. But how different are they really, considering that patriarchy is so well entrenched even in our own psyches!

However, without discounting the importance and pleasures of female spectatorship, and stressing that women are definitely not entirely colonized, I would like to focus on the gaze of the male audience, keeping in mind that most films are made by men for a predominantly male audience and to reflect on the relationship of the way men look at women, and the resulting power dynamics in society.

Using psychoanalysis to demonstrate the way the unconscious of patriarchal society has structured film form, taking Freud and Lacan as a basis, Mulvey says on the position of women in patriarchal society,

> ... the function of woman in forming the patriarchal unconscious is two-fold, she first symbolises the castration threat

> by her real absence of a penis and second thereby raises her child into the symbolic .... Once this has been achieved, her meaning in the process is at an end, it does not last into the world of law and language except as a memory, which oscillates between memory of maternal plenitude and memory of lack ..... Woman then stands in patriarchal culture as signifier for the male other, bound by a symbolic order in which man can live out his phantasies and obsessions ...by imposing them on the silent image of woman.....

According to her, narrative film is made for the pleasure of the male spectator alone, who seeks to control and "indirectly" possess the female figure through narcissistic identification with the main male protagonist, who controls the gaze and the events on the screen, thus giving the male spectator a reassuring sense of omnipotence. The gaze also provides another kind of pleasure – the voyeuristic one. The viewing conditions – dark, anonymous, the brilliance and the rapidly changing light patterns on the screen, and the narrative norms of constructing verisimilitude, of never returning the gaze of the audience, all add in giving the spectator an illusion of looking into a private world.

But since the woman also signifies lack, her image is also a source of anxiety (the castration complex), so the male seeks to nullify it by fetishism or over valuation. Therefore according to Mulvey, this ambivalence, where the woman is seen as a lure (object of desire) and a threat (woman seen as lack and therefore signifying the castration anxiety), impels men to worship and fetishize woman on the one hand (the goddess/mother), e.g., Ghatak's women characters, or to devalue, punish and save her, the guilty object (the whore/vamp), as in Guru Dutt's *Pyaasa* on the other.

While contesting Mulvey's phallocentric assumptions in corroborating Freud's signification of woman as 'lack of a penis', one cannot but agree that for man, woman is the Other. As Roland Barthes suggests: the Other is that which bourgeois (/patriarchal) ideology cannot recognize or accept, but must deal with in either of two ways – either by rejecting and if possible annihilating it, or by rendering it safe and assimilating it, converting it as far as possible into a replica of itself.

As Mulvey says, "In a world ordered by sexual imbalance, pleasure in looking has been split between active/male and passive/female. The determining male gaze projects its phantasy onto the female figure which is styled accordingly". The very assimilation that Barthes speaks of to render the otherness of the woman safe, seems to be achieved by using phallic imagery with the woman, turning her effectively into a phallus. I am not saying that this is the only way a woman is represented, but that this is a form of imagery used too often. To take as example, if one looks at Shilpa Shetty's song 'Aila Re' from *Jung*, it would become clearer, in terms of the way her body is shot, the way her body emerges on the screen, the use of the gun, which is again quite phallic. To take a more obvious example, consider the ads for beer, where the body of the woman is likened to the bottle, which is likened to, again the phallus. This is not merely a function of looking, but also of course, of the manner of representation.

But of course one is not suggesting that this is the only spectatorial position, or way of presentation of the woman. Spectatorial pleasure may even proceed from the viewing of the female figure as plenitude, or in identifying with the female figure, i.e. opposite sex identification, which Mulvey ignores. After all, we are all multiply gendered, and according to psychoanalysis essentially bisexual, thus a possible pleasure can be from the ability of the cinema to satisfy that need to overcome sexual difference, the wish to be both sexes temporarily through the mobility of multiple, fluid identifications.

To conclude, I would like to state that I do not intend to negate the pleasure in looking or being looked at, but one must remember that there is a power inscribed within that, and when predominantly one sex is constituted as the spectacle and the other as the bearer of the look, there is a cause for concern. While a large web of conglomerates producing consumer goods thrive on the anxieties this develops in women, one can only wonder at how much this costs women, including the actresses who live with the presence of the oppressive gaze of million of men, in terms of bad body images, inferiority complexes, depression and even pathologies like bulimia and anorexia. While we are taught that even our bodies are not our own.

Reference

Mulvey, Laura. "Visual Pleasure and Narrative Cinema," *Film Theory and Criticism* Ed. Leo Braudy and Marshall Cohen. 5th edition, New York: Oxford University Press, 1999.

4 Courting: Hindi Film Ishtyle

Malati Mathur

> *"I kissed her (to make her accept my proposal) but it didn't work. Do you think I should try rape now?"* - Govinda in the promos of the recently released blockbuster *Jodi No. 1.*

If you think that the above is a rare instance of the disgusting expression of male chauvinist swinism (and I hope pigs will forgive me for the insult), painful disillusionment awaits you. Courtship in Hindi films is invariably crude and insensitive, the hero frequently taking recourse to behaviour which our lawmakers have termed 'eve teasing', in his nightmarish fervour to win over the girl of his dreams. For every Rajendra Kumar whose wooside manner comes replete with soulful renderings of a romantic ghazal, there are the Dharmendras and Govindas who pursue the heroine and pester the life out of her, manhandling her roughly, pulling at her dupatta, pinching her cheeks and so on as all the while, the girl tries to get away from this boor who professes undying love as he tries his utmost to practically disrobe her in public. The marvel of this is that the heroine finally succumbs to the hero's dubious charms and is won over with his caveman-like antics. Is it any matter of great surprise then that the majority of our male youth appear to think that the way to a girl's heart is to make crude remarks and even cruder gestures? If the wondrously beautiful Aishwarya or Hema are themselves irresistibly attracted by the shenanigans that the average Hindi film hero's (or his director's) idea of courtship is a manifestation of, what proof then the ordinary girl next door or on the street or at the bus stop?

Time was when a film hero voiced his affection for the heroine in a surreptitiously delivered letter wherein he expressed his misgivings that she might be offended by his delicately articulated feelings. Or he might sing a paean to the moonlit night and star-studded sky, making subtle comparisons with his beloved all the while. Not so anymore. Our modern hero believes in letting it all hang out (literally) performing unabashedly in his song and dance sequences, those actions that any self-respecting man would confine to the privacy of the boudoir. While it is not my intention to appear a self-righteous, suffocating prude, I must confess at the risk of seeming hopelessly square, old fashioned and way, way not 'in', that the appallingly vulgar movements of certain so-called 'romantic' songs make me want to puke, upchuck, throw up... oh well, I'm sure you get the drift.

Inextricably bound up with this manner of wooing is the idea of masculinity. The more 'macho' a man is, the more compelling it appears for him to railroad the girl into accepting his proposals. The gentle, sensitive lover who quotes poetry and has exquisite manners is considered effeminate and has practically become as dead as the dodo – leastways in the esoteric environs of Hindi filmland. And as for uttering "sorry" or "thank you" or "please"???? What are you blathering on about? No self-respecting macho hunk would allow these words to slither out of his manfully clenched jaw, so help him god. Thus you have the girl slapping the boy for pestering her in one scene to be immediately followed by the boy walking 'masterfully' up to her and kissing her in a deliberate, provocative, least romantic way in public after which the duo breaks out into a song and dance sequence... (Sanjay Dutt and

Pooja Batra in *Hasina Maan Jayegi).* The idea of the 'punishment kiss' is one that our filmmakers appear to have borrowed from a whole plethora of Mills and Boon 'classics' which inevitably include this activity as an essential element of foreplay in the run up to the happy ending.

In an eminently offensive scene in another recent film – *Kuch Khatti Kuch Meethi* – the wife prepares to leave her husband's house again after the couple have been brought together by their daughters after a long period of separation caused by a misunderstanding. The husband watches helplessly as his children urge him to intervene and prevent their mother from walking out on them to return to the independent and comfortable life she has fashioned for herself abroad. So, what then, does the good man do? Does he apologize to her for having doubted her fidelity? Does he persuade her not to go away once again so that they can enjoy their new-found togetherness in the mellow light of middle-age bliss? Nah! As their grown daughters watch breathlessly, this erring husband delivers a resounding slap to his wife after which – wonder of wonders – she falls at his feet sobbing and demanding to know why he didn't use this technique earlier when she left the house all those years ago! Good Lord! shudder to think of all the gullible males (not to mention females brainwashed by stereotypes) lapping this up as manna from the heavens and applying this method to resolve marital differences in their private lives, smug in the belief that this is what the woman wants and – moreover – the only thing that she understands. And this in circa 2001 after all the brouhaha of women's rights and emancipation!

Another concept that defies all logic is the heroine flipping for the hero after he rescues her from the unwanted attentions of certain unsavoury characters. Now, after all, those slimy creatures are doing exactly what the 'hero' has been doing all along – spouting coarse comments, making uncouth gestures, blocking her path, trying to reach out and fondle her.... So why is it that the hero should feel such moral outrage and even more startling, the heroine feel grateful to him for delivering her from such a fate when she has experienced the same at his hands and will, doubtless, continue to do so???! ! !

And, what about the fate of the girl if she should, god forbid, be victim of rape? Apart from those films which portray such women as dervishes running amok in order to wreak revenge, there are the innumerable celluloid weddings arising out of this detestable act. The woman who has been violated is, willy-nilly, compelled to marry her assaulter in a shotgun wedding and no one ever bothers to find out whether the victim would like to spend the rest of her years in wedding bliss with the perpetrator of this horrendous crime against her psychological being. Tied up with this is the concept of a woman as property, a possession which needs to be passed on, unsullied, from one owner to the other. Within the patriarchal parameters, the man who has known a woman carnally brands her as his forever – much in the manner of animals being branded by their owners. Whoever dreams of asking a cow whether she wants to stay with the man who has bought and branded her? So, it would be inconceivable for a rape-victim to refuse to marry her rapist – an act which would immediately alienate audience sympathy. How can she even think of being intimate with another man?! What kind of a promiscuous, perverted creature is she, to refuse the man's offer of marriage when he could so easily have shrugged off the matter and got on with his life? She deserved what was done to her – would be the pious, self-righteous conclusion of more viewers than one would think. In such a situation, the rapist assumes an almost noble halo for, has he not, after all, been generous enough to accept a 'tainted' being as his wife, no matter that the taint has been of his own doing when he could have had the choicest of virgins (another macho concept) to choose from – and with a huge dowry in the bargain? And, has he not assumed responsibility for an act that cannot be proved and which he may vigorously deny and get away with?

Most Hindi films feature the scenario of poor boy meets rich girl, they fall in love they encounter opposition from all sections and finally marry after a great many trials and tribulations. The subaltern hero – a role perfected by Govinda – falls for an educated (English-speaking, no less!), wealthy young miss – no matter if he himself is a self-confessed 'fifth-fail' scholar (Govinda in *Pardesi Babu)* who can, at a pinch, recite a 'cow essay' in English. The fashionable, independent, pampered heroine is then gradually Indianized – which means she starts wearing saris, sporting a bindi and bangles, is compelled to perform degrading menial chores, dwindles into a wife who regards her man as her god in spite of (or because of?) all the humiliations he heaps on her and is finally squeezed into the traditional mould and made fit for public consumption as the quintessential *Bhartiya Nari*. Now, why on earth would an intelligent, educated young woman from the upper strata of society choose to completely annihilate her personality for a barely literate lout notwithstanding his proverbial heart of gold, is a notion that seems to have entirely escaped our estimable filmmakers. Are there no good men with a similar background who can measure up to her expectations and with whom she may be expected to have more in common and with whom she can lead a fairly happy life?

And, in an interesting reversal, the rich boy who marries far beneath his station is regarded as noble, generous and sacrificing while the rich-girl-marries-poor-boy syndrome is considered as a divinely ordained injunction aimed at bringing the shrew to heel. Or watch the theatre erupt in whistles and joyous cries when the educated hero, in dire straits which effectively conceal his academic credentials, is spoken to in English by the heroine and he turns around and replies to her in the same language, taking her completely by surprise! Oh English! That bugbear of the masses enmeshed in a love-hate relationship with it! Is there a young woman who walks around spouting this queen of languages? It is a grand conspiracy designed to destabilize the great Indian *parampara* and must hence be tackled on a war footing. In walks the hero fresh from the village, reeking of manure and radiating rustic simplicity who sets out to 'reform' the silly girl and bring her to her senses by gradually inducing in her all the great archaic notions of Indian patriarchal sensibility. That the hero who brings about this drastic change in the heroine is either already a jeans-clad dandy (if he is a town hick) or slowly changes into one, is a point that is conveniently ignored.

And woe betide the girl who puts career and ambition before family! While it is a virtue for a man to be a workaholic, the woman cannot and must not make professional commitments that would come in the way of her serving the great Hindu undivided family with all its masala of endless ceremonies to commemorate each rite of passage. Even if her husband is unable to provide for the family and she has to, of necessity, go out to earn her living, she must, at all times be careful not to crush his ego (Rekha in *Agar Tum Na Hote)*, put up with all his suspicions of her infidelity, observe the *karva chauth* fast religiously even if he is a philanderer and has given her hardly any happiness in this life leave alone think of the next seven rebirths (a wish that all *pativrata* wives make)...

Hindi films have, over the years, been the trendsetters in sartorial and beauty matters – almost being the benchmark for contemporary tastes. It is hardly surprising then that male youngsters should, in matters of courtship, ape the formulae that appear to work so well for the current rage at the box office. All the more reason, one would think, for filmmakers to be more sensible. But then, what would you expect of people who believe in delivering all manner of trash under the guise of offering 'what the public wants'? Wielding the camera is probably a more onerous responsibility than wielding the pen, as the visual medium is several times more powerful than the written one. Add to this the sway that tinsel town's charismatic heartthrobs have over the masses and the job of filmmakers as arbiters of taste and public opinion becomes that much more accountable. But is anybody listening.

5 Women in Indian Cinema: Fictional Constructs

Vrinda Mathur

Lights.... Camera.... Action.... the focus zooms in on a very spirited Basanti riding her horsewagon, mouthing four letter unprintables, whip in hand, talking consistently to her mare – Dhanno. The audience reacts with wild applause.

Lights.... Camera.... Action.... This time the focus shifts to a hyper-paranoid, petulant Zubeida throwing tantrums, because the man she loves has chosen to abandon her preferring to seek solace in the company of his 'oh so mature, so dignified Queen.'

Lights.... Camera.... Action.... The scenes go on and on.

Women in Indian cinema, ranging from cult movies and celluloid blockbusters like *Sholay* of the seventies to the more recent *Zubeida*, which engages itself with serious gender issues continue to be portrayed and presented as either damsels in distress to be rescued by knights in shining armour, or demented feminists, or just plain simple belly-shaking glamourous dolls, whose sole ambition in life is to attract the attention of accomplished males.

Events seldom catapult women characters of the Indian cinema to a white-hot spotlight. They are dumped into the quagmires of tension-packed fireworks of the home-prison or the ambitious exploitations of healers and killers, lovers and betrayers. The women are shown as having no sphere of their own, no independent identity, no living space. They go down in collective memory as organic imperfections, ramshackle, rickety, unhinged creations, mere fictional constructs of the 'fragile – handle with care' male ego.

'Truth of fact' and 'truth of fiction' are incompatible, yet they are curiously blended in Indian cinema to present a homogeneous reality which has the unmistakable stamp of male authoritative hegemony. The male characters of Indian cinema, i.e. the heroes (those knights in shining armour) and the villains (those over-energetic sharks) move around the space of the movie like players in a deadly choreographed game of chess – with the women characters as the sacrificial pawns. As the stories progress towards expected and anticipated endings, Indian cinema proves again and again that its women characters will always need something more than the brains which God Almighty has given them. Their loves, their dreams, their unexpected destinies shall always oscillate vacuously between the pluralisms of culture and traditions, paradoxes of progress and representational aporia.

The vitalizing power of the women characters is always absolutely ignored. The two areas on which I wish to focus attention are, firstly, the mother's role, inheriting all the power and status of the 'mother goddess' tradition of Indian culture and secondly, women characters trapped in secondary roles as somebody's wives, somebody's daughters or somebody's love interests but never their own selves i.e. never as women – individuals in their own right.

The mother's role, in Indian culture, enjoys a double inheritance as it encompasses the 'mother-goddess tradition'. "Mother goddess can be interpreted as expressing ideas of power, autonomy and primary in the widest sense of the terms..... she conveys a world view in which the creative power of femininity is central" (Ganesh 5), she is the combined energy of the Gods but she wields weapons and battles alone with hardly any male support. She is the benevolent 'shakti' – the actualizer of Gods latent power and the embodiment of His grace. She enjoys an independent status. "Even the popular Radha-Krishna couple is typically shown in a totally non-hierarchical relationship." Mahakali, Mahalaxmi, Mahasaraswati, Durga are portrayed alone, "This is the Goddess who exists in herself – by herself," (62). Ganesh goes on to point out, "The Goddess is a powerful symbol of linkages. She bridges realms and levels hierarchies and schisms; between the autochthonous and alien, conquerors and conquered begs to differ" (63).

The goddess image, however is represented through cardboard representations – either as a tyrant figure (of a mother-in-law) or a sacrificing mother, or even as the bloodthirsty Kali who asks for sacrifice.

Similarly, the role of a mother – a supposedly 'good mother' is absolutely trivialized in Indian cinema. This silent suffering, stoic species is so distressingly deified on celluloid that by the end of the movie you are convinced that these faces will soon be up on postage stamps. The positive impact and significance of this character is absolutely stultified with the result that the character just slips through the fingers and what remains behind is a pathetic caricature.

The Indian cinema does not place the mother within a realistic setting, instead it strives to contract this sphere into a limited area thereby turning this space into a place of isolation and confinement.

But the mother's maternal instincts can have a far-reaching effect on public life. The well known American writer (and feminist) Charlotte Perkins Gilman has observed, "Mothers with their natural characteristics of care, nature, provision and education can be shown to be ideal public administrators" (1898:3). They can have a strong impact on society with their natural habit of serving the interests of others and also the manner in which they bring up children.

This concept of 'social motherhood' which transcends the 'separate sphere' ideology can be exploited to positively tackle the repressions, suppressions and arbitrary conventions of society. Her characteristics of 'care', 'nurture', 'provision' and 'education' can enable the mother character to direct the resources of administration and society, away from competition and self interest thus aiding social advancement and progress. The politics of social motherhood can be directed towards aiding social advancement and not hindering it.

The projection of non-nurturing, well-intentioned but misguided mothers has a strongly crippling effect on social and cultural theory. A strong endorsement of the mother ideal could reveal the vast potential of this character. The lenient affection, compassionate attention bestowed by the mothers on their infant daughters to turn them into strong individuals or the daughter's memory of her mother's affection for her and the self esteem and strength of will it has generated in turn, is a sphere sadly misrepresented by the Indian cinema. In *Kya Kehna* the decisions of the heroine come very close to this ideal but then the glass ceiling appears again and the recurring concern for mass approval and erudite assent resurfaces repeatedly thereby overshadowing the essence and spirit of the character. The Indian cinema's failure to emphasize the significance of women participation in the general scheme of human advancement and progress is its singularly weak point. It continues to portray the 'Mother' character with such remote eerieness, well insulated by social histrionics, that she yearns to break free from the sterile omnipotence of the patriarchal network in which she is trapped, into another world, another time, another space.

The second domain which eclipses the position and powerful impact of the woman character is the manner in which she is depicted as purely a woman. This blasphemic caricature is trapped within stereotyped roles. The suppressions, the exactions and the dictatorial conventions of society tend to inhibit the 'autonomy' of woman as an individual. In the view of Zauderer, "Autonomy is not merely a liberal masculine ideal," but a basic need for freedom of thought and action (67). The liberation from the feeling of helplessness is the ideal of autonomy. Through the formative years of growing up, during the socialization process, the woman learns to submit to the tyrannies of the fraternal society at all the three levels – the emotional, the social and the financial. Woman characters are perceived and presented as socially inferior beings. Because they are socially inferior the female bonding is depicted as clearly distinct from the male bondings. Male bonding is always depicted in positive light songs like "*yeh dosti hum nahin chodenge.... chodenge hum magar tera saath na chodenge*", endorse that phenomenon. When it comes to female bonding, it is either depicted as women hurling hostilities on their own sex or the other extreme of physical closeness i.e. lesbianism as in Deepa Mehta's *Fire*. Women characters are always shown as divided amongst themselves. The harsh realities of life, perpetrated by the masculine world make her believe that obedience is security and therefore right. She is terrorized to accede to unreasonable demands in the name of security – financial, emotional and social. She learns to be a good daughter, a good wife, a good mother, a good love interest, but never a good individual at peace with herself, her world of her interests.

The experience of giving birth to herself, of being born anew, is mysteriously withheld from her. This feeling of being rendered helpless leads to the experience of anguish and at times, tests the inner strength of a women calling upon her to discover herself. Resistance defines the 'self', Gilman describes this feeling as a realization "I was realizing with an immense illumination that neither she, nor anyone, could make me do anything. One could suffer, one could die if it came to that, but one could not be coerced. I was born...." (Gilman 34). This is a sphere that is grotesquely misrepresented by Indian cinema. In *Guide* the heroine comes near to it in the song "*katon se kheench kar yeh aanchal, tod ke bandhan bandhii payal*" but she is coerced back by the sweet talk of the colonizer to be colonized once again.

The overcoming of the fear of helplessness is an experience that can liberate the women of Indian cinema from being coerced again and again. It is only after this experience that women can freely choose to accept authority. To accept authority freely and consciously would then make the woman character, truly an individual, not merely an extension of the male egotistical ideas. The recognition of the fact that she was able to draw upon her own competence and strength would redefine personal autonomy, and therefore redefine the woman character.

The present portrayal of women on screen merely perpetrates the Indian cultural devaluation theory. "I am a girl, therefore bad and therefore destined to suffer" is the message that is sent forth in movie after movie. This space between a strong woman real life and her portrayal on celluloid needs to be negotiated and the positive ambience foregrounded. Indian cinema has a double role to play in shaping the mindset of its people. It is loved greatly and has tremendous mass appeal but that is not enough. It must also set the stage for social change. Can woman be redefined and recategorized into 'I am a woman, therefore strong, therefore invincible'. Only then can the woman characters come alive on screen. Until then they shall continue to be what they are – mere fictional constructs and one dimensional figures who are distant from the ordinary, real life woman.

References

Dinnerstein, Dorothy. *The Mermaid and the Minotaur*: New York: Harper and Row, 1976.

Ganesh Kamala, "Mother who is not a Mother." *Economic and Political Weekly* (October 20-27, 1990).

Gilman, Charlotte Perkins, "The Best Form of Government" *The Woman's Column* V. XI no. 22 (Nov.5., 1898) in *The Living of Charlotte Perkins Gilman*. New York: D. Appleton-Century Co., 1935.

Zaudcrer, Naomi B. "Social Motherhood: Charlotte Perkins Gilman and Feminist Politics." *Journal of Contemporary Thought*, 6 (1996).

6 Bollywood Portrayals of Women With Disabilities

Meenu Bhambhani

It would be a cliché to state that women form the "marginal component" of society. And if we suggest that within this component there is another sub-group of disabled women which is all the more marginalized it would be an erroneous terminology as its use would lend existence and hence give this group some kind of recognition – like a species on the verge of extinction. What is ironical in case of this group which lives on the periphery of society is that it is virtually ignored and not spared a second thought even by their own able-bodied gender and tragically by disabled men too.

> Despite their significant numbers, women and girls with disabilities, especially in the developed countries of the ESCAP region, remain hidden and silent, their concerns unknown and their rights overlooked. Throughout the region, in urban and rural communities alike, they have to face the major problem of triple discrimination by society in general, not only because of their disabilities but also because they are female and poor. Prejudice prevails even within each of the three categories. Among women, the woman with disability is seen as inferior and even among other people with disabilities she is not their equal. In fact, women with disabilities find themselves in "Catch-22"

> situation, in which they are forced into being among the most isolated and marginalized. Thus they become the poorest of people.... (Mohit 25)

There is no doubt that a number of problems of girls and women with and without disabilities are common. In her foreword to the book entitled *Women and Disability* (1991), Mary Chinery Hesse says that, "EQUALITY OF OPPORTUNITY and treatment for women has yet to be achieved in many societies. A woman with a physical or mental disability faces a double handicap.... Although some progress has been made in improving the status of women in general, disabled women have remained a largely ignored group" (ix). Women with disabilities are more vulnerable to neglect and physical, sexual and mental abuse as they do not have time lag i.e. they are unable to defend themselves since the time taken to escape or protect oneself from possible physical and sexual abuses is not available to them which is not a problem with non-disabled women. This vulnerability in turn compels the disabled women to look for male protection and thus seek marriage. But unfortunately:

> ...the society regards disabled women as non-sexual. They are not considered suitable for marriage....In India, marriages are mostly arranged. A disabled woman gets disqualified for marriage on account of her handicap. If marriage ever takes place a number of compromises are made. Either they are married to much older men or widowers....In most cases non-disabled men get married to disabled women but the reverse is not true. The dowry demanded by men and offered by the families of the disabled women is exorbitant. Disabled women are considered incapable of bearing and rearing healthy children. Society undervalues women with disabilities. She is not considered an ideal child or an acceptable person as an adult, is unfit as an employee, unsuitable as a wife, incapable as a mother. (Baquer and Sharma 193-194)

Media and more importantly women's and disability organizations are also indifferent to the discrimination faced by them. Women all over the world, as it is are victims of a discriminatory system. Why is it that amongst them WOMEN WITH DISABILITIES are conspicuously missing? What relegates them to the fringes of periphery? In the Indian context, what societal, cultural and historical factors are responsible for their invisibility, reticence and chronic neglect?

To begin with, disabled women do not have any documented history. They have not set any precedence which some of the disabled men have although they too have been projected in a very negative light. Disabled people in Indian mythology as well as history have been depicted as cruel and spiteful, normally acting in connivance of some evil. There are only a couple of disabled women that one can find in Indian mythology, one being the one-eyed orthopaedically impaired maidservant of queen Kaikeyi in *Ramayana* called Manthara who was responsible for Lord Rama's exile and another is Kubja (meaning hunchback), a hunchbacked Gopi in Braj in whose name Krishna is teased by the Gopis. Lord Krishna used to address Kubja as sundari meaning a beautiful woman. Lord Krishna saw the inner beauty of Kubja and the gopis teased him for liking an impaired woman who appeared ugly owing to her disfigurement. Similarly in our mythological stories we have heard that women with disabilities are neglected even by Lords. According to a Katha recited during the month of Kartik Poornima, Goddess Laxmi had an elder sister who could not marry because of being dark and disfigured. When Lord Vishnu proposed to Laxmi she expressed her inability as her elder sister was still unmarried. Instead she urged him to marry her sister. Lord Vishnu refused saying that there is no place for such people in heaven. But he would help her solve her problem and married her elder sister to a peepal tree which he said was another form of Vishnu. Disabled men on the other hand have been shown occupying prominent positions such as the visually impaired king Dhritrashtra or orthopaedically impaired Shakuni Mama in *Mahabharata*. Both have been shown siding with evil. In our history there is just one disabled ruler i.e. Taimur Lang – Lang being his nickname derived from his malformed foot, which gave him a limp. Though he was a powerful ruler he has been projected as an insensitive and atrocious person. These negative images have had a deep influence on the psyche of the Indians who till today perceive disabled people either as objects of pity or personifications of evil.

In a patriarchal society there are different yardsticks of perceiving and judging disabled men and women and the treatment meted out to them is definitely discriminatory. Women have seldom been perceived as human beings but as objects of beauty and bestowers of services to their husbands and families, their contribution never having been calculated in statistical terms. They are producers of economy but have been projected as consumers and hence are considered a burden on limited resources. It is this perception of non-disabled women as beautiful objects delivering services free of cost, as commodities of consumption, which interferes with the development of disabled women. Globalization of economy has also played a major role in strengthening patriarchy as it has brought women on the centre stage of the sex market. The testimony to this fact is the increasing number of beauty pageants held even in remote and smaller towns of India. This process has aggravated the marginalization of disabled women as they are considered neither physically beautiful nor sexually marketable. In fact they are considered asexual. Their disability makes them lose the quality of looked-at-ness which the non-disabled women have. It also renders them inefficient, incapable, unwanted and undesirable. However hard they may try the disabled women hardly hold any attraction for anybody in society.

Societal response towards them is of utter neglect and demanding total submission. One can find this negative response in media, which acts not only as the mirror of society but also as a catalyst of change bringing in new ideas, values, and modes of perception in society. In a country like India, where 50 per cent of its population is illiterate, more than the print it is the visual media, which reaches easily, is popular and enjoyed by a wider audience. Even in visual media it is films which have a powerful and long lasting impact on people. Films are an important popular media, reaching out to the educated and uneducated alike. They also sensitize at times allowing one to delve into the psychology of the human characters.

The disabled people and especially women with disabilities are projected in a most unartistic and apathetic manner. Bollywood actors and actresses are not only matinee idols but also icons and role models who are imitated and emulated by the masses. The portrayal of disabled people in Hindi films relegates them to a parasitic dependent existence in society. They are usually the ones who are confined indoors pitying themselves and crying for escape from their dysfunctional physical state. The popular Hindi cinema has always been inspired by Hollywood and, as Madeline Cahill and Martin Norden have observed, like their counterparts reflect the discomfort of society in the company of disabled (*Hollywood's Portrayals of Disabled Women*). In Bollywood too one can conspicuously see the difference in construction of images of disabled men and disabled women. Let us first observe the similarities in both the genders. In both the sexes disability is rarely congenital. It is always acquired later making the acceptance of the difference digestible to the masses. Usually the disability is cured either medically or miraculously in the climax, which brings them back into the mainstream of society. Both lead a dependent life on their families and have seldom anyone to interact with except their immediate kin. They, more or less, belong to the upper strata of society blessed with facilities – medical, financial, educational – which helps in their integration in society. The similarities, however end here. As in Hollywood, in Bollywood films too the images of men with disabilities are more prevalent. In spite of their disability, which might be interfering with their machismo, they are loved and cared for by non-disabled females and above all remain desirable. But the reverse in case of women with disabilities is rare. They are objects of beauty desired and gazed at by mainstream males. This obsession with femininity makes the filmmakers bestow them with impairments, which do not interfere with their looked-at-ness. The disabled women who have severe impairments are always in character roles of mother or sister and seldom in the lead role of the protagonist. A brief analysis of some of the images of disabled women in Bollywood films in contrast to men with disability may be a proof of the way society responds to them.

At the cost of generalizations I would like to make some initial statements that there have been some sensitive portrayals which have aroused sympathies. Films like *Koshish* and *Khamoshi* have successfully portrayed hearing and speech impaired characters and were also successful in sensitizing the masses. However, to begin from the beginning, there are hardly any images worth analyzing as in the 1950s the disabled had a marginal existence. In the 50s films they were portrayed either as beggars or in other marginal roles which were totally inconsequential to the plot of the film. These films however abounded in images of blind mothers who were poor, miserable and were taken care of by their only sons, reliving the myth of sons bringing in salvation and being the caretakers. Disability was simply unacceptable and this made the disabled themselves negate their existence. To cite an example, in 1958 there was a film called *Hum Dono*. It had Dev Anand in a double role. In one of the characters he is portrayed as a disabled war veteran – a situation so unacceptable to him that he asks his own look-alike to present himself as his wife's husband. The fear of rejection by the societal institutions like family force him to lead a self-abnegated life. A situation of being dead is regarded far better and acceptable instead of being only half-alive.

In the 60s there was another film called *Aarzoo* which had jubilee hero Rajendra Kumar, named Gopal, in the lead opposite Sadhna who plays Asha. In an accident Gopal loses one of his legs and he tries to avoid Asha, as he believes his disability would make her life miserable and he will not be acceptable to her as he had been handicapped. Despite being a doctor by profession he regards himself to be of no use to anyone and consequently out of the matrimonial market. In one of the scenes Asha tells Gopal: "*Ek apahij ki zindagi jeene se to maut bhali hai*" (Its better to die than to lead a life as a handicapped person). This statement is reflective of society's perception of disability. She however continues to love him and in order to convince him of her love attempts to get one of her legs amputed. A sacrifice demanded from non-disabled women for disabled men is never reversed. If a woman becomes disabled she is left lamenting on her plight all by herself. There are two issues which could be focussed upon here: the acceptability of disability which is acquired as a result of some accident and acceptability of disabled men by non-disabled women. The concept of *pativrata* (devotion to the husband), concept of ideal love and ideal woman is so ingrained in women that they go on carrying the baggage of tradition and therefore there is an acceptance of men with disabilities without any qualms or quibbles by non-disabled women.

The 70s were the transitional period and one found quite a few impaired women in lead roles in Bollywood – established stars being the pioneers of change. Severe impairments were still the forte of character actresses like Farida Jalal who played the role of wheelchair bound sister of Amitabh Bachchan in *Majboor* or Naaz who has acted as Rajesh Khanna's orthopaedically impaired sister in the film *Sachha Jhoota*. They are no doubt loved but no effort is made to help them to become self-sufficient. In *Sachha Jhoota* Naaz who plays the part of Belu lives in the village with her brother Bhola and stepmother. To escape from step-mom's atrocities Bhola decides to leave for town so that he can earn enough money to marry off his sister. Belu is illiterate but adept at household work. On the death of her mother she comes to the town in search of her brother. Her disability leaves her sexually vulnerable and an attempt is made to violate her modesty but she is saved in the nick of time by Vinod Khanna – a police inspector. He gives shelter to Belu in his home. The Inspector's mother takes a liking to her and decides to arrange her match with her son. But before she decides she asks Belu if her disability was congenital or was it acquired later on. Again a reflection on society's attitude and its obsession with the perfection of human bodies. Had Belu not acquired her disability as a result of an accident and hence potentially curable, perhaps marriage would have eluded her. This again raises the myth of marriage as a means of empowerment of women. Women's empowerment lies in education, in skill and in financial self-sufficiency which is denied to them and even more so to women with disabilities. Custom has rendered such women dependent on their fathers, brothers or husbands – if they have one – for support and "unaccustomed to struggle with difficulty, unacquainted with any resource to supply an independent maintenance they are reduced to depths of wretchedness" (Spender 32).

There were four different films on disabled women and people in the same decade namely *Kinara* which had Hema Malini playing the role of a visually impaired dancer; *Anurag* which had Mausami Chatterjee as visually impaired orphan girl and a good singer in the lead; *Koshish* – a sincere and an honest effort by writer director Gulzar – in which Jaya Bhaduri and Sanjeev Kumar played the lead role of a deaf-mute couple and finally *Imtihaan* in which Tanuja played the part of a locomotor disabled woman. In *Kinara* and *Anurag* one finds the lead disabled women extremely charming, beautiful and bestowed with unusual artistic gifts. They are loved by Jitendra and Vinod Mehra – the male protagonists of the films respectively for reasons other than their disability. Hema Malini is shown acquiring visual impairment as a result of an accident partially a responsibility of the male protagonist who is all the time guilty of being the cause of her disability whereas blindness of Mausami Chatterjee in *Anurag* is cured in the end. For the first time a mainstream commercial film like *Imtihaan* showed the disability of the female protagonist which interfered with her quality of being admired and hence rendered her undesirable. Tanuja, who plays the character of Madhu in the film, walks with a slight limp, though once again she is beauty personified. The protagonist Pramod, played by Vinod Khanna, pities her for her disability and loves her for her extremely good and noble nature which is in sharp contrast to the nature of Bindoo, who plays the character of a vamp. Here again the disability is a result of an accident and not congenital which makes the mainstreaming or integration much more easy. Madhu apart from being beautiful is also a very good painter. Deborah Kent says, "If...a man finds a disabled woman attractive, it is because her disability draws him to her, making her mysterious, heroic or appealingly vulnerable....The disabled woman is often seen from the outset as a victim....Her disability may stand for helplessness, innocence or blighted opportunity" (*Women and Disability* 15). Disabled woman, thus, cannot be average, moderate, independent or an underachiever. She is always good to look at or she has no place in mainstream cinema. *Koshish* is a pioneering, sensitive and true to life portrayal of a speech and hearing impaired couple who are shown leading normal lives, with their struggles, desires and interactions with the non-disabled people. The film is a deviation from the run-of-the mill stuff of commercial crass. However, here too the disabled father is shown as imposing his will upon his non-disabled son whom he forces to marry a girl with hearing and speech impairment. The resistance on the part of the son and ultimate surrender to his father's will suggests the sham in society whereby even the sufferers or caregivers who are non-disabled find it difficult to accept persons with disabilities in their lives. Here he wishes to draw his non-disabled son into the world of the disabled by imposing this marriage on him. In spite of having close encounters with the disabled in their immediate family the non-disabled refuse to develop any sensitivity or empathy towards them and the disabled are forced to lead a life of seclusion.

In the 1980s there were two remarkable films on disability – *Naache Mayuri* and *Sparsh* – one being a commercial venture and the other belonging to parallel cinema. *Naache Mayuri* is based on the real life struggle of a Bharatnatyam dancer Sudha Chandran who, having lost one leg in an accident, achieved heights of glory in her chosen field with the help of an artificial limb thanks to her grit and passion. She herself acted the part of Sudha. In the film as soon as Sudha acquires disability her lover Shekhar shuns her, as he could not carry her burden for life. On the other hand there is *Sparsh* which has Nasiruddin Shah playing the character of a visually impaired principal of a Blind School. He is fiercely independent, highly educated and despises any display of pity. Shabana Azmi – a non-disabled teacher – working in his school, loves him. The two films suggest a contrast in male and female projections of disability in mainstream and parallel cinema and give a cue as to what is expected of women in society. A woman sans disability accepts disabled men without any qualms but the non-disabled men hardly have any compunction in rejecting women with impairments. These films further project that women are handmaidens. Their traditional role is that of service delivery for which there is no remuneration paid to them. If women become or are disabled their utility is reduced. Their selfhood is not realized i.e. society fails to regard them as persons and being women and that too disabled, requires them to be totally submissive.

It would be worthwhile to analyse here another 80s film *Barsaat Ki Ek Raat* which had Rakhi in the lead playing the character of a visually challenged woman. Her portrayal highlights the strengths of disabled women but at the same time reinforce the images which are a result of cultural myths. She is not financially independent but has expertize in all household jobs – she can cook, stitch, clean, do gardening in addition to being very charming. This makes her sexually vulnerable and desirable too. An attempted rape leaves her with a sense of guilt, blaming herself and suffering from a kind of victim syndrome. Inspector Anniruddh played by Amitabh Bachchan, proposes to marry her but she refuses at first for two reasons – firstly she has begun to consider herself sullied and secondly she feels that owing to her disability she will not be able to perform her traditional role of a housewife, of giving services to the husband. To quote Alice Walker, what she wrote about black women in her book *In Search of Our Mothers Gardens: Womanist Prose* is equally applicable to disabled women:

> Creatures so abused and mutilated in body so dimmed and confused by pain, that they considered themselves unworthy even of hope...they dreamed dreams that no one knew – not even themselves, in any coherent fashion – and saw visions no one could understand
>
> (Walker: 232)

But ultimately she accepts marriage and confers the status of God or an angel on her husband. Her portrayal signifies loss of self-esteem and also a confusion as to how she can best represent herself. The relationship then rests on inequality and loses the charm of mutual respect which is a pre-condition of any marital bond. Women in general are "caught in a world structured by man centered concepts" (Jones 359) and for disabled women it is all the more difficult to free themselves. The cultural values do not permit them to treat themselves at par with non-disabled men and thus shun all avenues of "individualizing their self" (Kannan 12).

One finds the process of disabled men being adored by non-disabled women or disabled women rejecting their lovers and pitying themselves being repeated in the 90s films. They have disabled men in abundance but disabled women are a rarity. For example we have Sanjay Dutt – a polio affected person – in *Saajan* loved by Madhuri, Rishi Kapoor in *Chandni* – a wheelchair user suffering from spinal cord injury, loved by Sridevi, but is subsequently cured, Sanjay Dutt again as a visually impaired person in *Dushman* and Mohnish Behl with his upper left limb impaired loved and married to Tabu in *Hum Saath Saath Hain.* They are all desired in spite of their disability – whether congenital or acquired at some later stage in life.

The year 1996 and 1999 had a film each on disability, which had a commercially viable starcast – *Khamoshi* and *Mann* – yet both failed to excite the masses and the experimentation of bringing the disabled centrestage ended in a fiasco. *Khamoshi* is a sensitive portrayal of a deaf-mute couple played by Nana Patekar and Seema Biswas. They are shown languishing in their own silent world and as misfits in the world of hearing people. Their only contact with the outside world is through their non-disabled daughter Anne played by Manisha Koirala. The world/society is indifferent to them and they are indifferent to the world – leading an isolated life. Like the couple in *Koshish* this couple is also shown imposing upon their daughter Anne and creating obstacles in the fulfillment of her dreams and ambitions. She feels that her dreams are impossible as with disabled parents they can never be realized. But at the same time the film has been successful in sensitizing the society. It is an attempt to project a human issue and has allowed one to see the psychology of a disabled person, as to how they survive in a world which is not ready to understand and empathize with them. They are possessive of their daughter having lost one of their children as they could not save him in times of crisis due to their hearing impairment. The child kept screaming for help and ultimately died. In order to prevent such a mishap from occurring again their daughter becomes their voice and shield.

Mann is a love story of Dev and Priya played by Aamir Khan and Manisha Koirala. In the film Priya meets with an accident and loses both her lower limbs. Like the 60s film *Aarzoo* or the 80s film *Barsaat Ki Ek Raat* she too finds herself unfit for love or marriage and feels she would be a liability on Dev owing to her disability. But Dev listens to his *mann*/heart and accepts her in spite of her disability. Again a male stereotypical image has been projected. Dev would not have fallen in love with Priya had she suffered from a congenital disability. Such a disability would have left her on the periphery of society. But because she was already a part of mainstream life prior to acquiring the disability it was possible to integrate/ bring her back to it. Here the behaviour of disabled woman is also questionable. She, "herself often strives to raise doubts in the mind of her lover. If she truly loves him, she must protect her man from taking on an intolerable burden. At the same time, in testing a man's commitment she is attempting to protect herself from the pain of future rejection" (Kent 14).

It is these negative images which go a long way in the formation of attitudes towards disabled women. The abilities of disabled women are rarely projected. Disability, in most of the films, is either ridiculed and made fun of in comedies or is pitied and patronized. Disabled are shown as vulnerable and at the same time undesirable which makes their integration in the mainstream world impossible. They have never been projected as economically self-sufficient or fending for themselves and making a positive contribution to the family purse. Indeed it is this aspect which helps in giving them a status at par with their non-disabled counterparts, who again lead a dependent life. Indian Committee on the Status of Women had established that "in order to release women from their dependent and unequal status, improvement of their employment opportunities and earning power has to be given highest priority" (Mitra 30-31). This is equally applicable to women with disabilities whose empowerment lies in their financial self-sufficiency which, in turn, would help them in making a shift from cultural and traditional bonds and they must be projected as such in all forms of media.

References

Baquer, Ali and Anjali Sharma. *Disability: Challenges Vs. Responses.* New Delhi. CAN, 1997.

Boylan, Esther. *Women and Disability.* London: Zed Books Ltd., 1991.

Cahill, Madeline and Martin Norden. *Hollywood's Portrayals of Disabled Women.* New York. (Unpublished)

Hesse, Mary Chinery. *Women and Disability.* Ed. Esther Boylan London: Zed Books Ltd., 1991.

Jones, Rosalind Ann. "Writing the Body: Toward an Understanding of *l'ecriture feminine*". *Feminisms.* Eds. Robyn R. Warhol and Diane Price. New Brunswick: Rutgers University Press, 1991.

Kannan, Laxmi. "To Grow or Not to Grow: That is the Question for Women". *Critical Practice,* Volume VII, No.2, June 2000 pp. 9-18

Kent, Deborah. "Disabled Women: Portraits in Fiction and Drama". *Women and Disability.* Ed. Esther Boylan. London: Zed Books Ltd., 1991.

Mitra, Jyoti. *Women and Society: Equality and Empowerment.* New Delhi: Kanishka Publishers, 1997.

Mohit, Anuradha. A Report on "The End of Long Silence". *National Conference of Disabled Women.* New Delhi. NAB-CBR Network, 1996.

Patel, K.A. *Women and Sustainable Development: An International Dimension.* New Delhi: Ashish Publishing House, 1995.

Spender, Dale, ed. *Living by the Pen: Early British Women Writers.* New York and London: Teachers College Press, 1992.

Walker, Alice. *In Search of Our Mother's Gardens: Womanist Prose.* London: Harcourt Brace Jovanovich Publishers, 1983.

7 Muslim Women's Identity: On the Margins of the Nation

Supriya Agarwal

On viewing the mainstream Hindi cinema between 1970-1990 we observe that despite the difference in approach and theoretical framework, the female protagonist is not projected from the woman's point of view and her role is projected through stereotypes as that of a woman as child, whore, wife, mother, vamp etc. The cinema presents women as an object of male desire and potential possession. Equally significant is the deification of women in certain social roles; the pure virgin, the loyal and obedient wife, the mother and on the other side the 'Pakeezah' prostitute. While woman is regarded as the moral guardian of the family and community, her moral strength is clearly not enough to protect her from the pitfalls of society. The chief characteristic of a female is her exploitability which in the opinion of the traditionalists has to be protected by the strength of the male.

In such circumstances when we view the projection of the Muslim women in Hindi cinema, we find that they stand doubly marginalized. First as women and secondly as members of a minority community which finds less representation on the whole. It is from this perspective that we seek to study the representation of Muslim women in the commercial cinema.

My study is mainly based on an analysis of the four films which have been most popular in the subcategory of Muslim-centred films – *Pakeezah* (1971), *Nikaah* (1982), *Bazaar* (1982) and *Umrao Jaan* (1982). In these films we notice that the female protagonists enjoy a key position as far as their roles are concerned, they are the central figures around whom the story revolves but what needs to be looked at is their identity as women. We realize that a secondary position is imposed on them by strong environmental forces of society which are under the control of men. They are on the margins both of society and destiny, placed in stereotyped slots with very little left to their choice. Such portrayal of women is applicable not only to the Indian cinema but throughout the world. Christine Glendhill in her essay *Recent Development in Feminist Criticism* remarks:

> A crucial issue of Feminist film criticism is the examination of the fact that "Women as women" are not represented in the cinema, that they do not have a voice, that the female point of view is not heard. Recognition of this fact unites all attempts at a Feminist critique of the cinema. (251)

Despite the prejudiced portrayal of women, this cinema is popular because it constantly poses question to the audience, especially those belonging to the lower middle classes and the process of questioning is carried out at multiple levels – through characterization, the narrative cinematic techniques used and through the different familial, religious, political and sexist modes. To ensure audience identification some injustice, exploitation and suffering is worked into the framework of the films taken up for discussion. It is noticeable that despite the pre-dominance of nawaabs and begums, the female protagonists have humble origins. In *Pakeezah* both the mother and the daughter are forced by circumstances to become prostitutes. In *Umrao Jaan*, Amirun belongs to a poor family, is kidnapped and sold in the flesh market, in *Nikaah* Niloufer belongs to an average middle class family, gets married to a nawab but is promptly divorced and in *Bazaar* both Najma and Shabnam are so poor that even their family members are willing to sell them to the highest bidder. Thus we see that not only is the female protagonist located within the subaltern class but she is also shown to have been wronged by society and suffers a great deal both emotionally and psychologically. In *Pakeezah* Nargis rejected and humiliated by her fiance's family had to spend the rest of her life in solitude. Sahibjaan is also abused and is not accepted by society. In *Umrao Jaan* Amirun who could not get a respectable status, is turned out of her parent's house by her own brother and finally has to come back to the life of the brothel. Niloufer in *Nikaah* is also portrayed as a helpless wife getting bored and yearning for understanding. In *Bazaar* Shabnam's innocent love is thwarted and she is then forced to marry an old man, resorting to take her own life to escape more misery. When Najma's own parents propose to sell her, she escapes by running away from home to marry the man she loves but has to reconcile by being his mistress.

Although the origins are humble and the misfortune and suffering intense, yet the female protagonists are not portrayed as completely supine. They because of their beauty, affection and morality are able to win the hearts of men and wield considerable power over them because of their personal personality traits. Men are shown falling in love with these heroines, even if this love is motivated by desire. What is noticeable in these films is that the protagonist who is wronged and oppressed by society, gathers courage and strength to raise her voice against oppression though it is another thing that soon she is projected as unable to continue the revolt and has to yield to various societal pressures. Discussing such an image of women, Fareed Kazmi in her essay "Muslim Social and the Female Protagonist" remarks:

> It is this image which helps in interpellating the audience, especially those women who belong to the subaltern classes and

> see in them a role model that they would like to emulate but cannot, because of their oppressive existential situation. In other words, this rebellious posturing of the female protagonists helps define and articulate the innermost desires of these women. (233)

When we understand and analyse the deeper structure of these films we find that the masses in general get a different message from these films. The woman projected as victim, tries to struggle but fails and is accepted only when she is ready to fit into the graded hierarchical social system and thereby reinforce the inequitable gender relation which they seem to be attacking. Rather than pose a challenge to the system, they help to strengthen it. Her role of self sacrifice is appreciated by the masses in general and any sort of assertion or rebellion by the protagonist is viewed grimly. The daughter who refuses to marry the man of her parents' choice is liable to be locked up, beaten and flung about the room without any shock being inflicted on public opinion. In these films the feminine is not juxtaposed with the masculine but is treated as a subculture. Their roles are pushed into the language and category of the victim and oppressed.

The story of these films is guided by middle class value structures about sex and respectability. Males are masters of themselves while the female protagonist is cast in a fixed canon. Women are seen and presented from the male point of view. They cannot have a respectable identity without being under the shelter of men, as daughter, wife or mother. So, if a woman in Indian films is dislocated from a family, she is fitted into the role of a courtesan or a prostitute. Umrao Jaan and Sahib Jaan gain popularity for their beauty and talent for dancing and singing but for the rest they have no identity. John Berger in his work *Ways of Seeing* points out that the social presence of a woman is different from that of a man, "While men act, women appear, while men survey, women are surveyed. Men look at women, women watch themselves being looked at. Thus woman becomes an object, an object of vision, a sight to be seen" (112).

In all the four films focused on, it is the men who are instrumental in deciding the fate of the women and the vulnerability of the weaker sex is stressed. Sagar Sarhadi's film *Bazaar* is a little different from the mainstream commercial film as it presents the plight of the women through their silence and eloquence of feelings and emotions. The film also gives the message that individuality can be gained only through economic independence.. Though the meaning lies enclosed and camouflaged, the film seeks to express that which has been submerged and suppressed. The focus on such social and feminine issues needs to move outside cultural and disciplinary boundaries. Films like *Bombay*, *Zakham* and *Fiza* concern themselves with the historical construction of Hindu and Muslim identities in India and the transformation of these identities in the colonial and postcolonial periods in the context of the rise of nationalism. Space and territory are the central elements in religious nationalism but the films I have taken up are more of Muslim socials which have posed more or less, the problems of the Muslim women's identity on the margins of the nation. As Peter van der Veer has discussed in his work, *Religious Nationalism, Hindus and Muslims in India,* "the nation is often imagined as a brotherhood of men protecting their women folk. Men are portrayed as strong and powerful, women as weak and powerless. But protection also implies the exertion of male authority to which women have to submit" (85).

The complexities and the ambiguities of religious discourse on femininity and the female body also need to be taken into account. Here comes the image of the purdah, as projected in the films taken up, where the stress is always on the physical beauty of the female protagonist and therefore on the veil which hides that beauty. The veil gives a certain kind of romance to the woman and hides what all men desperately want to see. The lifting of the veil therefore has many other connotations. It professes freedom, and demarcates the confines, and outlines the margins. These are the margins which confer anonymity and erase selfhood, the margins which limit and stultify and annihilate"(vii). In fact multifarious veiling devices are used in the social films to constantly forge new linkages, through the medium of plot organization and through verbal and structural patterns.

In the films, the female protagonist is presented more as an isolated, glamorous, sexualized object on display. In their traditional exhibitionist role women are simultaneously looked at and displayed, with their appearance coded for strong visual and erotic impact. As Laura Mulvey in her work *Visual Pleasure and Narrative Cinema* has analysed,

> There are two contradictory aspects of the pleasurable structure of "looking" in the conventional cinematic situation. The first developed through narcissism and the constitution of the ego, comes, from identification with the protagonist. The second scopophillic, arises from pleasure in using another person as an object of sexual stimulation through sight. In film term it implies a separation of the erotic identity of the subject from the object on the screen. In a world ordered by sexual imbalance, pleasure in looking has been split between active male and passive female. (218)

For Umrao Jaan and Sahib Jaan their profession is such that they have to perform before men. But as the narrative progresses they fall in love with the male protagonists and become their property and the men assert their right on them by fighting or by paying a large sum of money, which is approved by the general audience as an act of benevolence. A woman's desire to be possessed by a man and her emotional dependence on him has been focused on. The contest is also between domesticity and prostitution. In *Bazaar* both the heroines crave for fulfilment of their love and marriage with the men of their heart. B.R. Chopra's *Nikaah* also portrays the helplessness and dependency of the female protagonist on men who accept and reject her at their will. While trying to understand the married status of Niloufer, I couldn't help recalling Simone de Beauvoir's work *The Second Sex,* wherein she comments:

> The only difference between women who sell themselves in prostitution and those who sell themselves in marriage is in the price and length of time the contract runs. For both the sexual act is a service, the one is hired for life by one man, the other has several clients who pay her by the piece. The one is protected by one male against all others, the other is defended by all against the exclusive tyranny of each. (569)

The female protagonists in these films although portrayed by well-defined speech, dress, appearance, social and religious practice, we notice that real-life-like men and women with different class positions, social backgrounds and individual dispositions are ignored. The women characters are treated more in terms of abstractions and the basic projection centres round the need to be loved and accepted. The protagonist is subordinated both as a woman and as a Muslim, within the family and in society. A woman has to face many social prejudices, orthodoxies and beliefs, yet none of these problems are articulated or challenged in the films under discussion. Besides we observe that there is a basic dichotomy between the overt and the deep structure. To formulate a counter-hegemonic feminist discourse it is necessary to locate the problems within the temporal and spatial realities of the average Muslim woman's world with a stronger sensibility and a sharper perceptibility of the viewer, which somehow has not happened so far.

References

Berger, John. *Ways of Seeing.* Harmondsworth: Penguin, 1985.

Christine, Gledhill. "Recent Developments in Feminist Criticism". *Film Theory and Criticism.* Eds. Leo Braudy and Marshall Cohen; New York: Oxford University Press (1974), 1999.

de Beauvoir, Simone. *The Second Sex.* (1953), London: Vintage, 1997.

Jain, Jasbir and Amina Amin, eds. *Margins of Erasure.* New Delhi: Sterling, 1995.

Kazmi, Fareed. "Muslim Socials and the Female Progagonist: Seeing a dominant discourse at 'work'." *Forging Identities: Gender, Communities and the State.* Ed. Zoya Hasan, New Delhi: Kali for Women, 1994.

Mulvey, Laura. "Visual Pleasure and Narrative Cinema". *Screen,* Vol. 16 No. 3 London University Press, 1986.

Veer, Peter van der. *Religious Nationalism: Hindus and Muslims in India.* Oxford University Press: New Delhi, 1999.

8 Towards the Radicalization of the Indian Family

Veena Singh

With the release of *Masoom* in 1982, which did quite well at the box office, a new note was struck in the history of Hindi cinema. Prior to this, the films that made to the box office were primarily films either with a religious theme *(Jai Santoshi Maa)* or films portraying some event from history *(Rani Roopmati, Jahanara, Taj Mahal, Mughal-e-Azam)*. However, films with social themes also drew great crowds. Some of the films had themes like division of property *(Sansar, Avatar)*, dowry *(Shubhkaamnaein)*, untouchability *(Sujata)*, tussle between generations (*Kal, Aaj aur Kal*), or class disparity (*Julie, Bobby, Do Aankhen Barah Haath*). In addition to these, some films which were love stories also have been very popular. To name a few: *Sangam, Amar Prem, Kati Patang, Ankhiyon Ke Jharoke Se, Ek Duje Ke Liye.*

But *Masoom* is a film which deals with the issue of a child born outside marriage. Its uniqueness lies not so much in the subject as in the originality of its treatment. Earlier, in the late 50s, *Dhool Ka Phool* and later on *Dharamputra* dealt with the same issue but in these more than illegitimacy, the ideals of secularism and humanism were highlighted.

For the purpose of this paper I have selected four films, *Masoom, Kabhi-Kabhi, Sajan Ki Saheli* and *Rehaee* as the narratives of these films highlight a social problem – the acceptability of a child born out of wedlock but each film problematizes it differently. If in *Kabhi-Kabhi* wifehood is foregrounded, in *Sajan Ki Saheli* it is the concept of motherhood and how tradition defines it. The four films interrogate how the Indian family is undergoing a change. The obvious transforma- tion from a joint family to a nuclear family is not the only change but psychological and emotional changes shaping the human being affect the joint family, nature of sexuality and moral values as well. Till now, the threat to a family has been perceived as coming from the entry of a new member especially a daughter-in-law. But now the aberrant sexual act is also seen as a threat.

After the rise of feminism in the 70s there has been a noticeable departure from the old orthodox way of looking at the question of illegitimacy. In the earlier films the illegitimate child was either abandoned, left to the mercy of nature or given away to an *ayah* for fear of social stigma but *Kabhi-Kabhi* released in 1975 is perhaps one of the first movies which looks squarely at this social problem. But as *Masoom* which came five years after the release of *Kabhi-Kabhi* projects the issue more sharply, I intend to take it up first.

This is how the film *Masoom* begins: a hospital room with a female patient who has consumed an overdose of sleeping pills (the reason being the other woman in her husband's life) is being consoled and comforted by Indu and Chanda (Shabana and Tanuja). But immediately the focus shifts to a happy family – D.K. Malhotra (Nasseruddin Shah), Indu and their two daughters.

Ironically, soon after this D.K. is informed about his illegitimate son, who ultimately comes to live with him since the mother, Bhawana (Supriya Pathak), is no more. The coming of this child, Rahul, to live with the legally wedded wife of his father and their children brings into focus several issues: (a) the issue of relationships – extra-marital and between husband and wife; (b) the woman as mother and as wife; (c) and the importance of a male child in the Hindu family.

Fidelity is the basis of every relationship, specially marriage. The presence of the child Rahul, born outside marriage is a symbol of breach of faith and trust. By way of part confession, part explanation and part self justification D.K. tells Indu that his relationship with Bhawana was a very transient one. He had met Bhawana when he went to Nainital for an Old Boys' function. Bhawana was very lonely, sad and depressed. Flashbacks show D.K. and Bhawana amidst the scenic beauty going out together and getting drawn into a romantic relationship. On D.K.'s part, the relationship is primarily a carnal one, devoid of any emotional involvement. The marked difference that D.K. has set between his physical self and his emotional self becomes evident as the film unfolds itself. One notices how, when in Nainital his holiday mood included having sex with a stranger but once with his family the memory of Nainital is perhaps erased till brought back by the school master's telegram. Later when Rahul is with the family, D.K.'s conflict is how to absorb the child in his family without disturbing the family happiness.

Rahul's entry into their lives disrupts the husband-wife relationship. Indu's faith in her husband and in her marriage gets a rude jolt. In her words "*Mujhe tum par aitbaar nahin raha*" (I no longer have faith in you), and in a conversation with her friend, Chanda, she observes how unstable and fragile relationships can be, as a relationship can be established both within and outside marriage. Indu resorts to a daily dose of sleeping pills as the conjugal harmony is broken. She forbids her husband from touching her and when her husband tries to talk to her she either goes up to her room or comes downstairs.

Acceptance of Rahul by D.K. is not so much of a problem, for he is his son but for Indu he is the "other woman's" son. He is the symbol of her husband's disloyalty and infidelity towards her and her children; an affront to her self-respect as a wife. D.K.'s faithlessness is also an indication that Indu's role as a wife is minimized. The husband is free to have a son through another relationship. Although Rahul's arrival punctures the marital harmony yet Indu, for the sake of her children and the integrity of the family, acts with great restraint and decorum.

Indu, however, distinctly demarcates the area of inclusion and exclusion where Rahul is concerned. On his arrival his baggage is put in the study and when the elder daughter resents this, she comforts her saying that it is a matter of a few days only. For her Rahul is an unwelcome guest. The wife in her is so violent that she is totally indifferent to the demands and needs of childhood especially of a child like Rahul whose anchors are all gone. For instance, at the dining table she gets up and goes away without eating when Rahul sits next to her. She serves food to her two daughters but does not serve Rahul. In this film and also in *Kabhi-Kabhi*, the dining table image has been used as a symbol with added significance, for it is a token of order and concord in the family. It also stands for celebration and reunion. At another time when Rahul talks to her she curtly stops him and goes upstairs to her room. On her birthday she is happy when her children come to wish her in the morning. Just as she is responding to her husband's greetings, she sees Rahul through the half open door and she at once withdraws, for Rahul is a painful reminder of her husband's infidelity. But when Indu is alone she silently admires and appreciates the wooden box that Rahul has made for her birthday. Once, at night, she tiptoes into Rahul's room and draws a quilt over him but the sight of the photographs of Rahul and his mother agitate her. She rushes back to her room, throws the box and asks D.K. to take the child away. On another occasion when Rahul calls her "Mummy" she retorts, "I am not your Mummy".

However, it is not her hatred for the child which forces her to behave in this manner. In fact it is a manifestation of her protest against the male-defined environment and values. No wonder she says, "*to jo man mein aayega, karoge? Meri bhi feelings hai*". (So you will do what you feel like? I too, have feelings). Thus while emphasizing the idea of individual's feelings and the worth of the individual she is also articulating the idea that the existing ideological and social constraints are questionable.

As a woman, no doubt, Indu resents Rahul's presence but the mother in her wins over the woman. Rahul then acquires an identity of his own and is no longer merely the "other woman's" son. On the morning, when Rahul is missing from the house, she is visibly upset and frantically looks for him in and around the house. On his return she scolds him saying that children are kidnapped and should anything happen to him what would they do? This is the moment when the mother supercedes the woman, the human problem transcends sexual limits and the other woman's existence or connection with her husband recedes into the background. Also Chanda's return to her husband and son acts as a catalyst. These feelings are further reinforced in her, when in the taxi, while going to drop her daughters to the school, Indu notices Rahul's parting gift, his drawing book, with Mini. While flipping through its pages, she notices how the child had drawn the family picture including himself, but then scratched his figure out. This and the love that has developed between her daughters and Rahul help dissolve the tension and lead her to accept Rahul.

The two daughters' acceptance of Rahul is instant, though the elder daughter had initially resented a guest in her study. Rahul helps her with her homework, makes a wooden box and soon a deep intimacy and the bond of kinship is established. "Rahul bhaiya" becomes a part of everything the daughters do, plan or celebrate.

The last scene of the film shows Indu, the two daughters, Rahul and D.K. in the car. This is also the first time in the film, that all are shown together as a family, looking happy, ready to drive back home – literally and symbolically with D.K. in the driver's seat. Indu's acceptance of Rahul raises her in stature, for, had she been a barren woman accepting the "other woman's" child would not have been a big deal but to accept Rahul in the present circumstances does mark her out.

If one recollects the beginning of the film one would realize that the background for Rahul's acceptance has already been built. The first time we meet D.K.'s family, the talk is about a male child – if Mini had not been Mini "Munna hota", "bhaiya hota". Indu playfully pointing to her husband says, she has a son. D.K.'s reply is "but I don't". Thus the psychological desire for a male child and the importance of a male child in a family is hinted at. According to the Hindu scriptures when a man begets a son he is a complete man and also *moksha* is obtained through a son. Amongst the Hindus, marriage is necessary because the continuity of the family line is very important and essential and this continuity depends on the male child, as a daughter is considered to be "*paraya dhan*" (another's property).

But unlike *Masoom* in both *Kabhi-Kabhi* and *Sajan ki Saheli* the illegitimate child is a female and in both these films, it is the woman who has had a pre-marital relationship. Anju (Waheeda Rehman) in *Kabhi-Kabhi* and Kunti (Nutan) in *Sajan ki Saheli* do not disclose the truth about their failed love affairs and their pre-nuptial motherhood to their husbands till it becomes imperative for them. The question then is, does the past matter? How much does it matter?

For both Kunti and Anju it is the societal compulsions that act as deterrents. Our society follows two models of behaviour, one for men and the other framed for women. Under the traditional culture a woman is given no space between sexual maturity and pre-marriage. For her, sex outside marriage is a sin. She is expected to enter marriage as a virgin but if the pre-nuptial chastity is lost and especially if she has borne a child it becomes a source of great danger and a threat to her later life and such a woman is branded as a "soiled woman" *(kalankini)*. Both, Anju and Kunti do not meet this demand of virginity in the woman and thus have to hide the truth.

The illegitimate daughter Pinki's (Neetu Singh) arrival on the scene threatens Anju's social status as a wife. As a consequence she neither acknowledges her illegitimate daughter nor allows her to address her as "Mummy". The age old image of revered and ideal women like Sita and Sati Savitri upon which the Hindu female psyche has been fed, have taught Anju the denial of selfhood. She runs away from herself and distances herself from her guilt. Although Anju explicitly does not acknowledge or shower her motherly affection on Pinki, yet there are gestures suggestive of her maternal love for her illegitimate daughter. For instance, she makes Pinki sit at Sweetie's place at the dining table much to the chagrin of both father (Amitabh) and daughter (Sweetie) or during the match she encourages Pinki while her husband cheers their daughter, Sweetie. Perhaps the helpless woman can dare to do no more than this. Ultimately when she accepts the truth, her husband angrily refers to it as 'paap' (sin) but ironically Anju does not question her husband when she comes to know of his past.

Amit in fact secretly feeds himself on his past memories, it is not surprising that his house is called "Atit" (past). His family environment is stiff and cold sans companionship. He is not a lover to his wife but merely a lawfully wedded husband. The film *Kabhi-Kabhi* begins with Amit (a poet) and Pooja's (Rakhi) love affair. Amit is depicted as a romantic lover but does not approach Pooja's parents when they arrange a match for her. Later when he confronts Pooja and her husband (Shashi Kapoor) he talks of the 'intense pain' *(kasak, dard)* that he has nurtured in his heart and the sacrifice he has made in love. Would it be wrong to say that he had been more in love with the idea of love than in love! Amit's kind of passive romanticism is perhaps a subject for ridicule and the whole idea of romance has been critiqued in this film.

Amit, in words and deeds lives for his daughter alone and the love situation in which his daughter Sweetie is caught (falling for the same boy Rishi Kapoor, who loves Pinki) is an eye-opener for him. It is after this that for the first time he fondly thinks of his wife. Memories that had imprisoned him are all gone. He accepts Anju's daughter only after his own daughter has made peace with Pinki and has accepted her.

Anju's predicament poses the question, what does marriage imply? Is it only being a mother or only being a wife? The dilemma faced by the foster parents of Pinki, Dr. Shobha and her husband (Simi Grewal and Parikshit Sahni), whether or not to disclose the truth about Pinki's birth to her prospective in-laws when she decides to marry her lover (Rishi Kapoor) also brings up the question of the legitimacy of a parental legacy for a woman.

Like *Kabhi-Kabhi*, in *Sajan ki Saheli* also Kunti's lover is a poet and in this film also, love neither culminates into marriage nor in a lasting relationship. But unlike *Kabhi-Kabhi* the husband, Avinash (Rajendra Kumar) is a very sensitive and a caring husband. It is in fact, the wife (Kunti) who has a materialistic bent of mind. To her a big car, a bungalow and other luxuries matter and these concerns are perhaps her reason for marrying Avinash. Throughout the film Kunti and Avinash, on most occasions are shown arguing, talking, standing against the backdrop of a life size poster of them together. The poster underlines the meaning of marriage.

For Kunti, the life of an Indian woman begins after marriage – an implication that a woman's past is to be cut off, buried and forgotten lest it should hamper and dampen her married life. She once says that to save her home she would do anything. Little wonder then that she not for a moment suspects that Munmun (Rekha) who pretends to be someone else's illegitimate child could be her illegitimate daughter. On the contrary, she hurls abuses on Munmun calling her "*paap ki aulad*" (born in sin) "*kichard se sane*" (littered with filth) "*ma kalankini*" (mother with a bad reputation) which are but echoes of the patriarchal system. On the other hand Avinash accepts Munmun at once.

In Avinash (who knows fully well that Munmun is his wife's illegitimate daughter) the paternal feelings are ready, waiting for a recipient as he has no children of his own. Thus his acceptance of Munmun comes very swiftly and smoothly. Both Avinash and Munmun pretend to be lovers in order to arouse maternal feelings in Kunti. When the truth about Munmun dawns on Kunti she confesses to Avinash, "I am a woman, I am weak. I hid the truth for fear of losing you".

In both *Kabhi-Kabhi* and *Sajan ki Saheli* the illegitimate daughters, Pinki and Munmun, have to struggle very hard to reach out to their mothers but the fear of society and conformity to the traditional norms compel the two mothers to be unmotherly. What the society wants is juxtaposed to what an individual wants. For both Anju and Kunti, the moral issue takes a hold over their lives and the individual's desires are pushed back and suppressed. In both these films fidelity is not the question as both the women, Anju and Kunti, have been faithful in their marriages. It is their past which threatens the peace of their homes. Whereas in *Masoom* in spite of violation of fidelity by D.K. (as his is an extra-marital affair) the question of faithlessness is nowhere focused upon in the film. In fact, during the cricket match D.K. with fatherly pride applauds Rahul's game. A woman has limited choices. She can either resort to sleeping pills or kill herself or silently announce to herself the severance of links with the past. The three films are very much gendered. No doubt, in these the rehabilitation of an illegitimate child into the family is a step forward but tradition is reinforced despite images of radicalism. There is still no breaking away from the belief of the docile body and women as objects and subjects.

But *Rehaee*, released in 1988, treats the subject a little differently by presenting an alternative image of a woman. The story hinges around a change from silent endurance to expression of the self which changes the status of women from submission to equality. In this film prospects of employment drive most of the menfolk to urban areas, leaving behind their wives and children. Very meaningfully, the position of the wives in the village is juxtaposed with their men in the city. The men visit brothels to satisfy their physical urges and some return home with venereal disease.

In the village, some women like Sukki (Neena Gupta) and Takoo (Hema Malini) have extra-marital relationships and as a consequence get pregnant. For Takoo, love is what gives happiness and her relationship with Mansu (Naseeruddin Shah) gives her this happiness while her husband is away. If a woman like Sukki aborts out of fear of her husband: a woman like Takoo insists on having the child as it is her baby – her flesh and blood, in spite of her husband Amarji's (Vinod Khanna) insistence to terminate the pregnancy. His assertion that he is the provider and his order to abort should be carried out, only makes Takkoo more resolute. She tells Amarji, if she is the cause of his embarrassment, he need not talk to her.

During the panchayat meeting, Roopji (Mohan Agashe) whose first wife has been burnt alive by him (because of an aberration ending in pregnancy) insists that Takoo must pay for her 'sin' because a woman cannot thrust her '*paap*' on her husband and also that, punishment to Takoo will act as a deterrent for the other village women. No doubt, for Takoo, all this has been a most trying experience, but she is neither exhausted nor crestfallen. She does not succumb to the woman's legacy of pain and submission. In the panchayat, Takoo does not defend herself presumably for she does not owe an explanation to anyone. However, an elderly woman stands up and speaks fervently in support of women. This is perhaps for the first time in the Hindi films that the sisterly solidarity – a bond of shared experience – of women is foregrounded.

Once again questions like, what is marriage? What are masculinity and feminity? How is *maryada* defined? What *is paap?* are tacitly raised. Takoo provides a different example of a woman who recognizes her right to her body. Through Takoo and the elderly lady, the film highlights the fact that women need love and support for they are also human beings and that the male dominated society should be fair to them. In this their sexuality is also recognized. If the man-made society requires them to be like *Sita*, men better be like *Ram*.

It is Takoo's integrity of character and moral courage that makes her tell her husband that a woman does not want the freedom to sleep with men but it is a woman's legitimate right to bear a child, the right that nature has gifted her with. A woman thus, has a right over her child: it is her flesh and blood, therefore it is her decision to keep it or not. Takoo thus shatters the male canons which construct, ascribe and prescribe roles for women. She refuses to suffer the fate of a woman's lot like the other women and fulfills a need for feminist freedom thus shouldering the responsibility of her action and rendering the father irrelevant. Briefly the body is freed from the mind and physical love, bodily pleasure and emotional love are separated.

Ultimately Amarji (Vinod Khanna) is moved by her reasoning to realize that the acceptance of Takoo and her unborn child is the only rational solution to the crisis in his family. Like Lord Shankara he too should take the good with the evil for this is true manliness. Obliquely it is also a realization of the inadequacy of the social system.

Undoubtedly in *Rehaee* the question of acceptability of an illegitimate child is approached in a very radical manner but the fact remains that the characters are all villagers belonging to the working class, whose concept of morality is different from the moral concept of the middle class people. Also, one cannot overlook the prediction of the astrologer about a male child. Although in the film this is not further developed, Takoo is happy to hear this forecast. Is then Takoo's determination not to abort her child also because of this thought that perhaps lies embedded in her subconscious mind? The conventional idea of the significance of a male child is certainly a step backward, but the issue of the right to the body is so strongly projected in the film that it overshadows everything else. Another film which needs mention in this sequence is *Kya Kehna* released in 2000. Here again the woman Priya (Preity Zinta) refuses to get her pregnancy terminated on the ground that it is her child, even when her lover Rahul (Saif Ali Khan) refuses to marry her because of class disparity. Betrayal by Rahul makes the muted female self of Priya speak out. Ultimately Rahul repents and offers marriage to her but is rejected, for Priya does not respect him. Priya's acceptance of another friend, Ajay (Chandrachud Singh) as a husband, who has not only been a support throughout, but who has appreciated her strength and dignity as a woman, defines marriage – marriage acquires meaning only if it is a relationship based on mutual respect, love and sturdy support. To such a couple a child within or without marriage can cause no disruption in life. Maturity in marriage which recognizes the need for a greater understanding than the mere physical relationship is significant.

All these films, each in its own way, question the social norms which deny the individuality of the woman and discriminate against her on grounds of morality. Thus the normal structure of the family is radicalized.

9 Crossing the Boundaries: Woman in Search of Self

Anshoo Sharma

" 'Imaginatively she is of the highest importance practically she is completely insignificant, she pervades poetry from cover to cover; she is all but absent from history'. This quotation from Virginia Woolf's *A Room of One's Own* expresses the ironical paradox of a woman's life. Men need her, love her, worship her and write about her but they do so in relation to their own selves" (Jain 1).

This statement represents exactly the position of women in society whether urban or rural. These two issues of subjection and emancipation have often been the subject matter of filmmakers – both male and female. For the present paper I have selected four films – *Arth, Mrityudand, Aastha* and *Paroma*, placing the last directed by Aparna Sen at the centre. The first three are directed by Mahesh Bhatt, Prakash Jha and Basu Bhattacharya respectively. Spanning the period of 80s and 90s these films can be categorized as parallel cinema except perhaps *Mrityudand* which was a commercial success and contained elements which carried mass appeal. The other three films were received very well by the female viewers, the upper middle classes and also the upper classes but they failed to reach out to the masses. These films make a very strong statement about a woman's perception regarding her body and herself, juxtaposed with a man's perception about her. In *Paroma* especially, this is highlighted throughout the film.

Paroma as the title suggests is the name of the central character played by actress Rakhi who is portrayed as a middle class Bengali housewife. The movie opens with the Durga festival – the deity known for its "Shakti" the female counterpart of the male *Shiva*. The name *Paroma* suggests completeness and being best, being first, as *Param* is a superlative which means 'The Best'. Among the Hindus it is also used as a prefix to show respect and reverence. But to realize her individuality she has to go through myriad experiences. The film traces this path and its bylanes.

The film begins with a questioning of the role of a woman and her place in a household – whether she is a Bhabhi Ma, a Kaki or someone else. The given name which gives a person an individual identity is lost somewhere among these different roles. It is the foreign-returned young photographer Rahul Rai who initiates her into the discovery of her 'self'. He refuses to cast her in the role of Bhabhi, Kaki or Ma though Paroma tries to make him address her as Bhabhi if not Kaki indicating that she also feels safe within these roles which form a protective barrier around a woman inhibiting an outsider from trespassing the boundaries of decorum. But this barrier at the same time limits the female from expressing herself and draws the parameters which she is prohibited from crossing. Going back to the Hindu epic *Ramayana*, one can see that if Sita dares to cross the Laxman Rekha she will surely have to face Ravana's illicit desires.

In the very beginning of the film there is a focus on the female body and the male gaze. During a lunch scene the director's camera focuses intensely on Paroma's lips while she nibbles her food and takes miniscule bites of a chillie. Rahul's gaze gets riveted and it is almost as if he is observing a very personal act. Later during the photographic session she is quick to pull down her saree to cover her ankles indicating that she is aware of his gaze. Slowly over a period of time there is a shift in this awareness when she starts viewing herself through his eyes. A woman frames her identity according to the way a man looks at her which becomes socially acceptable. It is the normative pattern set by patriarchy. It is primarily a moving glance similar to that of a moving lens of a camera framing a picture. It is the male gaze which constructs female identity and the woman learns to look at herself through the man's eyes.

Sen has shown the existence of a conscious interest in Rahul towards Paroma. Initially his interest is professional as he wants to capture the image and essence of an average Indian housewife and he is encouraged in this venture by Paroma's family members including her mother-in-law who feels that it is their duty to accommodate a guest in every possible way. Slowly over the photo-sessions a sexual undercurrent builds up when Rahul's interest in Paroma becomes personal. Paroma also finds herself attracted towards him because he is the first person to make her realize that she is still desirable. It is her own worth which is reflected in Rahul's gaze that makes her desire him. The director purposely chooses a photographer as protagonist rather than a person belonging to any other profession. It allows him to shift 'frames' wherein she is placed, to look at her as a 'body' in a different sense. For the family hers is a serving, procreative body, for him a sexual artifact, an object of beauty. There are two distinct ways of framing her physical presence. And the narrative by contriving to take her out of the domestic space allows this shift of space. It is her refusal to continue to be shaped by his perception, to be used, to be photographed, which becomes the means for her awareness of herself as a person. She crosses over from the 'role frames', from the 'key-carrying housewife' to a woman who desires reciprocal relationships and to be valued as a person in her own right.

Over the years of married life and motherhood playing different roles of a wife, a daughter-in-law, a sister-in-law and a mother, her own self, her own desires are lost somewhere. During one of the photo-sessions Rahul asks about her interest in sitar and poetry. She had been interested in them before marriage but now no one was concerned about her tastes or interests. Her education had also come to an abrupt end with her marriage. This we come to know later in the film. A similar theme is found in Jane Austen's novels as well where women's education was not given importance and the so called drawing room arts were merely practised to ensnare an eligible match and even if a woman was interested in them seriously they were soon forgotten in the whirlwind of married life and childbearing and rearing (Jain 3). As Laxmi Kannan writes "Women are trapped in cultural 'values' that offer no scope for individualizing the self" (Kannan 12).

Coming to childbearing the four films *Paroma, Aastha, Mrityudand* and *Arth* focus on the concept of motherhood from two different angles. The first, as is apparent in *Paroma* and *Aastha*, the woman's role is to provide hot food for her children, educate them and be there for them whenever needed. The other angle which is dominant in the later two films (*Arth* and *Mrityudand*) is that which is related directly to the experience of their bodies. In *Arth* which is about the married life and the extra-marital affair of the protagonist Inder, both – the wife Puja and the lover Kavita – desire a baby. The idea of a child gives them a sense of completeness making the bond of love stronger towards their man. As Sudhir Kakar writes:

> Whether her family is poor or wealthy, whatever her caste, class or region, whether she is a fresh young bride or exhausted by many pregnancies and infancies already, an Indian woman knows that motherhood confers upon her a purpose and identity that nothing else in her culture can. Each infant borne and nurtured by her safely into childhood, especially if the child is a son, is both a certification and a redemption. (Kakar 1981: 56)

Towards the end of the film Puja adopts the girl child of her maid but refuses to share her life with another man. The idea of motherhood in itself becomes more fulfilling than a man- woman relationship. There is in this a silent rejection of marriage. Similarly in *Mrityudand* when Bari Bahu, the elder sister-in-law, realizes that she is pregnant she experiences extreme happiness. Her body becomes a means of self-realization. The ability and capacity to conceive and give birth to a new life gives her a sense of self and of power. Through the act of procreation there she experiences regeneration which indicates her womanhood. She says ecstatically:

> *"Hum banjh nahin hain ab pani hamen gala nahin sakta, aag jala nahin sakti, hawa hamen baha nahin sakti, pavitra ho gaye hum"*
>
> (I am not barren, the waters cannot dissolve me, and fire cannot burn me or the wind blow me away. I have become pure).

Later when her younger sister-in-law asks her about her pregnant state, she admits boldly that it was the result of her will and that it belonged to her alone, she says:

> *"Sab niyam tod diya hum"*
> *Choti bahu: "khud apna marzi se?"*
> *Bari Bahu: "Han apna marzi se... paheli bar to apna marzi kiya hain. Kab tak sahen yen niyam?"*
> *Choti Bahu: "Kiska hai?"*
> *Bari Babu: "mera!!"*
>
> ("I have broken all rules", Younger daughter-in-law: "By your own will" Elder daughter-in-law: "Yes, my will... It is the first time I have followed my wishes. For how long shall I bear these dictums?" Younger daughter-in-law: "Whose is it?" Elder daughter-in-law: "Mine!")

Until now she has led a deprived life, weak in body and weak in spirit, having frequent bouts of illnesses whenever she is under emotional stress, and ultimately rejected and left by her husband. But now, having conceived, she comes into her own. The younger sister-in-law who is herself pregnant supports her and their father-in-law too feels happy for her. He is old and weak and had to give in to his sons' wishes even if he felt that they were making wrong decisions. Now in the elder daughter-in-law's case the means may be wrong and tinged with adultery but the end seems to be right and he feels happy in her happiness. According to Sudhir Kakar, "the head of the family, or other elder males who feel themselves entrusted with the family's welfare, gently but firmly seek to mitigate the excesses of the mother-in-law and the elder women" (76). Here it is not the mother-in-law's but the son's excesses which he tries to mitigate by his gentle acceptance of her firm decision.

Coming to extra-marital relationships the first thing that strikes one is that they take place when the husbands are away. In absence of their overshadowing presence a woman evolves as a different being--a separate individual who is not a mere shadow of her husband. In *Paroma* the husband is away on a business tour when her relationship with Rahul develops a close intimacy. He encourages her to see life from a different perspective. This is symbolically shown when he makes her cross the railing of a narrow parapet from where one gets a bird's eye view of the whole city. It is very symbolic when he says – learn to live life dangerously, because it is only when one is ready to experiment and take chances that there is a possibility of gaining something valuable in the process. And in a woman's case that 'something' is realization of oneself as a separate entity – complete and whole and not a mere extension of the rib of Adam.

But for Paroma to cross the boundary is not an easy step. Time and again she tries to deny herself, but ultimately realizes that Rahul complements and completes her both mentally and physically.

Similarly in *Aastha* the circumstances which lead to the woman overstepping her boundaries happen when the husband is away. One is almost reminded of Ravana who under an innocent garb beguiles Sita to cross the Laxman Rekha. A simple obligation of a few rupees to a woman named Reena leads her into a vortex from which she is unable to save herself. She gets carried away by the passion of the moment, seduced against her will by the sexual expertize of the other man. It reminds one of the bee and the spider who spins a complicated web, once trapped into which the bee finds it difficult to escape. At first viewing, the turn of events seem difficult to accept, as it is an unfamiliar theme for the Indian psyche but we cannot ignore it as false because such incidents do happen. Her physical relationship with her husband has been one-sided. She is a mother of a daughter yet her body's capabilities of pleasure have been untapped and undiscovered. As Ann Rosaland Jones writes "women, historically limited to being sexual objects for men have been prevented from expressing their sexuality in itself or for themselves" (358). It is initiation into this passage of discovery that becomes irresistible to her. Emotional love and physical love have been placed here as two different things. Emotionally she is never unfaithful to her husband and even on the physical level at the very first opportunity she gets she shares her newfound self with her husband. The pleasure at the discovery of her body's heightened perceptions she wishes to share with none other. Sexuality, as pointed out by Kakar, is the creation of the two-person universe where the affirmation of her female body and the recognition of her feminine soul take place simultaneously (Kakar 144).

Her relationship with the other man is neither a conscious one nor a personal one. Simone de Beauvoir has expressed this feeling in her *Memoirs of a Dutiful Daughter* and Madhuri Chatterjee has summed this up. I quote "To exist happily in a conservative world requires an element of fantasy and make belief. Sexual love, transitory and falsely constructed though it may be, seems a necessary step to female maturation" (Chatterjee 149). There is also a subconscious attraction towards the monetary benefits which are spent either on her daughter or on her husband. When Reena tries to convince her that it gives her freedom there is this heart-rending cry of her soul – "*Kya karoongi main aise aasman ka jo meri zameen mujhse cheen le, jo mera ghar mujhse cheen le*?" (What will I do with the sky that snatches away my earth from me, takes away my home from me?)

In this film the theme of adultery has been used in order to redefine love. Here the ordinary middle class housewife discovers herself and at the same time rediscovers her love for her husband. The body which is culturally and traditionally undermined and taken for granted, used as an object or a receptacle, suddenly acquires a consciousness of its physical response and desire. And through the portrayal of the husband's character the director tries to convey the all-encompassing quality of true love which is all-accepting – accepting vices along with virtues of the beloved. In this case it is the man rather than the woman who proves a true feminist. The eternal longing of a woman for a feminine identity seems to be fulfilled here.

In *Mrityudand* once again it is only when her husband steps out of her life that Bari Bahu has a relationship with another man – a relationship which is based on respect and consideration. She crosses the boundaries of caste and social norms by falling in love with Ram Bharan a man who comes to her rescue at the lowest moment of her life. After her husband leaves her the emotional trauma takes a toll of her physical health as well. She has to be taken to the hospital. On the way a heavy rain storm breaks out and the wagon in which they were travelling is damaged. Ram Bharan carries her almost in a half-dead state to their destination. Over a period of time he proves to be a caring, compassionate person who recognizes her as an individual. In their relationship her body becomes the medium and he the mediator. It is through motherhood that she gains power and confidence which come from the realization that she has a right to take decisions regarding herself and her body. Her pregnant state gives her a sense of freedom. Earlier all the decisions had been taken by her husband. Their life together was never a fulfilling one. Though he was impotent, it was she who bore the allegation of being barren – a blatant example of the unfairness of male patriarchy. Again it is he who decides to leave her in order to become a *Mahant*. She pleads with him not to take away the dignity of wifehood from her which was all that was left to her. But his response is similar to Inder, the protagonist of *Arth*, who categorically states that *he* has made the decision to live with Kavita – his lover, and his wife Puja's repeated pleadings to give her one more chance falls on deaf ears. Why is it that men take all the decisions and it is the women who have to suffer their consequences?

If one goes on to reverse the situation it is to be noted that men react very differently if put in a woman's place. They vent their anger, shun the women and make them feel guilty. They are never shown to be in a compromising position – grovelling or pleading with their women. Later, in *Arth* when rejected by Kavita, Inder wishes to be accepted back by Puja. At this juncture, Puja poses the hypothetical question to him, that if she had done the same, would he have accepted her back and the answer is obviously 'No'. Thus it is clear that the socially acknowledged set of norms vary widely for men and women.

Similarly in *Paroma* when Paroma's relationship with Rahul is discovered by her husband Bhaskar Chowdhury, there is a complete isolation of her by the entire family. The mother-in-law falls critically ill, the daughter and husband stop talking to her and when she confronts him he alleges that it is due to her wayward behaviour that his mother fell ill and ultimately calls her 'a whore'. Once again the double standards of the male attitude become apparent, when, just a few days ago during his business tour, his sexual advances are checked by his secretary and he has no compunction in calling her 'a bitch'. Considering this example one realizes that a man looks upon a woman as a body to be possessed and not as an individual having emotions or intellect. "How strange it is that even in the context of this most intimate relationship between man and woman, in which they both ought to be equal partners giving and receiving pleasure from each other, women are looked upon as mere instruments of joy..." (Harish 215). Even in the role of a wife he does not love her for herself as an individual, but rather as a proud possession belonging to him alone. She is there to fulfill all his needs and is supposed to have none of her own. In *Mrityudand*, *Aastha*, and *Paroma* the men lay claim on a woman's body without any consideration to their willingness, let aside their pleasure. Their actions are mechanical, focused just on their own gratification. Here one is reminded of Kamala Das's *My Story* where she compares the husband to a chieftain and the wife to a vassal (98). The ground root of experience remains the body (Gupta 143) – which has been given prime importance in these films. It is the woman's body which is the focus of the male gaze and which circumscribes them in a stereotypical role. Therefore in these films the women are shown to begin their search for self through their bodies. Whether it is Paroma or whether it is Bari Bahu in *Mrityudand*, they both rebel and the rebellion begins with their bodies.

Closely related to the idea of self-dependence is the concept of education and career. The two are interlinked and are an important means of gaining freedom. One is reminded of Virginia Woolf when she refers to Aphra Behn – a woman forced by circumstances to earn her own living and work "on equal terms with men". And "here" she says "begins the freedom of the mind..." as quoted by Jain. She further says "Freedom means to breathe freely, to meet people, to have *an openness of experience*" (Jain 3).

Both Paroma (in *Paroma*) and Puja (in *Arth*) want to earn their own living rather than depend on any male support. There is a new hope and confidence in them when they contemplate economic independence. In *Arth* towards the end of the film, Puja is not only capable of fending for herself but also for her adopted girl child. She requests Raj (who has become a friend and moral support in her life and also the one who loves her for herself – unconditionally) to let her go and says "*Aaj tumhara sahara mujhe kamzor bana dega*" ("Today your support will make me weak"). It indicates two things firstly that she has discovered her self-sufficient individuality and secondly that she is not ready to compromise it in any way, nor for any one – not even for the love of a man who has helped her discover it.

Similarly Paroma also opts for a job and her sense of wonder is apparent when for a meagre sum of rupees six hundred, she says "*Maine kabhi itne paise kamaye hain*?" ("Have I ever earned so much?") She too rises above the need of male support. This is depicted symbolically when her hair is shorn-off for the medical tests – which indicates widowhood (the husband does not actually die but is dead for her in a way). And Rahul she lets go, again symbolically shown in the film, when she drops the paper containing information regarding him through the window pane. She has evolved into an individual identity and is no longer dependent on others for her well-being. The emotional and psychological selves are discovered through the physical.

Talking of symbols one comes to the point of dreams "which become a vehicle to express hidden desires" (Jain 8). Paroma throughout the film has a recurrent dream of a mad woman locked in the attic – who is her paternal aunt Sudha Bua who keeps asking her "*Sankal khol degi*?" ("Will you open the latch?") and Paroma's continual inability to reach the latch. This is juxtaposed with the claustrophobic strains of her married life (again the sexual implications are indicated). She almost comes face to face with her dream when she witnesses an errant mad women being forcibly caught and taken back to the confines of a lunatic asylum. This is parallel to her situation where her unconventional behaviour has been labelled as sin and madness, where every effort is made to confine her within the defined roles of a wife, mother and a daughter-in-law.

When Paroma withdraws into herself after an abortive attempt at suicide, everyone including her doctor wish her to see a psychiatrist. Every effort is made to bring her back into the "normal" role of a *bhabhi*, a *kaki* or a mother. No one realizes that she has evolved as an individual – separate from these roles. She undergoes a metamorphosis. And this transformation is apparent to the viewers when she asks her close friend Sheela (another emancipated woman who has opted out of marriage – though a good cook and seamstress) for "*kagaz aur kalam*" (paper and pen) and to write and express oneself is an act of courage. It is an act of self-definition (Jain 8). This self confidence and strength is also reflected in her confessional statement before her entire family when she says: "*Mere mann mein apradh ki bhavana nahin hai*", ("I do not have any feeling of wrong-doing in my heart") thereby absolving herself of the feeling of guilt.

Finally another important metaphor that runs through the entire film and which cannot be overlooked at this juncture is that of a plant. It is a particular species which Paroma recollects from her childhood and keeps searching for. Ultimately Rahul gets the plant for her at the point of time when he is about to exit from her life. Initially the plant stands for a continuing relationship with Rahul but later it becomes an identity for herself. In the end while looking at the plant she remembers its actual name – *Krishnapallavi*. She says "*Woh patte*! Callendula *kaise*? *Haan*, Euphobia contenopholia – *Krishnapallavi*!?" ("Those leaves! Not callendula! Yes, Euphobia contenopholia"), thus indicating recognition of her new-found self.

In conclusion one can say that like a phoenix she rises from her ashes – stronger, more capable. It is the rebirth of Durga, the Paroma who has realized her '*Shakti*' but in a new form, a different context.

References

Chatterjee, Madhuri. "Simone de Beauvoir's *Memoirs of a Dutiful Daughter.*" *Women's Writing: Text and Context.* Ed. Jasbir Jain. Jaipur: Rawat Publications, 1996.

Das, Kamala. *My Story*. New Delhi: Sterling, 1988.

Gupta, Santosh. "The Epistemology of Inequality: A Look at *The Second Sex*". *Women's Writing: Text and Context.* Ed. Jasbir Jain. 1996.

Harish, Ranjana. "*My Story*". *Women's Writing: Text and Context.* Ed. Jasbir Jain. 1996.

Jain, Jasbir. "Reading Women's Writing". *Women's Writing: Text and Context.* Jaipur. Rawat Publications, 1996.

Jones, Ann Rosalind. "Writing the Body: Toward an Understanding of *l'écriture féminine*". *Feminisms.* Ed. Robyn R. Warhol and Diane Price Hernell. New Brunswick: Rutgers Univ. Press, 1991.

Kakar, Sudhir. *Intimate Relations: Exploring Indian Sexuality.* New Delhi: Penguin, 1989.

– *The Inner World: A Psycho-Analytic Study of Childhood and Society in India.* Delhi: Oxford University Press, 1981.

Kannan, Laxmi. "To Grow or Not to Grow: That is the Question for Women". *Critical Practice,* Vol. VII, No. 2, June 2000.

10 Body as Text: Women Transgressors and Hindi Cinema

Jasbir Jain

Women's issues are central to every society, primarily because they go on to define all human relationships and social constructs. In India, for a variety of political and cultural reasons, women's position has been centre-staged in various ways, ways which are not necessarily pro-feminist, instead very often they tend to influence socialization processes and reinforce subordination or compliance to the norms defined by patriarchy.

Cinema is a medium which has a much wider catchment area than any written literature or political debate. It cuts across class and caste boundaries, is accessible to all sections of society and in order to be financially viable needs to incorporate within it all those ingredients which may contribute to its success at the box office.

Where Indian cinema is concerned song and dance, fights, pursuits and rhetorical dialogues are almost indispensable to the film's success. In its threefold task of providing escape (through romance and fantasy), entertainment (through fun, laughter and visual pleasure), and engagement with social issues (by reflecting upon contemporary problems), the Indian cinema is perpetually engaged in a balancing game. But within this threefold thrust the placement of women remains central (where the visual element is concerned) even if their roles may be secondary or peripheral.[1] The focus remains on their beauty or their bodily exposure. For a while, in the seventies, there was a spate of films variously classified as art films, parallel cinema or new wave cinema, but these too were a continuation of the 'development agenda' so evident in Mehboob's *Mother India* (1957).[2] The women images they projected were conventional and the experimental shift was towards low-budget films and issues of exploitation in the feudalistic village set-up, a move as it were toward realism[3] which required a more active engagement from the audience.

But this movement tapered out giving way to multi-starrers on one hand and a continuous strand of serious movies which work across the distinct boundaries (art and commercial) and raise issues of significance within mainstream cinema on the other. Many of these films may not succeed at the box office but they do reflect the reality of middle class life and make a significant intellectual statement.[4]

A number of directors like Basu Bhattacharya, Gulzar, Rituparno Ghosh, Aparna Sen, Mahesh Bhatt, Prakash Jha carry on the tradition defined by Satyajit Ray, Ritwik Ghatak and others. Movies like *Mirch Masala*, *Tamanna*, *Aastha*, *Astitva*, *Rehaee*, *Paroma* even if they use formula situations, handle them with great sensitivity and shift from clichéd symbols and statements to create detonative signs which generate complex responses.[5] They too use the female body but use it differently. It is not possible to avoid the body, for as Susan Bordo has said, "The body is not only a text of culture. It is ... a *practical*, direct locus of social control, it is a metaphor of culture" (Bordo 13). Therefore, specially in a visual medium, it is important how women look at their bodies, how men look at them, how they dress and behave, the manner in which they are used by the director, by the narrative and by the women themselves. The body, the will controlling it, its sexuality or the violation of it through seduction or rape, its procreativity or barrenness, its location within space, all acquire meaning which can either reinforce conventional perspectives, or produce a counter discourse.

For the purposes of the present paper, I propose to consider in some detail Basu Bhattacharya's *Panchvati* (1987) and *Aastha* (1997), Deepa Mehta's *Fire* (1996) and Mahesh Manjrekar's *Astitva* (2000). These were movies which met with varying degrees of success but none of them was a major hit. *Panchvati* did not even get a theatre release. Contrasted with them are Prakash Jha's *Mrityudand* (1997) and Raj Kumar Santoshi's *Lajja* (2001), both of which have met with substantial success. Peripherally I shall be referring to a couple of other movies like *Purush* and *Kya Kahna*. I also make a distinction between the portrayals of women as victims, rebels and as transgressors. Even as the three categories overlap in the sense that victims mature into rebels or transgressors, each one of them highlights different character qualities and consciousness levels.

Movies which project victimhood tend to focus on oppression and violence and reinscribe patriarchal value structures, often located within larger frameworks like the development project, they highlight the qualities of sacrifice and traditional heroism where women are concerned. Victimhood becomes part of a survival struggle, or embodies the concept of an 'ideal womanhood', the *pativrata*, or is placed within a domestic power struggle between the mother-in-law and the daughter-in-law. Such portrayals attempt to construct Indian femininity along conventional patterns.

Rebel women are often portrayed through ridicule and comedy. Rebelliousness need not always be conclusive or even approved within the narrative structure. At times it may be part of the discourse on modernity and perceived as a potential threat to patriarchy through the values of education/ westernization/independence. But at times these images may be located outside the middle class, and there may be positive portrayals of the questioning of the rebels as in *Mirch Masala*.

This also happens in films like *Damini, Pratighat, Purush, Zakhm, Zubeida* and several others. But very often the rebellion itself upholds traditional values and the courage or heroism displayed falls within the Durga/Kali image, that is the image of the vengeful mother-goddess.[6]

In contrast to these two conditions of victimhood and rebelliousness, transgressive behaviour violates the norms of traditional morality and constitutes a deviation from the socially approved moral norms of sexual relationships. Women in these movies trespass into zones not acknowledged as legitimate and define a new relationship with their body and self (bridging the separation between the two). They call into question issues of fertility, mother-right and right to body.

In the main women's issues are part of a larger social debate and men often enough are also victims, rebels or transgressors, only they are not seen as such. Moreover some of the tools of oppression are wielded by men as they occupy a position of power in gender equations. Also it is to be seen that the endings of films which deal with transgression have a special significance. Very often there are no solutions and hence no closures. At other times, when there is a solution, it foregrounds the role of the forces which help bring it about. Multiple forces are at play which allow the narrative to open out in multiple ways to reach different viewerships. Such a narrative strategy – of widening the frameworks, of working at multiple levels and providing open-ended endings – emphasizes the interconnections between religion, patriarchy and morality and their impact upon the socialization process of the girl child.

Panchvati is apparently a bold movie. Based on Kusum Ansal's 1976 novel *Uski Panchvati*, it sharpens the narrative to make a radical personal statement.[7] It is a comment on the institution of marriage even as class factors and individual inclinations are brought into play. There is transgression but no rebellion, the options are clearly stated and any attempt to alter them would damage the social fabric. The hero Vikram (enacted by Suresh Oberoi) is an artistically inclined businessman, in fact a poet who wants to remain in touch with his inner being. An adopted son of the family, he has willed everything to his younger brother Jatin. During a visit to a painting exhibition he is attracted towards the young philosophically inclined woman artist Sadhvi and invites her to his house.

Contrasted with this scene is the scene back home where Vikram's wife Neera is discontented with the life he has made for her, and refuses to postpone her card-playing session for his visitors. The wife is otherwise portrayed as a considerate woman who has been alienated by her husband's single-minded pursuit of business interests.

Subsequently a marriage proposal is conveyed to Sadhvi on behalf of the younger brother Jatin. But as the future unfolds itself, it is a marriage between incompatibles. He values her only as a body, as a beautiful woman, who should now fall into the life-style of a rich man's wife and keep herself engaged like his bhabhi, Neera. He is equally contemptuous of her middle class background and her artistic pursuits. Despite Sadhvi's desire to be her husband's confidante and friend, the marriage is a disaster. Psychologically the two artistically inclined members of the family gravitate towards each other, unable to resist the initial attraction that each had experienced. This is an act of transgression in more ways than one. Not only is it extra-marital, it is a relationship between the husband's elder brother and the wife of the younger brother, a relationship otherwise forbidden (Minturn 76 and Kakar 13)[8] and the boundary is emphasized in the film by Jatin herself when he tells his brother not to mediate between him and his wife.

Nevertheless, the two – Vikram and Sadhvi – gravitate towards each other in a moment of shared regret and sense of affinity and the result is that Sadhvi conceives (Neera's childlessness is thus foregrounded). Sadhvi now takes up residence with her 'guru' outside both her natal and her marital home. This retreat is very much like that of Sita's retreat to an ashram where she is placed outside worldly life. Sadhvi frees her husband from the marriage bond and tells him that the child is not his. Vikram cannot marry her, all he can do is to provide her financial security and enable her to be independent. True to the *Ramayana* motif which is indicated by the title *Panchvati*, she gives birth to twins.

Throughout the film the attraction between Vikram and Sadhvi is held in delicate balance and the final moment of coming together is not a moment of temptation. Instead it is worked towards steadily by juxtaposing contrasts. Vikram's quiet restrained character is contrasted with Jatin's aggressive possession of his wife at a moment when he is himself unwilling to stay home for her painting exhibition, and Vikram's recognition of her separate individuality with Jatin's ceaseless efforts to fit her into a mold. There is also a contradiction in Jatin's approach. He refuses to share his business concerns with her but wants to use her as a medium of arriving at his business negotiations. There is also the attitude to space. Vikram wants to live in open spaces, Jatin in enclosures. For Jatin, Sadhvi is only a body, for Vikram she is a person in her own right with a distinct individuality.

Vikram himself is trapped within a marriage which has more silences than communication. The psychological roots of this distancing are only passingly referred to and the blame is laid at Vikram's door. It is his need to build a business, to pay his debts as an adopted son that has created a rift between them.

In the Sadhvi-Vikram relationship, several questions are raised – the distinction between marriage and a union of love(*shaadi* and *suhaag*), the difference in the nature of love and of desire, the need of self-expression even as it is located within a physical relationship. But even as her future life is defined by a transgressive act, she is projected as a very traditional woman, modest, self-effacing, rooted in inherited cultural values, wanting only for her personhood to be recognized within domestic space and when this does not happen, then to opt for a life of abstinence.

This debate about the nature of love and marriage is continued in *Aastha*, a later film of Basu Bhattacharya. It is also a story of a transgressive act, but a transgression not consciously willed as in *Panchvati*, but yielded to due to external pressures. It works through the strategies of seduction. And in this case desire itself is momentarily separated from love. The narrative is set in Mumbai (as contrasted with Delhi and Kathmandu in *Panchvati*) and within an ordinary middle class household. Subtitled *In the Prison of Spring*, the film opens with a classroom scene where the play *Romeo and Juliet* is being discussed, and tales of other lovers form a parallel discourse. The lecturer Amar (played by Om Puri), asserts that love is not defined by dying together; it is defined by facing the challenges of life, by living together. (Interestingly Sadhvi in *Panchvati* had also defined love not as a 'sleeping together' but a 'waking together'. Thus there is an intertextuality at work in several of these films).

The narrative discourse at a literary level is continued throughout the film through a variety of devices. There is a subsequent discussion on Othello's murder of Desdemona for suspected infidelity. Amar again considers it unjustifiable. Desdemona was not a possession which he owned, but a person he loved. He had no right to sit in judgment on her.

Other discussions which take place on the nature of love are between the girl student and her boy friend, and between Mansi (Amar's wife played in the film by Rekha) and the socialite who runs a call girl racket. There are also two embedded narratives in the film encapsulated as scripts for theatrical performances. One of these is based on the Kamli episode, which Amar and his friend (played by Dinesh Thakur) witnessed during their visit to the Ahmednagar fair and the other on Mansi's relationship with the rich businessman (played by Navin Nischal), a relationship based on money transactions. By unfolding the happenings as part of the main narrative, then enfolding them within spoken and framed narratives by an observer in each case, the strategy is to select the incidents which require attention as also to place them in the same category as *Romeo and Juliet* and *Othello.* This strategy also postulates a test for Amar – does he believe in what he states? Thus we have the earlier discussions being reflected in the performance scripts at the two ends while the Amar-Mansi relationship constitutes the central portion.

The Kamli tale is of a rural woman's experience of being an object of exchange between her father and her husband in the first instance, and then between her husband and the 'other' man to whom she is sold in exchange for money. Her husband needs the money and in order to meet this need, he encashes his wife. This act has the approval of society. Now when the husband has come back to buy her, the second owner is not willing to sell her. Kamli is pregnant with his child. The dispute between the two men is being tried by the local panchayat. The question is who owns the woman and who owns the child? And can a mother be bought and sold just as a wife can be ? The panchayat asks the woman as to which of the two men she prefers. At this the woman laughs. Later this is turned into a script and the mediating agency is that of the lecturer's mind who comments '*Purushon ki takat pe, aurat rani naukrani banti hai, Chulha badalti rehti Hai*' (It is male power which decides the status and position of a woman forcing her to serve new masters). Kamli's laughter is in itself an act of rebellion. She laughs at the absurdity of being asked what she wants as if that has any value.

As the mediating voice of the girl student shows, is Mansi's case any different ? Is she not being pushed into hiring out her body to meet the economic needs of the family ? Middle class constraints are there, but there is also a subtle juxtaposition of Amar's self-absorbed attitude. He does emerge as a sensitive and a creative mind who has made his choices. But there is also an underlying selfishness. He can afford to go for a 3-day holiday with a friend, to take a taxi to the bus stand, but is unwilling to take a tuition or two to supplement his income or to economize on himself for the child's needs. He is fairly matter of fact and unromantic in bed and takes his wife for granted. It is Mansi who is worried about meeting the family's requirement, and it is she who does all the housework while he rehearses with his students in the sitting room. The relationship is not based on any equal partnership, it is an unequal one. He appears to be a person who is caught in the image of his own creation - a self-sufficient intellectual, the head of a family and indifferent to the pressures of consumerism. In fact, at one point Mansi says *"shehar hamare beech aa gaya hai"* (the city has come between us).

Slowly and steadily a conspiracy of silence is built up around him as the child goes for an outing with a friend and peer group pressures are met. And just as secretly does Mansi slide into a relationship with a business magnate. Surprisingly, the experience itself even if it leaves her with a sense of guilt, releases her untapped sexual desire. Mansi brings this awareness of her body to the site of her legitimate desire, and through this asserts her identity. It expresses her need to know herself in relation to the 'other' and step out of the role of the sexually passive female.

It is true that the choices are never so clearly defined. Mansi experiences both guilt and fear, and finds herself retreating just when on the verge of making a confession. The opportune moment eludes her. Also the money she earns allows her for the first time to indulge those she loves - her husband and her child. Otherwise she has not much to call her own - not even enough space in the house to keep her possessions.

Thus as the two stories are narrated, the similarities in the two women's situations become clear, Amar is called upon to sit in judgement and he is of the opinion that if the deviant wife still wishes to live in the family, she has a claim on it because true love accepts not only the strengths of the loved one, but also their weaknesses. The ending redeems him and absolves him of his earlier self-centredness as it brings together his intellectual ideas and his emotional response. The conventional *agnipriksha* is thus dispensed with.

In *Panchvati*, if on the one hand the husband's proprietorial rights are proclaimed, "*Yeh meri patni hai, wohi karegi jo mein chahunga*" (she is my wife and will act according to my wishes), on the other the wife's right to her own body is also established. In *Aastha*, the extra-marital relationship is only of the body, not of the heart. The husband–wife relationship is able to withstand it, because for Amar, Mansi is more than a body.

Both the films manage to do without violence (except for a wife-beating scene in *Panchvati*) and without songs, there being only some background poems in *Panchvati* and none in *Aastha*. Together they provide two kinds of endings. In *Aastha*, the story comments upon itself as a beautiful love story (*ek bahut hi sunder prem kahani*), while *Panchvati* can also be treated as a sad love story. Community intervention through same sex friends also features in both the films. Yet despite these sensitive portrayals, they failed to appeal to the imagination of the masses.

Another film, Manjrekar's *Astitva*[9], met with a similar fate at the box-office despite some very good reviews. *Astitva* is also an exploration of the institution of marriage, its one-sided expectations and the claustrophobic existence it thrusts upon the woman confining her within domestic space. It also comments on the confines of a family and on the mother-son relationship. Patriarchy is represented by the husband, the son and the lover (the music teacher). All of them proclaim their ownership and claim the loyalty of the central woman character Aditi, played by Tabu, in different ways. The outside world is represented by the husband's friend Ravi and his wife Meghna, who happens to be divorced and has two daughters from her first marriage, and the son's fiancé, Revati. These two women – one twice married, the other young and unmarried – provide a contrast to the submissive domesticated wife Aditi who is contained within the home. Suddenly her world is disrupted when a letter arrives announcing a legacy for the wife (and conferring upon her economic independence) which sets her husband thinking. Even as the husband talks loudly about his college flings and later affairs thus separating the moral limits of men and women, he begins to work towards exploring the reason of this legacy.

We are taken back in time, to the early years of their marriage, the long spells of separation and the frustrated desires of the young wife. Marriage and romance are separate for the man, not so for the woman: finally she is swept off her feet by the desire of the moment and she conceives, the music lessons are terminated, she ends all connections with Malhar Kamath, the music teacher, attempts a confession, fails, and as the years pass by, she increasingly allows herself to be housebound.

Now the husband works through his diaries and the dates and confronts his wife with the fact that their son is not his. And as a consequence he rejects her (but not the son) condemning her to a separate existence within the house. It is at this point that the son's fiancée comes to her help. The woman has transgressed but is really not guilty, the blame lies more with the husband as he has refused to take cognisance of her desire, of the needs of her body and also because he concentrates on building high walls around her. But it is she who is treated as guilty, humiliated and rendered homeless. There is nothing and none she can claim as her own.

As contrasted to these movies, there are others which have dealt with acts of transgression but have met with better fate at the box office like *Kya Kahna*, *Fire*, *Mrityudand* and more recently *Lajja*. The reasons for this again are manifold – the framing of the narratives, the liberal use of other ingredients like dance, song, violence, rhetoric and even more than these the dominant presence of a counter discourse within the films often provided by recourse to a simple polarity between good and evil, the Ram-Ravana separation and often the rehabilitation of the women within conventional morality.

A brief reference to *Kya Kahna* which foregrounds both romance and the class issue. But once the heroine finds that her trust is misplaced she regains her respect by asserting herself. She decides not to abort the child and she also decides not to marry the man rejecting the two conventional options. Thus she moves away from conventional behaviour which would mean getting rid of the child in someway (by abandoning or giving it away), or marrying the father of the child. She establishes her right to motherhood without making any concessions to paternal claims.

The other side of this story is projected in *Fire*[10] which offers a complex study of human relationships where heterosexual relationships have failed or become meaningless and are juxtaposed with masturbation on the one hand and lesbianism on the other. The lives of the two women, Radha and Sita, are caught up within the confines of domesticity which interacts with familial and religious frameworks. There is Ashok's relationship with Swamiji which is based on giving the Swamiji obedience, financial support and physical comfort. Ashok occupies a womanly role where devotion and the massaging of Swamiji's feet are concerned but a masculine role where economic support is concerned. Contrasted with this is Jatin (the younger brother) relationship with Julie, his Chinese girlfriend. Like Ashok he is shown tending her feet and polishing her toe nails. In reversal of these positions, both the brothers occupy superior male roles in the household where the women do all the caring and the tending. The two daughters-in- law are still governed by the paralyzed mother-in-law who constantly demands attention and are expected to follow conventional behavioural codes. They are both sexually deprived. Ashok lies next to Radha testing his own self-control and Jatin takes Sita brutally in order to fulfil his duty to the family by fathering a child.

Jatin resents the family. It is because of the joint family that Julie has refused to marry him. He is insensitive to Sita's desire for love or her romantic ideas of a married relationship. Instead her first sexual experience is marked by brutality and indifference. He turns his back on her and goes to sleep. In a subsequent scene again he wants to perform the act as part of the baby making project, but this time Sita rejects him.

Sita's entry into the family acts as a disruptive force, she tries to adapt herself but her urge for freedom, her newly discovered sense of her body push her to explore it sensuously. Radha finds her own repressed desires responding to her. Their relationship is reminiscent of Ismat Chugtai's short story "The Quilt"[11] where the wife, deprived of her husband's love turns to lesbianism. There is all along an emphasis on the importance of physical touch so underplayed in a conservative society. Throughout the relationship with their men, it is this which is missing. And when it is there, it is without any tenderness.

The film thus goes on to make an important statement as it seeks to reverse the concept of abstinence which has been seen as an enabling factor in women's lives. The model Indian woman is one who is able to control and sublimate her desire (through prayer and fasting). But Sita moves away from this ideal and refuses to be treated like an object. There is a scene when Radha is portrayed oiling and combing Sita's hair, symbolising a comforting, caring relationship, at once nurturing and intimate.[12]

Contrasted with the congested space in the house and the kitchen down below is the life on the terrace which the two build together, and the flashbacks related to open spaces from Radha's childhood help focus attention on their present state of conferment. Little acts of rebellion allow them to make a change from the agoraphobic ideal and move towards self-nurturance.[13]

The crisis occurs when Mundu's self-indulgence in the act of masturbation is discovered and his lapse and the Radha-Sita relationship become oppositional to each other as well as to the centre. Mundu sneaks on them. Desire is seen as a dirty word. Ashok seizes her and kisses her as if to sully and use her. Radha sends Sita away promising to follow her after having talked to

Ashok. It is at this juncture that the theme of wifely devotion, deviation and trial by fire surface again. The performance of the Ram-Lila had earlier formed a backdrop to Swamiji's discourses. Now Radha's clothes catch fire, a fire which engulfs the whole house. Ashok is seen leaving the house with his mother in his arms while Radha is engulfed in the flames. This is a kind of coalescing of both the act of *agnipriksha* and of *sati*.

The film has two endings. The fire episode provides the first ending and with this many movie-goers would start leaving the hall. The scene itself is a long drawn one. Then follows the real ending when Radha in her half-burnt clothes finds her way to the Nizammudin shrine where Sita awaits her. The shrine of the Sufi saint also represents the presence of a humanist faith outside self-denying rigid religious structures. The narrative moves away from constricting frameworks and patriarchal institutions to render the acquisition of agency possible for both Radha and Sita.

As compared to all the movies discussed above, *Mrityudand* and *Lajja* unhesitatingly use all the formula motifs and ingredients of mainstream cinema – song, dance, violence and rhetoric – in liberal measure and yet try to problematize women's issues. Of the two *Mrityudand* does it with more restraint and therefore with more effect while *Lajja* takes up a large number of issues and uses conventional frameworks and tends to be melodramatic. The two are not alike, the directorial approaches are different but both fall back on earlier models of feudalistic societies. Tirpat Singh in the first and the Thakur in the second represent the corrupt power centres. Both films have an interpretative community which is sympathetic and intervenes to help the women, and both project their endings through women's solidarity across caste and class. Yet the two are very different.

Mrityudand opens with a male crowd chasing a highly pregnant woman to her death – a punishment for sexual transgression. Sex continues to remain a central issue as the village women are used and exploited by the politicians and the mafia group represented by Tirpat Singh, the contractor. The decadent aristocratic families continue to remain issueless for the time being.

It is a story of two brothers, the elder one has been married for seventeen years (played by Mohan Agashe) but is issueless. The blame has been passed on to his wife (played by Shabana) while in actuality he himself is impotent. Power becomes a substitute for sexual potency. He has the 'Mahant' of the 'Math' murdered and gets himself appointed as the Head thus condemning his wife to widowhood. The younger has just got married and is caught up in the financial affairs of the family. He realizes that he is no match for the corrupt ways of officialdom and soon finds himself a prey to Tirpat Singh's offers of help. His wife (played by Madhuri Dixit) tries to restrain him but fails.

In the meantime the elder brother's wife falls ill, has to undergo a long treatment in the neighbouring town and has a relationship with the lower caste man who had come to their help. She conceives and wants to keep her child. Back home the younger brother is murdered and the younger Bahu staves off Tirpat Singh's attack on her purity in a Durga-like manner.

In the scene when Chhoti Bahu finds out about the elder one's pregnancy, she asks her whether it was of her own will. Bari Bahu replies yes, it was the first act she had ever done in accordance with her own will. Towards the end all those patriarchal forces represented by religion, wealth and power descend upon them to hound the guilty woman to her death, reproducing the first scene. But these forces are thrust back when all the women get together, women who have a shared memory of their oppression. This kind of a neat victory of good over evil makes a very conclusive ending but it also subtracts from the artistic quality. The redeeming features of the film lie in the dialogue, the manner in which woman to woman relationships are developed and the interpretative forces represented by Om Puri who is a marginal, shrewd and practical man but is not corrupt like the others. Besides the transgressive act exposes the hypocrisy which is part of patriarchy by attacking the stigma of barrenness which the woman has been forced to live with. Once again it is the right to one's body which is established – and within it mother right. The father does not matter. The child belongs to the mother.[14]

Lajja has a very interesting motif as the main strand – the motif of a picaro heroine, forced to flee from place to place not because she is in pursuit of adventure but because she is homeless, like every woman. Neither her husband's nor her father's home belongs to her or can offer her protection. But this interesting motif is made to carry a heavy mythological burden. All the main women characters bear the names of Sita – Vaidehi, Maithili, Janaki, Ram Dulari. All of them also remain within the socially approved norms of sexual conduct, except for Maithili and she has to pay the price for that through the loss of her child. Yet even while adhering to social forms of behaviour, each one of them finds herself confined and threatened by death, neglect or insecurity. Power seems to be concentrated not merely in men, but in father figures who are either active or passive, Vaidehi's father-in-law is aggressive, her father submissive, Maithili's father goes on yielding to unfair demands while the groom's father makes unreasonable claims. Men use women not only to exploit them but also to sacrifice them.

Husbands do not necessarily offer protection. Vaidehi's husband thinks of her as an incubator which can be dispensed with at will, Maithili's suitor is a puppet in his father's hands, Janaki's lover Manish suspects her of infidelity and asks her to choose between him and the unborn child. Other women like Lata and Sushma are also victims. Lata is married to Purshottam, a man much older than her, and Sushma is pursued by her father and uncle for having desired to marry a man of her choice.

While the women continue to live upto the ideal of 'Sitahood', men fail to come up with an appropriate concept of masculinity. The model projected by Ram is a flawed one as the performance of the *Ramayana* reveals. If Sita has to face the trial by fire, Ram also needs to stand the same trial. The *Ramayana* motif is a recurring one in Hindi cinema and strikes a responsive chord in the audience, but the critiquing is equally significant for it refutes the simple polarity between good and evil. Chidananda Das Gupta while commenting upon this motif in *The Painted Face* points out that it offers one of the most "glaring instances of parental violence towards offspring" (174).[15]

In each of the subnarratives the women are seen as losers. Vaidehi is on the run, Maithili may never find a husband, Janaki has a miscarriage and Ram Dulari is raped and murdered. They rebel only when all limits of tolerance have been crossed. And in the end they are rehabilitated within normative patterns with the men having undergone a change of heart. Thus the structure is not challenged only the inequality in it, its failure to value the life of the mother along with that of the child. Of the two men who act as mediators one is a petty thief, the other a social victim turned Robin Hood.

Again, like *Mrityudand*, the film has a double ending – one when the women beat back the Thakur, the other when Vaidehi, now the proud mother of a daughter (this is of significance) and a suitably transformed husband meets the reformed thief as taxi driver. The woman is entrapped in the oversize mantle of motherhood. The reinforcing of traditional symbols, the exposure and exploration of the female body, the inclusion of the hipswinging, pelvic gyrating dance numbers all place the film firmly within mainstream cinema with a very strong eye on the mass audience. Janaki's sensible perception of the need for bodily freedom does not make a significant dent. In *Lajja* scenes of intimacy are missing, while in *Aastha* and *Panchvati* they abound. The debate of the body is mainly between exposure and intimacy, between rape and desire, between sex and love. In this debate, the cinema uses the female body for a variety of purposes. For visual pleasure is a strong element in cinema as Mulvey has emphasized, "In their traditional exhibitionist role women are simultaneously looked at and displayed, with their appearance coded for strong visual and erotic impact so that they can be said to connote to-be-looked-at-ness" (Mulvey 837). But the directorial gaze even while framing the female body for exhibition and erotic impact can still code it differently. Thus when there is an act of sexual transgression it is not merely a defiance of the normative moral code, it also raises other questions related to self, being and personhood. No act of oppression or of rape can in itself evoke sympathy. And every such portrayal carries within it sado-masochistic possibilities specially where stereotypes are employed. In several movies, despite strong feminist statements, the images are cast in stereotypical molds as in *Pratighat* and *Purush*.[16] Both deal with rape and injustice, but both also use the image of the vengeful Kali.

The question then arises what relationship do the stereotypes have with (i) box office success and (ii) the women question. Apparently loud melodramas state the case more simply and appeal to both who perpetrate violence and those who resist it. They challenge nothing, they only expose the other side of the story. When the message is coded in subtler shades, it is not merely erotic pleasure but the mind which is engaged in the film's interrogation. Most of the films which deal with transgressive acts raise questions regarding the boundaries imposed upon the female body. Is it only women who transgress and never the men? Questions which are raised when women transgress are never raised where men are concerned. A woman is rendered homeless, it is her body which is her home, her present and her future, her possession, her capital and her labour. An act of transgression breaks the control of others over the body and compels society to reformulate its boundaries in whatever limited measure. It draws attention to the nature of human will. It is not the act but the questions it raises which acquire significance in the larger social discourse.

Notes

1. Very few movies project strong women characters. Women are used to play romantic roles, molls or other decorative roles, or the mother who controls the lives of her children. Even sensitive directors like Raj Kapoor and Guru Dutt have given us male centred films while fully exploiting a woman's physical beauty and sensuousness.
2. In the late fifties and early sixties there was a spate of developmental films which propagated the Nehruvian ideal of socialism. These films – like *Naya Daur*, *Paigham* and a host of others – believed that elimination of poverty, social reform and technology would help relieve oppression. *Mother India*, though different in several ways, also belongs to this phase. Note the inauguration of the dam with which the film begins.
3. This realism can be seen as being generated by the ground realities, and having a close relationship with the earlier social realism of the thirties. There were various strands and various phases. If on one hand films like *Do Bigha Zameen* were realist movies, so were Benegal's films like *Ankur, Manthan* and *Nishant*, Mrinal Sen's *Bhuvan Shome* as well as Satyajit Ray's trilogy. As I understand it, realism would also imply side-tracking of the girl-meet-boy romance on one hand and the 'grow rich quickly' story on the other. It grappled with everyday problems, which perhaps had no solutions. But the woman question was not central to this realism.
4. M. Madhava Prasad in *Ideology of the Hindi Film: A Historical Consciousness* uses the term 'middle class cinema' to describe the urban centred films directed towards (i) asserting the national role of the class (ii) construction of an exclusive space of class identity (163-164).
5. These movies are very different from a film like *Sholay* which went on to create cinema history but which does not make any of these finer statements. Male friendship, resistance to tyranny and quotable phrases remain its major strengths.
6. This is a common enough association in India. For further details see Jasodhari Bagchi's article "Representing Nationalism" (*E&P Weekly*, Oct 20-27, 1999). Bagchi writes, "Of all the forms of Shakti worshipped in Bengal the darkest and the most terrifying was Kali, the female energy that stands on a male corpse" (WS 67).

7. The main story, along with the names, is borrowed from the novel. I am not sure whether the film acknowledges this debt or not. But the novel is more crowded. There are three brothers, Vikram has three grown up daughters and there is a mother-in-law as well. In the end Sadhvi's confession to her husband is complete. It involves Vikram and disrupts many lives and Vikram offers to support her as a mistress. In all these concerns the shedding off of the extra baggage enriches the film. The absence of guilt, however, is common to both.
8. One of the reasons for the purdah tradition within the Hindu family was to avoid contact of the young bride with the older men of the family. Minturn writes "Jaiths and Susurs were seen as potential seducers". The relationship with the husband's younger brother has traditionally been viewed as more free, and in the custom of casting the mantle the younger brother can marry the elder's widow but not vice-versa. Kakar dwells upon this in *Intimate Relations,* pp. 11-13.
9. I am not devoting too much attention to *Astitva* as there are other papers in this volume which discuss it at great length.
10. My references are to the English version of *Fire.*
11. Chugtai's "Quilt" is not necessarily about lesbianism as a natural impulse but about lesbianism as a result of sexual frustration.
12. There is a similar scene in *Rudali.* This action embodies a nurturing relationship between mother and daughter as well as between friends.
13. See Bordo for a detailed discussion of the agoraphobic phenomena. It represents a "reassertion of domesticity and dependency on feminine ideals". When career opportunities are denied and women are placed in roles of dependence, women begin to live it literally (17).
14. There are strong resemblances between this film and *Mother India* – the feudalistic structure, the notion of development, the fear of sexual assault and the male predator patiently on the watch for the right opportunity – all are common to both.
15. See Das Gupta 172-176 wherein he looks more objectively at the character of Ravana and traces the reasons for Sita's rejection to the rise of patriarchy. He is critical of the "insidious way the epic is being used to reinforce the values of an aggressive, resurgent Hinduism" (174).

16. *Purush* has a strong resemblance to a Finnish novel titled *Manrape* (by Maria Tikkanen) which was later filmed as *Men Cannot be Raped* where a woman who has been raped decides to punish the man and ties him down just as he had done her and forces him to have sex with her against his will thus reversing the idea of violation. Such revenge films do foreground a woman protagonist but they also lend "novelty to an old relish for violence", as well as provide "fresh excuse for a rape scene" (Das Gupta 161).

References

Bordo, Susan R. "The Body the Reproduction of Femininity: A Feminist Appropriation of Foucault". *Gender/Body/Knowledge: Feminist Reconstructions of Being and Knowing*. Edited by Alison M. Jaggar and Susan R. Bordo, New Brunswick: Rutgers University Press, 1989.

Bagchi, Jasodhara. "Representing Nationalism: Ideology of Motherhood in Colonial Bengal". *Economic and Political Weekly*, Oct 20-27, 1990.

Chugtai, Ismat. *The Quilt and Other Stories*. Trans. by, Tahira Naqvi and Syeda S. Hameed. New Delhi: Kali for Women, 1990.

Das Gupta, Chidananda. *The Painted Face: Studies in India's Popular Cinema*. New Delhi: Roli Books Pvt. Ltd., 1991.

Kakar, Sudhir. *Intimate Relations: Exploring Indian Sexuality* (1989). New Delhi: Penguin, 1990.

Minturn, Leigh. *Sita's Daughters: Coming Out of Purdah*. New York. Oxford University Press, 1993.

Prasad, M. Madhava. *Ideology of the Hindi Film: A Historical Reconstruction*. Delhi: Oxford University Press, 1998.

Mulvey, Laura. "Visual Pleasure and Narrative Cinema". *Film Theory and Criticism*. Ed. Leo Braudy and Marshall Cohen. New York: Oxford, 1999.

Tikkamen, Maria, *Manrape* trans by Alison Weir (Virago 1978), London: Corgi Edition 1979.

11 The Working Woman in Three Bengali Films: A Retrospect

Dipendu Chakrabarti

Bengali cinema has at last woken up to the fact that stereotyping women as objects of male desire is being challenged by a growing consciousness of gender issues. The result is a number of films critiquing the patriarchic suppression of female identity after the *succès de scandale* of Aparna Sen's *Paroma.* Even the mainstream cinema nowadays makes occasional concession to this new perception of women's traditional role-playing. This change in perspective has been possible due to the increasing activities of some women's organizations, expansion of women's studies in the academia, and, above all, extensive coverage of women's problems by the print and electronic media.

The situation was different when Satyajit Ray, Ritwik Ghatak and Mrinal Sen dominated our parallel cinema. They did not face any pressure of the kind of feminist discourse that compels today even male directors to rethink the women's question, yet they each made a film that foregrounded the vulnerability of a working woman operating within the parameters of male hegemony. Ritwik's *Meghe Dhaka Tara*, Satyajit's *Mahanagar,* and Mrinal's *Ekdin Pratidin*, though each is separated from the other by a number of years, have a shared concern for the dilemma faced by women when they have to reconcile their traditional feminine image with their role as breadwinner.

Meghe Dhaka Tara by Ritwik Ghatak addresses two issues simultaneously: grim struggle for existence of the people uprooted from their homeland by the partition of Bengal, and the supreme self-sacrifice of a refugee girl for the survival of her pauperized family. Dire economic necessity compels Nita, the heroine of the film, to combine two roles – she is the protector and at the same time the victim of a family that is fast losing its sensitivity due to the dehumanizing effect of post-partition economic crisis. Though Nita's father is still sympathetic to his eldest daughter, her mother's nature has been so warped by grinding poverty that she always treats Nita harshly for not doing enough for the family and at the same time pampers her younger children. The only other person in the family who feels for Nita is her elder brother who is unemployed but determined to be a singer, and Nita, too, reciprocates by encouraging his musical aspiration. Nita is betrayed by her lover when he falls in love with her younger sister and marries her ceremoniously with the full support of her mother. When Nita's elder brother comes back home after his initial success as a singer in Bombay he finds Nita suffering from tuberculosis and living like an outcast in a corner of their house. He sends her to a sanatorium at Shillong where she dies, a victim of brutal exploitation legitimized by the so-called familial values upheld by the Bengali middle class even after the traumatic experience of the partition.

Though Ritwik claimed that Nita is best understood in terms of Jungian archetype as an incarnation of Uma, the daughter of the King Himalaya, his film clearly contradicts this authorial intention. *Meghe Dhaka Tara* is too realistic a film to allow such archetypal configuration. The central concern of the film is the suffering of a working woman destined to be exploited by her family which is itself haunted by economic insecurity, a fall-out of the partition of Bengal. Nita's stoical endurance, however, is not dictated by a conscious choice of altruism, unlike Sonia's in Dostoevsky's *Crime and Punishment*. It is the inevitable response of a woman forced to play a role that silences her voice and puts under erasure her own identity. Nita herself realizes towards the end of her life that it was a crime on her part not to protest against injustice. Ritwik was obviously not interested in a frontal attack on patriarchy; indeed, he has pitted mother against daughter, sister against sister to suggest an internecine struggle in the feminine world. Whether this is the outcome of the politics of patriarchy is not made clear. For Nita's father is more supportive than her mother, and her elder brother accuses the whole family of being unjust to her. Obviously the film does not adopt a feminist perspective, but the tragedy of Nita as presented by the director, underscores the paradox that a working woman in a poor family, instead of achieving economic freedom, only perpetuates her enslavement.

What Nita cannot do is done by Arati in *Mahanagar*. Satyajit Ray makes her protest against the callous treatment of her Anglo-Indian colleague Edith by their boss, and when warned of the consequences of her action, she defiantly hands over her letter of resignation. Her concern for another woman victimized by the arbitrary decision of the boss is doubly significant: (a) the boss has been very nice to her, so she could easily have ignored the case of Edith; (b) Arati's husband has lost his job, the whole family now depends on her, yet she forgets all this when she stands by her colleague.

But, like Ritwik, Satyajit, too, adopts a perspective for his thematic concern that stops short of a feminist critique of patriarchy. For Arati's husband assures her at the end of the film that she has done the right thing, something he would not have dared to do, and we see them walking together with an expression of a newly achieved understanding. Here, too, the working woman has to combine her traditional roles (as wife, daughter-in-law and mother) with the new role of a breadwinner, and silently suffer non-cooperation from her in-laws and husband. Since Arati is a married woman, Satyajit takes the opportunity of exposing the opportunism of male dominance. Arati's father-in-law has from the very beginning opposed her decision to work for money, a typical reaction of old Bengali middle class conservatism. But her husband's response is more complex; more liberal than his father, Arati's husband at first co-operates with her, but her growing competence as a salesgirl make him jealous and even suspicious about her interaction with the boss or any male client. He persuades Arati to resign from her job, though he blames it on his father. Ironically, when Arati is about to submit her resignation, she is informed by her husband over the telephone that she should change her mind because he has lost his job. Narendranath Mitra's short story, on which *Mahanagar* is based, brilliantly exposes the hypocrisy inherent in the male-dominated society, for there not only the husband but also the in-laws regret Arati's decision to resign her job. How opposition to a woman's decision to work in an office is swiftly turned to a condemnation of her decision to resign when her husband has to depend totally on her job – this inversion of the situation from the husband's position is highlighted by Satyajit who leaves out the reaction of the in-laws. The result is the bringing into sharper focus male dominance in marital relations. But Satyajit, like Ritwik, did not accept the conflictual relation between the male and the female in feminist terms. At the end of *Mahanagar*, Arati's husband compliments her for showing courage, an appreciative gesture suggesting a common space that transcends the male/ female binary.

There is another issue in *Mahanagar* which is often overlooked – the question of race. Edith is a victim of racism. The boss cannot trust her because she is Anglo-Indian and he has a low opinion of this community, particularly their women. Race and gender are linked up in a way that has never been witnessed in the Bengali cinema. Aparna Sen's film *36 Chowringhee Lane* also deals with the Anglo-Indian community and there is at the center of the film an old Anglo-Indian woman who is exploited by her ex-pupil. But it is concerned more with the loneliness of the woman than with any linkage between race and gender. *Mahanagar* very boldly brings together two women from two different communities, striking up a friendship in spite of the language barrier. It is Edith who teaches Arati to use lipstick, and lipstick has a very important semiotic function in the discourse of patriarchy that controls a conservative Bengali family. So Arati's husband makes a sarcastic comment on her use of lipstick which provokes her to throw it out of the window. She does not want to assert herself at home where she has always tried to be an ideal woman, like Nita in *Meghe Dhaka Tara*. But at her office she can act more freely and it is there that she chooses to support Edith when she is insulted by the boss. In fact, Arati, a Bengali woman makes a supreme sacrifice for Edith, an Anglo-Indian woman. This is a moment of solidarity that can be fully grasped only in feminist terms. In the original story, Arati's fight for an Anglo-Indian woman is ridiculed by her husband who also has a racist attitude. It is more realistic than the ending of *Mahanagar* that suggests a sudden change of heart in the husband.

Compared with Ritwik Ghatak and Satyajit Ray, Mrinal Sen is more seriously engaged with the gender issue. In *Padatik*, one of the political films that set a new trend in the Bengali cinema of the 70s, he linked up the suffering of a Naxalite activist with that of a separated woman. It was the first Bengali film that exposed the hidden patriarchal values of revolutionary politics and suggested that a revolutionary agenda cannot ignore the question of women's rights. His *Ekdin Pratidin* is a full-scale study of female identity as a cultural construct. The theme is once again an unsympathetic treatment of a working girl, but Mrinal's penchant for experiment focuses on the issue from a different perspective. One day, a working girl who, like Nita or Arati, feeds her family, does not come back home. There is a frantic search for her, but she is not found anywhere. Her parents, brothers and sisters spend a sleepless night, their neighbours express their concern and at the same time their suspicion about the morality of the missing girl. The most interesting thing about the film is the physical absence of the central character, Chinu, and the varying reactions of people to this fact. It is like looking at the problem of a working woman from the standpoint of the spectators who represent our society. The sudden disappearance of a working girl evokes in us anxiety as well as suspicion about her morals. The girl's family goes through a heart-searching, the younger sister Minu accusing mother of being unfair to Didi, mother blaming father, and when the girl comes back in the wee hours even the youngest sister looks at her with suspicion. The landlord who stays on the top floor makes damaging insinuations about the whole event, then there is the predictable fracas involving him and the girl's brother. An ailing old woman's comment reverberates throughout the film: To be born as a woman is a curse.

Mrinal Sen's tour de force is the deliberate withholding of information about the whereabouts of Chinu. In fact, coming back home she first tries to explain why she had to stay the night outside, but nobody is willing to listen to her. This silencing of the female voice has a symbolic significance. It shows the absolutist nature of patriarchy functioning in the conservative Bengali society. *Ekdin Pratidin* with its gripping sense of suspense forces us to wildly speculate about the reason why Chinu has not come back home and deliberately draws out the hidden patriarchic reaction from the audience. The anguished waiting for the missing girl not only heightens the sense of mystery that keeps the audience on tenterhooks, but also reveals the unpalatable fact that all this hullabaloo is due to the fact that the person who spends the night outside home happens to be a woman. *Ekdin Pratidin* is the first serious attempt in the Bengali cinema to critique the patriarchic surveillance for the subjugation of women. It prepared the ground for a deeper involvement with the gender issue in Aparna Sen's *Paroma* where a housewife, tired of playing different roles in relation to her family and in-laws, makes a desperate bid to redefine her own identity by flouting the discriminating rules of sexual morality. Since then there has been a spate of films for the big and small screens made by both male and female directors, all focusing on the problematic of man-woman relationship in different historical and social contexts, and inviting us to challenge the stereotyping of women in popular fiction and film. Looking back one feels sure that the present tilt towards a near-feminist discourse in the Bengali parallel cinema owes not a little to the three great films about working women by the three great masters of the celluloid – Ghatak, Ray and Sen.

12 Comedy and Gender: A Study of *Katha* and *Chashme Baddoor*

Jyoti Bhatia

There has been a tradition of comedy in Indian cinema since its inception. But in earlier cinema, comedy was specifically used for amusement and diversion. Comic sequences were stuck in at odd points to relieve the tension of feeling and to move the spectators to laughter. To arouse laughter, stereotypical, at times crude, farcical methods were employed. The comic artist entertained and amused because of his corpulence or gluttony or tipsiness or miserliness or horseplay or by projecting the henpecked husband, the fat, domineering wife. "Humour was then essentially concrete" (Cazamian 1). Gradually there emerged a class of filmmakers who besides entertaining wished to say something. They perhaps realized that comedy could be used as an agent of social change, that it could be used for more than mere entertainment and that it need not be always based on the physical. And the element of "consciousness and reflection" (Cazamian 26) were superadded to the popular comedy and the comedy became purposive – "Comedy, in this style amused men and made them resigned to their lot, thus fulfilling both a social and an ethical purpose" (Cazamian 28). Humour then also came to be suggested through understatement and not merely displayed by overstatement and exaggeration –

"a conscious restraint of speech, an appearance of unconsciousness that sets off a hint more forcibly, and a comic element, ...resulting from the contrast between the actual meaning and the words" began to be used in Indian cinema (Cazamian 13). Comedy thus gathered force with the depiction of both realism and ridicule.

Like most other genres, comic films too were usually made by male filmmakers. *Chalti ka Naam Gaadi* (1958), *Half Ticket* (1962), *Shagird* (1967), *Padosan* (1968), *Chupke Chupke* (1975), *Golmaal* (1979), *Damaad* (1978), *Angoor* (1981), *Jaane Bhi Do Yaaron* (1983) – are all, to name a few, a result of the male romantic, comic imagination. Does it then mean that women filmmakers do not have a sense of humour or that they do not have an ability to display it?

It is true that most women filmmakers have made serious films with women at the centre – concerned with women's issues, women's concerns and marital relationships. These films had a purpose and were made with a view to bring social awareness and change. But in this paper, I attempt to show that women filmmakers have a sense of humour, though it is rooted in a different kind of sensibility from that of men and they display it in a different manner. This sense of comedy manifests itself through the projection of the ordinary, familiar aspects of life – concern with food, domestic work, children, gossip, scandal, jokes, jealousy, love, marriage, pretence, disguise, fashion, appearance, snobbery, as also the inhibitions, aspirations, dreams, vanities, follies of the common man. The style and treatment too is different. Everything is dealt with minutely, finesse and tact. All this is a part and parcel of our everyday existence. But because we observe the human situation by being out of the game, we realize the similarity and also the absurdity of our actions, manners, habits, pursuits and thoughts, "Comedy then is a suitable technique; it can infiltrate ideas into heads that would reject them in any other form" (Rodway 15).

In this article, I propose to examine two films directed by a woman director – Sai Paranjpe – who presents this comedy of human life in her films – comedy which is "anchored in ordinary daily experience", and the comic effects "depend upon forays into the unexplored territory of wish fulfillment and fantasy gratification" (Charney 4).

Paranjpe realizes that to be human is to be inherently comic. Her films rooted in the day-to-day experience of life project the world inhabited by ordinary men and women pursuing their simple dreams and aspirations with occasional flights into the world of fantasy where the dreams are realized, the stars achieved, but also show the return to reality and the sudden deflation of expectations. Paranjpe knows the real world and the men and women well enough not to expect too much of them. She, therefore, presents life in the original and finds the ordinary rife with comic possibilities. And the comedy in her films arises because she exposes the gross difference between wish and reality.

Her film *Katha* (1982) is a story of a Bombay chawl – a microcosm of Indian society, inhabited by a number of families who take an active interest in each other's affairs, share each other's happiness and sorrows and rejoice and celebrate like one big family. There is no privacy and everybody knows every thing about the others. Paranjpe's sharp eye for detail records all the happenings in this chawl – from the children playing cricket in the compound and creating disturbance, the people talking to each other loudly across balconies, the curiosity aroused by the arrival of a new person in the chawl, the whispered love making of a newly-wed couple, to the reported activities of the cat, the give and take of milk and sugar that takes place in a close-knit Indian community, the different arrangements people make to fill water early in the morning, people hurrying towards the common toilets, the pride experienced by the family which owns a television, a refrigerator and other foreign gadgets and whose son is working abroad, the perpetually complaining and demanding wives and the harassed husbands.

And it is the picturization of this that lends a touch of comedy to all these everyday, routine activities. Paranjpe captures all the images and presents them in a very realistic but at the same time amusing manner. The cinematic treatment makes the comic element very vivid – as we see and realize the facetiousness in our day-to-day work. Like Henri Bergson, Paranjpe, perhaps sees a human being as a puppet or a piece of pure mechanism and uses laughter to show that man is 'an automatum' – all men when observed from a distance, appear to be performing similar acts and it is this similarity, this resemblance that makes all human beings 'comic figures'. Bergson says, "any arrangement of acts and events is comic which gives us, in a single combination, the illusion of life and the distinct impression of a mechanical arrangement" (105) and goes on to elaborate:

> the comic is that side of a person which reveals his likeness to a thing, that aspect of human events which, through its peculiar inelasticity, conveys the impression of pure mechanism, of automatism, of movement without life. Consequently it expresses an individual or collective imperfection which calls for an immediate corrective. This corrective is laughter, a social gesture that singles out and represses a special kind of absentmindedness in men and in events. (117)

Katha has its origin in the fable of "the hare and the tortoise". Paranjpe weaves the fable into the story but also makes a serious comment by subtly inverting the end. The film begins with the Dadima narrating the fable to her grandson. Paranjpe makes the narrative interesting and funny by incorporating 'a cartoon strip' (And this is a typical feature of Paranjpe's films). In the cartoon strip, it is the hare that wins the race. And this change makes the grandson question the end. The grandmother replies that "Times have changed and in today's world – it is the escapists and cunning people who actually win the race."

In the film too, it is not the slow and steady Rajaram (played by Naseeruddin Shah) who wins the race in reality – it is the sly, smart, stylish, eloquent, charming, sociable Vasu (played by Farookh Sheikh) who enjoys himself, deceives everybody with his sugary words, basks in the love and the attention bestowed on him by one and all and in the end shirks all responsibilities, breaks the trust and heart of a lot of people especially Rajaram's and Sandhya's (Deepti Nawal – the girl to whom he is engaged) and escapes in the pursuit of more fun and pleasure without any compunction. It is he who actually wins the race leaving the drooping flowers for Rajaram.

The cartoon-strip at the end of the film shows the tortoise winning the race (according to the accepted convention) but it also focuses on the meaninglessness of this victory for the flowers wilt as soon as the tortoise receives them. Paranjpe seems to be saying that this victory then is not a victory but a compromise. And that life is a series of compromises. Rajaram who loves Sandhya but is not bold enough to confess his love to her, finds her in love with his friend Vasu. And Sandhya who wants a handsome, smart life partner finds herself getting married to the shy and simple Rajaram in the end. But all through the film Paranjpe has also focussed on the morals and ideals of the protagonists. By pointing this out she is telling us that what we are running after is not a reality but a dream. She is gently mocking at the attitude of contemporary society, which gets impressed by the outward appearance but does not value the qualities of goodness and uprightness.

Paranjpe then is also using comedy as a corrective tool. She holds a mirror up to society to reflect its follies and vices, in the hope that they will as a result be mended. And the reality in her films becomes acceptable because she is observing life through the lens of a comic vision. Frame after frame, episode after episode is infused with the spirit of comedy. Rodway writes, "Most art, and comedy in particular is functional in society, whether it purports to be or not . . . . Comedy tends to integrate man's nature within itself or with the nature of his world, so that he can swim in his sea of troubles . . . " (Rodway

12; 22). Paranjpe, too, in her films, shows how comedy reconciles man to the chaos that exists in society, to fate, to his limitations and thus restores a balance.

Another film by Sai Paranjpe very rich in the comic element is *Chashme Baddoor* (1981). A very light-hearted and frothy film (*Times of India*, 25 July 1999), it revolves around the life of three friends Siddharth (played by Farookh Sheikh), Chimu (Ravi Vaswani), and Omi (Rakesh Bedi) who share a flat. They are wonderfully supported by Lallan Miyan (Saeed Jaffery) and Dadi (Leela Mishra).

While Siddharth is the sincere, sober, studious guy, who stays away from girls and wants to get a good job, the other two are frivolous - always following girls, trying desperately but unsuccessfully to woo them. Lallan Miya, the panwalla acts as their kind confidant and loans them cigarettes in their economic crises. Chimu and Omi are the laughing stock of the film. They are absolutely irresponsible, perpetually preoccupied with girls, flashy clothes and cigarettes. The walls in their room display revealing pictures and posters of girls. Pursuing good-looking girls is their hobby and they are always cooking up schemes to attract their attention. This singleness of purpose concentrates their energies. Their activities are a source of immense drollery in the film. They build up grandiose, heroic and eloquent visions of themselves and beguile both their own selves as well as others. But Paranjpe's handling of the visual medium is masterly and she regales us by making the play (impersonation) and the factual move side by side in the film and thus acquaints the audience with the pretence and the reality.

When Neha (Deepti Nawal) comes to live in their neighbourhood, Chimu and Omi seek to win her attention and gradually her love. They both visit her house separately and while Omi is mistaken for a plumber, Chimu is thrashed by the brother. Now it becomes a matter of pride and therefore they weave false stories and brag about their successful meeting with Neha. The contrast between the reality and the fantasy is the source of comedy here. Paranjpe, in both these films exploits the dream and flashback techniques to show the difference between wish and reality. And through this contrariety she always manages to stimulate humour.

In *Katha* too, comedy arises again and again out of the audience's awareness of the feigned (pretended) persona of Vasu against the backdrop of reality. Vasu's habit of exaggeration (overstatement), his attempts to draw wool over the eyes of the world is a source of endless mirth.

When Vasu takes Rajaram to a restaurant, he tells him of his past jobs. Paranjpe delights the audience by showing the reality moving side by side with Vasu's narration of absolutely fabricated stories. Vasu boasts of having worked as an officer at a hotel's reception, as an advertising and publicity person, in a film's directorial unit but it is the reverse which is true. He had worked not as an officer but as an attendant; not as an advertising and publicity person but as a roadside vendor who tries to attract the attention of passersby not exactly in the directorial unit but as a clap boy. He further bluffs and says that he left all these positions because he was not satisfied with the work. Again, it is the opposite which is true - Vasu is always dismissed - thrown out rather unceremoniously. But Vasu is Vasu - he believes in living life king-size and he knows how to get things moving in his favour. He tells Rajaram that one does not need to search for a job, it falls in one's lap, straight from the skies. He understands the inherent weakness of human beings around him and capitalizes on it, pretence with him "becomes a lifestyle that replaces any moral, ethical or religious commitments" (Charney 161).

In this context, Charney makes another important statement that "Pretenders are not only deflated in comedy but also displayed and celebrated" for:

> they help us to cling to illusions even when we know they are wrong, not only cling to them but actively pursue them against

> our own better judgement. Truth and morality are suspended as we watch the fascinating spectacle of con men magnificently conning us. The justification is in the magnificence. All the memorable comics pretenders are great talkers: inventive, hyperbolic, grandly absurd. They are superlatives after their own kind, non pareils, extra-ordinary men.... We would like to believe that the pretenders merely suffer temporary setbacks and will emerge again in full flower. (Charney 62-63)

Vasu, the pretender in *Katha* too is witty, dashing, energetic, forceful, colourful, casual and tremendously natural, functioning outside conventional morality, brilliantly manipulating men and situations but never offensive. Vasu flatters, entertains and impresses everybody – young or old and like a magician he is able "to manipulate chance and conjure up desired situations" (11). He "is a master of disguise, who cultivates illusions and false appearances" (12) and beguiles others easily when their defenses are down. Two examples in the film where Vasu bluffs and succeeds are when he befools the restaurant manager and later the Footprints shoe company's owner. And he actually gets a managerial job in the office where our sincere and hard working Rajaram works as a clerk.

Life is full of such ironies, Paranjpe seems to be saying and also that we feel good when we are praised and flattered. Most of us are ready to be taken in by people like Vasu who confuse, mislead, trap and beguile us with their deceptive ways. And in a way Paranjpe is showing the deceived man and the world as comic, their gullibility is treated as funny. She appears to sympathize and inspire sympathy in us too for this anti-social protagonist and her comedy is only a wooden sword of pseudo-criticism because at the changed ending of the conventional fable she had made Dadima say, that it is the escapists and cunning people who win the race in today's world. We both laugh with and at Vasu because he outsmarts or outmaneuvers the world that we find so troublesome. We suspend judgement about his morality because of our delight in his freedom.

Contrast is also a source of comedy in the film. The absolutely different personality of the two male protagonists – with Rajaram as a sincere, simple, shy, naïve, humble, honest, benevolent, generous and idealistic person and Vasu as deceitful, smart, bold, confident, cunning, selfish, flirtatious and completely self-indulgent. Although, it is Vasu who is Rajaram's guest, he acts as the host. He sleeps on the bed while Rajaram sleeps on the floor, he gets up late and demands tea, hangs around aimlessly while Rajaram works in the office and at home also he carries out his orders; Rajaram loves Sandhya but Sandhya falls prey to Vasu's charm. Paranjpe has treated Rajaram's simplicity and earnestness as laughable. When Vasu had come and imposed himself on Rajaram, he had promised to give him Rs. 300 a month and had made him dream of sending a money order to his parents in the village. But there is a large credibility gap in what Vasu says and what he actually does. And this contrast is presented by juxtaposing the dream sequence and the reality.

Use of dreams and projection into the future are two very important tools the director uses to produce comedy in her films. The dream technique as Charney has written:

> allows for a fluidity of movement that is not possible in everyday life. Displacement of real to imagined experience, distortion of visual images, substitution of dream logic for rational sequence and causality, endless repetition and variations of fixed patterns can all be freely used to emphasize a certain mood or turn of thought. Suddenly, everything is possible, and from this unlimited freedom comes the startling puns and new associations out of which comedy is created...(155)

Rajaram, the comic hero, of *Katha*, a very down-to-earth and practical person has modest desires in life of becoming 'the head clerk' in his office and of marrying Sandhya, the girl next door whom he loves but has never found the courage to tell her so. And it is only in dreams that he is able to triumph over his bashfulness, his fears, and act confidently. In one episode of the film Rajaram invites Sandhya to come and have 'samosas' with him. And while he is warming the samosas, he dreams – in the dream sequence he brings the plate of samosas and places it before Sandhya who tastes one and says "*Chai saath hoti to mazza aa jaata*" (Had there been tea with it, it would have been more enjoyable) and our Rajaram very confidently replies, '*Memsahib, chai chahiye to uthiye aur banaiye, khud bhi peejiye aur hame bhi pilaiye*' (Madam, if you want tea, then, get up and prepare it for yourself and me as well).

But this is a dream and the reality is very different. In reality, Rajaram's reply was '*Chai..? haan abhi lo*' (Tea? Yes, right away) and he gets busy, pumping the stove, to prepare tea. And the comedy is further enhanced when Vasu acts in the way Rajaram had wanted to. Comedy results because "...the same scene is reproduced with groups of different characters" (Bergson 120).

In another dream sequence, rather "a comic nightmare", Rajaram is pursued by the girls who work in his office. He is being teased, tormented, cajoled and forced to eat an apple. Rajaram tries to escape from their evil, dishonorable clutches and cries, "Are you not ashamed to behave in this manner, don't you have brothers and fathers at home?". And in the end Sandhya comes to his rescue in the dream. The whole dream is a comic one because the situation is reversed and the roles inverted. It is usually men who harass, tempt and seduce women and women cry out "Don't you have sisters and mothers at home?". But in the dream it is the opposite. Again it is a girl (Sandhya) who acts as Rajaram's deliverer from the mischievous persecutors. Paranjpe understands the specific links that exist between comedy and dreams. And she uses the dream sequences in her films to enable her comic hero to express his preoccupations.

Comedy in Paranjpe draws on the humble materials of daily life, but this is the base on which the structure is constructed. The making of comedy is:

> an imaginative activity that seeks to recombine and refashion the raw materials of experience into something different, something created by the mind, something essentially metaphorical.... As in dreams, the facts are thoroughly transformed by distortion, overemphasis, imaginary dialogue, wordplay, incongruity, and other personalising devices.... To put it simply, the objective reality is fundamentally changed by the churning and turbulent processes of wish fulfillment and fantasy gratification. (Charney 155)

Another important and major highlight of Paranjpe's films are their songs, dance, community celebrations and play-acting. They give a happy glow to the films in totality and delight, entertain and amuse at the same time. In *Katha* we, who are so occupied in pursuing the busy schedules of our lives take vicarious pleasure in the chawl festivities. Again it is a reminder to us that our lives, our interests are getting too narrow and to enjoy life in reality we need to broaden our areas of attention and interest. Comedy needs an inbuilt audience as well, and the community provides thus all norms of privacy and personal space are related.

Songs are an important feature in *Chashme Baddoor* too and are fitted appropriately to cause humour. The words, situations and picturization - all make the songs quite funny. The first song in the film which Neha is shown practicing '*Kali Ghodi Dwar Khadi*' becomes comic when we find Siddharth waiting at the gate of the music school on his black motorbike.

Another song happens when the love birds (Siddharth and Neha) are sitting in a public park. They wonder at how songs transpire in films instantly, with appropriate words and situation, where nobody is around the hero and the heroine. They too invent a song as they go along by rhyming words together like *pagal-badal*, *kajal-payal*, *deewana-mastana*, *anjana-pehchana*, *tapka-manka*, *bhatka-atka*, *aagosh-behosh*, *madhosh-khamosh* and the result is an absurd and meaningless song. The humour is further enhanced when they forget that they are sitting in a public park. They can even hear the music, are oblivious to the people around them and sing and dance around the trees with abandon as in films.

Rivalry and misunderstanding too can be the subject of comedy. When Siddharth gets a job, he also tells his friends about his love affair. And the first reaction this news generates is of jealousy but after that comes unbounded enjoyment and celebrations and takes the three friends into the world of dreams once again. And in the song '*pyar lagawat*' they imagine themselves in the guise of bridegrooms. *Teen yaar mein eek ki jam gai, do ki bhi umeeden jag gai* (Of the three friends, one found a mate and the hopes of the other two were also revived) – the song and the music are funny and diverting but again it is the picturization (the visual medium) that arouses laughter.

While following girls in the park, Chimu and Omi chance upon Siddharath and Neha sitting together. They feel betrayed and in a dejected mood sing '*Dost dost na raha*'(A friend, is a friend no more) and vow to save their friend from the clutches of Neha. Neha is the same girl with whom their earlier attempts of friendship had failed. Both know the real motive behind their jealousy but do not wish to get exposed and therefore plan to create misunderstanding between Siddharth and Neha. And here pretence, disguise, misunderstanding and eventually reconciliation are all treated in a comic manner, centring as they do on courtship and marriage.

Both Omi and Chimu weave false stories about Neha's character and create a rift between her and Siddharth. Later when they see poison in Siddharth's table drawer, they both acknowledge the truth and plan to reconcile them. The film ends happily with all the conflicts resolved and the lovers reunited.

Both *Katha* and *Chashme Baddoor* end with marriage, feasting and revelry. And again as Charney has observed:

> Just as tragedies end in death, so comedies typically end in marriage.... So the end of comedy is also a ritual ending, which makes it a beautiful and nostalgic moment that more than justifies any grossness or any excess.... The climactic moment of comedy is an exception, a holiday mood in which the rules are suspended and anything goes. (88-89)

The happy ending is achieved regardless of what precedes it and its conclusion with marriage, punishment or reform – usually implies a fresh beginning.

Paranjpe has the extraordinary knack of capturing microscopic details of our mundane existence and of putting them into the comic frame. Let us examine a few incidents in both the films to show the minuteness of Paranjpe's observation and her ability to capture it through the camera-lens. She realizes the impact of the visual medium and therefore focuses and concentrates the camera on 'real' scenes from life. And this ability to capture the nuances of everyday life, of domestic experiences, of ordinary men and women; the ability to delineate all this convincingly, bringing out the 'comic' but at the same time not harshly ridiculing those who are treated as 'comic' subjects, simply making us aware of our limitations and follies. And it is here that the woman filmmaker has excelled and shown her achievement.

In one of the initial scenes in *Katha* we are shown children playing cricket in the chawl compound – the ball accidentally flies into somebody's quarters and breaks an earthenware pot full of curd. This rouses the ire of the lady. And when the children request her to return their ball, she to spite them and satisfy herself halves the ball and throws it back with a pleased glint in her eyes, feeling avenged. But Paranjpe succeeds in making the whole act 'a comic one' – we as viewers, identify with the situation and realize that most of us cut ridiculous figures when we lose our sense of proportion. It reflects our immaturity, intolerance and littleness.

The representation of the conversation/interaction between Rajaram and Bapu (a physically handicapped resident of the chawl) creates a lot of humor in the film. The relatively innocent indifference and absentmindedness of Bapu to Rajaram's good news; his holding on to Rajaram, whenever he comes to him and getting all his work done is a source of great amusement.

In *Chashme Baddoor*, a significant episode of the film is when Neha come to the flat of the three friends in the guise of a salesgirl, and Chimu and Omi recognize her. They run away and hide themselves to save face and leave Siddharath to open the door and encounter the 'Chamko washing powder' salesgirl. The demonstration, the subsequent repetition of the advertisement's refrain, the clumsiness and simplicity of Siddharth, who gives her a clean towel to wash and opens the door immediately when the radio plays '*Hum tum ik kamre mein band hon*' (me and you together in a closed room) all bring a smile to our face because the situation's familiarity helps us to relate both to the situation and the actors.

Both *Katha* and *Chasme Baddoor* are fresh, gutsy, sparkling comedies, which thrive on human whimsicalities. They entertain and amuse even as they stress the need for the preservation of human values like friendship, love, honesty, truthfulness and kindness (Sengupta *Times of India*).

Paranjpe has put her films in the comic mode either because she finds the spectacle of human life amusing or absurd or because she wishes to satirize, mock, scorn or ridicule this spectacle or because she wishes to correct or reform it or because she feels that it cannot be corrected. And we as spectators laugh when we perceive that the relationship of anyone to himself, to society and its conventions, to nature, or natural law is very different from our own, or from what we pretend is true of ourselves. We laugh, when established roles or patterns are altered, and some one behaves like a God, animal, an inanimate object, or some one very different from himself. We laugh "at" a comic character in detachment or scorn, or if we feel somehow allied with him, and laugh "with" him recognizing common human feelings – the tall and short, fat and thin, clever and dull, formal and informal, brave and cowardly, idealist and realist frequently occur together. Her comedy is secular and earthbound and concentrates upon the local, established, and familiar, upon problem solving and the probable.

Paranjpe is, like Meredith's comic spirit, which when:

> contemplating men... luminous and watchful, never shooting beyond them, nor lagging in the rear... closely attached... has the sage's brows, and the sunny malice of a faun lurks at the corners of the half-closed lips... the slim feasting smile... finely tempered, showing sunlight of the mind, mental richness... its common aspect is one of unsolicitous observation, as if surveying a full field and having leisure to dart on its chosen morsels, without any fluttering eagerness. Men's future upon earth does not attract it, their honesty and shapeliness in the present does, and whenever they wax out of proportion, overblown, affected, pretentious, bombastical, hypocritical, pedantic, fantastically delicate, whenever it sees them self deceived or hoodwinked, given to run riot in idolatries, drifting into vanities, congregating in absurdities, planning short-sightedly, plotting dementedly, whenever they are at variance with their professions, and violate the unwritten but perceptible laws binding them in consideration one to another; whenever they offend sound reason, fair justice; are false in humility or mind with conceit, individually or in bulk; the spirit overhead will look humanely malign, and cast an oblique light on them followed by volleys of silvery laughter. That is the comic spirit. (47-48)

That is Paranjpe, the filmmaker. Comedy is said to be female in principle. This statement becomes more meaningful when we see Paranjpe's films – her films are episodic in structure, interruptive and congenial, reflect the chaos and disorganization of human existence, deal collectively with laughter, sharing, ribaldry, reconciliation, bonding, forgiving, qualities usually associated with women. The comedy in her films rises from the incongruities, hidden dreams, illusions, facial expressions, contrast, eccentricities, imitation, physical deformity, disguise, gossip, jokes, sex, food, dress, songs, dance, inversion, animation, by the use of the flashback and projection into the future technique. Paranjpe attempts to show the world its face in the mirror with its perfection and imperfection, virtues and vices. Her films are a refreshing change from the usual farcical movies and celebrate the sheer fun and vitality of life. They also celebrate the power and wit of women.

References

Bergson, Henri. "Laughter". *Comedy*. New York: Doubleday Anchor Books, 1956.

Cazamian, Louis. *The Development of English Humour*. New York: AMS Press, Inc. 1965.

Charney, Maurice. *Comedy High and Low: An Introduction to the Experience of Comedy*. NewYork: Oxford University Press, 1978.

"Hanste Huey, aate hai sab". *The Sunday Review, The Times of India*. 25 July, 1999.

Meredith, George. "An Essay on Comedy". *Comedy*. New York: Doubleday Anchor Books, 1956.

Rodway, Allan. *English Comedy: Its Role and Nature from Chaucer to the Present Day*. London: Chatto & Windus, 1975.

Sengupta, Ratnottama. "The Big Man of Middle Cinema", *The Times of India*. 5 Nov. 2000.

13 Questioning the Confines of Marriage: *Khushboo* and *Arth*

Bandana Chakrabarty

Ours is a cinema obsessed society. Films act largely as social mirrors. It is believed that films are a true reflection of society and social values. It would not be wrong to say that Hindi films have had a deep impact on the changing scenario of our society in such a way as no other medium could ever achieve. Would it be hyperbolic to say, "Without women there would be no cinema"? The answer is an emphatic "No" but the portrayal of women in Hindi films has not extolled womanhood. Rather it has denigrated it. Society, being single dimensional, it has created the one-dimensional film heroine – that of a pretty face perched on a snow-white pedestal of virtue.

In this world which has always been dominated by man, there has been a long history of oppression against women, more so in India. The history of Indian cinema presents a woeful picture of discrimination and marginalization of women. Whether it is a film of the 50s or of the 90s there has been little difference in the image of the celluloid woman. Commercial films are not going to change overnight in their attitude towards them, an attitude marked by discrimination and exploitation.

Women in Hindi films have been portrayed as devoted housewives, sacrificing mothers and dutiful daughters-in-law.

This image has been so constantly drilled into the Indian female psyche that women themselves have started believing in this 'self-portrait.' And no one can disagree with the strong subconscious influence and hypnotic effect that films have on our minds. The makers of these films (mostly men) emphasize that they are simply catering to what the audiences are accustomed to seeing. There is a strong resistance to the image of the woman who is articulate, vocal and independent.

The celluloid lady has always been shown as a secondary, subservient figure. Though the woman of the twenty-first century has entered and excelled in jobs that were once the prerogative of men alone, the heroine in contemporary films continues to be an outdated image with an unrealistic set of values. It is a different form of enslavement.

Hindi films represent women's, 'lack of status,' and have relegated them to silence and marginality. Consider the latest modern hits which most of us are familiar with. In *Hum Aapke Hain Kaun* the heroine's sister (played by Renuka Shahane) is a perfect '*bharatiya nari*', cooking and feeding the entire family, decking herself in pretty clothes despite being accomplished in computers. She has no time nor inclination for enhancing her knowledge. In *Hum Saath Saath Hain,* we have a modern day Ramayana where the three women have no ambitions or interests "beyond dressing upto the nines for their beloveds or stepping out of their four walls once they've ensnared their spouses and who derive joy and pride in serving their in-laws, looking after their precocious children and queening over the kitchen" (Ahluwalia *Tribune*, 10 Jan. 2000). Similarly *Biwi No 1* portrays a married woman who is ready to forgive her errant husband who has fallen for another woman. She observes the 'Karva Chauth' fast, praying for his long life despite being cheated by him. What are these popular films trying to portray? As Mahashweta Devi says that "even after fifty years we're at a point of no return. Today India has an extension of a medieval value system" (quoted by Ahluwalia).

From *Main Chup Rahungi* to the very recent *Hum Saath Saath Hain*, we have had women who have no voice or as Luce Irigaray has suggested in *Speculum de l'autre femme* that Woman is silence. At the same time there are films where women have been characterized in a traditional way and gifted with tremendous inner strength to overcome heavy odds. There have been films with strong women characters who remain in our memory for a long time like *Bandini, Mother India, Aandhi, Pratighaat*, and the more recent *Mrityudand.*

Of the many memorable women characters in Hindi films the two films that this paper discusses are *Khushboo* and *Arth* and the focus is on the betrayal of the women within the institution of marriage. Marriage and family are patriarchal constructs. Social conventions have tended to cooperate on behalf of the dominant group in the society, that is, Man. Although social customs and the circumstances work against these women yet they are able to face their situation boldly.

Khushboo is based on a story by Sarat Chandra Chatterji, himself a rebel and known for portraying strong women characters. The film is directed by Gulzar. It is the story of Kusum leading a quiet and uneventful life with her brother, Kunj, who sells toys and earns a living. She was married at a young age but was rejected by her father-in-law as a result of a family feud that occurred years ago. Kusum still honours that marriage believing in its sanctity and has not married again. When the film opens, we find the hero, Brindaban, the man to whom Kusum was married, coming to the same village as a doctor. Brindaban, in the meantime, had married but had lost his wife. He has a son from this marriage.

Brindaban and his mother try to rectify the earlier mistake by trying to win Kusum back. Once Brindaban's mother visits Kusum's house and hands over a pair of gold bracelets (kangans) without offering her any explanation. She takes it for granted that Kusum will only be too willing to accept the bracelets signifying her acceptance of Brindaban as her husband and lord. On the contrary, Kusum's self-respect receives a jolt and she returns the gold bracelets the very next day as she is unable to digest this humiliation.

The hero as doctor fulfills his duties towards society by caring and looking after the people of the village and Kusum deeply respects him as an individual and as a human being. The hero is forced to ask Kusum what is lacking in his personality that is keeping them apart. She tells him that he lacks the conviction to deal honestly with their relationship. In the final scene of the film it is only when Brindaban applies '*sindoor*' to her parting and requests her to be his wife, does Kusum consent to accompany him as his wife.

In the film we see that though Kusum is an ordinary village girl of pre-independence days, she is in complete control of her life and refuses to see herself as a helpless victim. There is a rebellion of a quiet kind in her. In spite of her bold dismissal of one set of behavioural codes, Kusum is unable to break free from her adherence to a few core values. Her expectations from the institution of marriage are based on her own terms of equality and dignity. In an earlier scene in the film, when her bosom friend teases her by asking whether she would return to her husband if he came to take her, Kusum retorts *"suhaag bhi loongi to bheekh mein ?"* (Shall I accept marriage as alms ?) Kusum accepts the bonds she wants. For her, self-dignity and individualism are inherent human values.

In *Arth* we come across a different situation where the heroine is trying to find the meaning of life after being betrayed by her husband. Pooja who belongs to modern Indian society finds that after seven years of her marriage she is totally alone. Inder (her husband) leaves her for another woman, Kavita, – an event for which Pooja was totally unprepared. She comes from an orphanage and is not economically independent. A shattered

Pooja makes every effort to save her marriage and put it back on the rails but fails miserably. Inder is adamant and has made up his mind to desert her. Gradually Pooja pulls herself out of this state of limbo and starts working at her life all over again. She enrols herself in the Working Women's Hostel and in due course gets a decent job with the help of a friend named Raj. The film depicts the realization that economic independence for a woman is a great asset in any given situation.

In *Arth* the concept of female bonding also has been explored. In the backdrop of the Pooja-Inder relationship there is the character of the maidservant. She is going through a similar phase in life – her husband is a drunkard and has deserted her for another woman. This illiterate woman has a mission in life – of bringing up her girl child and providing good education to her so that she may have a better life as compared to her own. On learning that her drunkard husband has stolen her savings which she had kept aside for paying her daughter's school fee she murders her husband in a fit of rage and lands in prison. Pooja, then, adopts this girl and realises the true 'arth' or meaning of her life.

There is another angle to the story about Pooja's relationship with Raj. He is a singer struggling to make a career in music. He is highly impressed to see Pooja humiliate Inder before everyone when he enters a party with his new love Kavita. Raj gives Pooja all kinds of moral support to enable her to overcome her problems. During this struggle they develop a strong bond of friendship. Raj becomes a star overnight and Pooja also is able to earn a decent position. He wants to marry Pooja but she refuses his offer as she feels that marriage is not the only meaning of life for a woman. She makes him understand that the selfless motherhood that has been bestowed upon her by her maid servant makes her life meaningful in the real sense. Her refusal to be a second fiddle to a man makes her character a memorable one. She has a point when she says that education alone can provide women with the necessary armour to protect themselves.

The most poignant scene of the film is when Inder returns to Pooja after being rejected by his mistress, Kavita. Pooja refuses to accept him again. Inder feels that since he is a man, all his injustices will be pardoned. He also feels that Pooja being a woman will only be too willing to accept him. Pooja simply questions him, "Had she done the same as he had and then returned to him, would he have accepted her ?" Inder says a very emphatic 'No'. In *The Second Sex*, Simone de Beauvoir has commented, "Marriage has always been a very different thing for man and for woman. The two sexes are necessary to each other, but this necessity has never brought about a condition of reciprocity between them" [446]. The husband is free to do as he pleases whereas the wife will always be subordinate, secondary and parasitic in her dependence on him.

Towards the end of the film Pooja tells her friend, Raj, that she wants to live her life by doing away with all other names except hers. Like Kusum in *Khushboo*, Pooja, too, accepts the bonds she wants and rejects those that stifle her growth. She does not require any man's support or help. Raj finally tells her, "*Jo saahas tum mein jaga hai, ab tumhe kisi Malhotra ya Raj ki zaroorat nahin*" (with the strength which has woken in you, you no longer need a Malhotra or Raj). Pooja then utters the quintessential verdict; '*Apne naam ko har naam se alag karke jeena chahti hoon*' (I want to dissociate my name from all other names).

Pooja is not portrayed as a woman who has no options but as a socially evolved individual who chooses and works out her own resolution. She chooses an independent strategy of survival, rejecting marriage which as Beauvoir observed is the only option offered to women, "Marriage is the destiny traditionally offered to women by society" [445].

In both the films the women protagonists, Kusum and Pooja, have questioned the prescriptive constructs of social institutions such as marriage and wifehood. Kusum accepts marriage on her own terms. Given her background and historical context, marriage for Kusum has a sanctity. But for

Pooja marriage is not all that important. She rejects the idea of settling down with a man. With social and cultural changes, a change has also come about in the ideas and thoughts of women. Each of the two women in these films has revolted in her own way. Kusum and Pooja react against and thus transgress the male discourse which entraps them. They are the women who "do not sweep aside the existing order. Rather they assert their own discourse in the face of the male one by breaking it up; subverting it and in a sense, re-writing it" (quoted by Mulvey 182).

Films are a very emphatic medium which influence our society. The films that project women in the right perspective from a humanistic and rational point of view need attention and appreciation. Even women artists must challenge the dictum: "In the film industry women are seen and not heard". They must not conform to the norms set by Hindi films of systematic cultivation of women as objects of desire. One looks forward to the film-maker's construction of strong, self-reliant and purposeful women protagonists who are able to step out and rise beyond their conventional concerns. The recurrent portrayal of marriage as being the only source of honour and achievement in a woman's life should be a matter of the bygone era.

References

Ahluwalia, Preet Mohan S. "Still Cast In A Mould". *Tribune,* 10 Jan. 2000.

de Beauvoir, Simone. *The Second Sex*, Trans and ed. H. M. Parshlay, (1953) Harmondsworth: Penguin, 1986.

Humm, Maggie. *Feminism and Film*. Bloomington and Indianapolis: Edinburgh University Press, 1997.

Mulvey, Laura. "Feminism, Film and the Avant-Garde". *Women Writing and Writing about Women*. Ed. Mary Jacobus: New York; Barnes and Noble, 1979.

14 Symbolism and Space in Aparna Sen's *Paroma* and Deepa Mehta's *Fire*

Mini Nanda

Paroma, as the name signifies, stands for excellence in beauty and attributes. In the opening scene against the looming statue of Durga – the symbol of Shakti, is Paroma at the center of the Puja Celebration in a traditional Bengali house in Calcutta. Which is a contrast with Satyajit Ray's *Devi* where the image of Durga at the beginning, full of adornments and finery, is worshipped in all her splendour. And towards the end, Durga shorn of everything, marks the movement from splendour to simplicity. Paroma is an equally beautiful and accomplished daughter-in-law, wife and mother, the epicenter of the family. She is responsible for everything – taking care of the family members, the guests, of the needs of her mother-in-law, who in turn stands for authority, the doyen of the family. Everyone consults her on both important and trivial matters, whether it is the purchase of a new flat or outings, or food on the table. In this traditional milieu the photographer is the exotic outsider, from America, equipped with war photographs of Lebanon. Rahul, the photographer, is a welcome guest for he happens to be the friend of a nephew.

On his next trip, there are photographs of Paroma at the Durga Puja, followed by Rahul's request to shoot Paroma as the quintessential Indian Bahu for *Life* magazine. The resistance is surprisingly not from the mother-in-law who is very supportive as is the husband; it is Paroma herself who resists the offer. The round dining table emphasises the equal status of each member of the family. The young daughter ironically chides her mother "You will live a secondhand life through baba", the elder son pipes in "Why don't you become a model?" and the husband responds typically, "No, no I won't be able to show my face".

The visual effect that the film creates is beautiful. We have charming vignettes of an Indian household – spacious porches with potted palms, settees, elegant cabinets and aesthetically arranged rooms. The scenes unfold Paroma holding court with the servant, planning the day's menu, meticulously counting clothes to be given for wash to the dhobi. She is, as Rahul tells her much later, a "guriya" in the household. At another level a puppet that doesn't have much life of her own. Her sitar lies rusting in a corner. She seeks permission from her mother-in-law to visit her friend, as she plies her with sweets. A counterpoint is provided by her friend Sheela who is a teacher in a spastic children's school. Sheela is divorced and is holding her own in the bursting metropolis. An interesting point is that this role is played by Aparna Sen, the film's director. Friends gather around Sheela and discuss their monotonous lives while Paroma's revelation of modelling assignments creates quite a stir among them.

In fact it is Paroma's placid life which is set rippling with the jaunty entrance of the photographer who places the camera in the center of the porch and the lens seem to focus on her very soul. "What do you think and do the whole day?" he asks a very flustered Paroma. The question is as unnerving as is the photographer's presence. She replies, "I do not know what I think". The application of *alta* on her feet by the photographer adds a different shade to their relationship. Paroma rubs it clean and declares to her family that she doesn't wish to be photographed as a "traditional beautiful housewife".

When the photographer takes her out into the open high spaces of the metropolis from the closed domestic space, a certain vibrancy enters her life. Symbolically Paroma treads on dangerous ground as the photographer guides her high up on the iron grid for a breathtaking aerial view of the city. Paroma seems to leave the mundane world below as she takes a fresh look through the camera and breaks into poetry, "*Bhool gaya hai shahar hamara jeevan ka shrotra*" (The city has forgotten the sources of our life). This seems to be the first connection with her forgotten past. The second connection is in her mother's dilapidated house. As the two – Paroma and Rahul – ascend the spiral staircase and enter the empty attic, childhood seems to rush up in a flash of happy children running up the steps. He becomes the catalyst of change for Paroma who emerges from her cocoon and talks about her aunt – Sudha Bua – who used to be locked up in the attic. There was a "scandal" about her and she would implore the children to open the door. They were forbidden to talk to her.

The visit to her mother's house reveals Paroma as a lady surrounded by material wealth and comfort as contrasted with her mother's dismal penury. On the other hand the photographer's visit to his old house is full of fun and laughter. He weaves a fantasy as he tells the new owners, who are simple and trusting people, that Paroma and he live in a caravan. She plays the sitar while he takes photographs. He is again the outsider who fascinates the young and old alike with the account of his life as a nomad. For Paroma there is the fear of her own untapped passion being unleashed and in distress she implores her husband on the telephone to return.

In stark contrast to Paroma's dilemma is her husband's unsuccessful overture to his young secretary in the office, who politely rebuffs him. And the husband's response is an abuse which he mutters after she leaves.

There is the inevitable storm that rages outside, as Paroma gets intimate with the photographer inside. The cinematic camera moves to the montage of scattered clothes, watch, shoes and the silent camera on the stand. The third eye of Durga in Ray's *Devi*, becomes the third eye of the camera in *Paroma*. As Rahul develops photographs, the present mingles with Paroma's past, the marigold fields and Sudha Bua's call for release. The song in the background "*Radhe dheere dheere nikalna gali se*" seems to cast a cautionary note.

The mirror image becomes significant in the shot when the daughter questions her mother: why she keeps buying new perfumes? Is it that she has complex about her age? Or when Paroma looks for moral support from her friend Sheela, she is questioned again, "Are you hurting anyone with this relationship? Do you need to have this affair?"

Paroma resumes playing the sitar, she even breaks into a song now and then. The lover leaves for foreign climes, they keep in touch through letters. Paroma is confident that her privacy won't be violated and asks him to write to her at her home address. But the arrival of the magazine by post shocks the family and a storm bursts. The husband is appalled by the intimate photograph of his wife accompanied by a fond note from the photographer.

The outside world of children, enthusiastic about their cricket, the world of fun and laughter is sharply contrasted with the inner world of adults – withdrawn and stern. The mother-in-law turns her out of her room. Her husband withdraws from her; he removes his clothes, the servants and finally the children from Paroma and asserts, "I don't want my children to be taught by a whore". Paroma's world is shattered; she raises a very pertinent question, when she asks her husband, "*Kya tumne kabhi koi galti nahi ki*?" which echoes the wife's question, in the film *Arth*, "If I had committed the same mistake would you have accepted me", and the husband's brutal "No" answers everything. (Incidentally the viewer is also reminded of the advances he made toward his secretary). Denigrated from Paroma to a whore emphasizes the whole process as it moves from the veneration of a woman as a deity to her denigration as a whore, hardly perceiving her as a woman, with feelings or desires of her own.

Paroma is completely alienated in her own house. She waits for Rahul to admit responsibility, but her friend Sheela informs her that he is untraceable. She requests her friend to find a job for her as she refuses the money her husband sends for her, which her daughter flings on the table. Poised at the crossroads of her life, at the traffic signal, Paroma is rudely shaken to see her disheveled aunt Sudha Bua, cry piteously as the mental hospital staff pull her away. Here we have the reflection of the self in the other. This is followed by Paroma's nervous breakdown.

At the nursing home, the family rallies round Paroma. Her hair is shaven off for an X-ray, prior to surgery. Her daughter breaks down at the news that her mother's hair will be tonsured. Tonsuring of her hair seems to be a process of sloughing off her past, the pain and the humiliation as well as thrusting a widowhood on her. Her blank expression, in the meeting with the family, changes to quiet resignation as she pours her feeling into her diary. Belated recognition comes for her precious plant, gifted by her lover, which she had nurtured. In a flash she remembers its name "Krishnapallavi" as she carelessly drops the papers announcing the whereabouts of Rahul and makes a final break with her past. She turns to her friend for help for an opening and asserts herself by accepting a humble job of a sales person in a Khadighar. When the neurosurgeon patronizingly suggests psychotherapy to erase her sense of guilt her calm reply that she has no sense of guilt signals a sense of freedom from the values of patriarchal judgment. From a housewife to a dependent mistress to a rejected wife and mother (poignantly shown in the scene where she hugs her younger son and cries as he gets impatient to run off to school) to a woman who asserts herself; rejecting the pin money from her husband, she takes small steps towards realizing her own potential. Her growth is like that elusive childhood plant she had searched for in vain. When she finds it, she fails to recall its name. Her final connection with her childhood past is established as she recovers her memory and remembers the name of the plant. Her life takes root like the sapling as she discovers her own self free of male framing and recognition. The cinematic qualities are very effective as Aparna Sen directs a film which is a slice of human life, revealing the fragile foundations of any human relationship, and the thin margin between acceptable and unacceptable values; the power structure in the family and at the same time bonds of friendship, especially between Paroma and Sheela, a friendship which is not dramatic but stable. Sheela passes no judgment on her friend but helps her in small and significant ways.

Deepa Mehta taps deeper waters as she explores feminine space in *Fire* shot in shadowy interiors as she questions traditional family structures that confine women to stereotypical roles like those of a dutiful wife or daughter-in-law. Her deeper needs and aspirations are unexpressed to say the most and unfulfilled to say the least. The young bride Sita is taken on a routine round of "honeymoon" to Agra where the guide extols the beauty of the Taj, the symbol of external love. The unconcerned husband refuses to answer whether he loves his wife for as he says they have barely been married. Home is situated in some old part of Delhi, where the elder daughter-in-law Radha takes care of the kitchen, cooking and serving the family, washing and dressing up her invalid mother-in-law. Radha has spent thirteen loveless years with her husband who had taken a vow of celibacy. Characters are sharply etched and contrasted in satirical pattern. As the elder son Ashok presses his Swamiji's feet, who mumbles a lecture on "Desire night" - love of power (sic) and "aspiration night" "power of love", the younger brother kisses the feet of his Chinese mistress and applies nail paint on her toes.

The elder brother needs to test his sense of control by ordering his wife to sleep by his side, as part of her duty to aid him in his quest for higher pleasure. The younger brother has a wham, bang, and thank you mam relationship with his new bride. He patronizingly asks her to find other interests in life, best served by embroidery or in taking up beauty culture as he returns to his mistress (a hair dresser?) who cuts his hair and preens him.

The juxtapositions are hilarious at times, the elder brother hands out money to each member and at the same time keeps money aside for Swamiji, whose pictures adorn his bedroom walls. At other times the contrasts are ironic and painful when Jatin stands against the film posters of "Hum Dono" and coolly tells his wife that his love interest lies elsewhere, or when Ashok tells his wife that the younger daughter-in-law must be pregnant, as she is looking very happy.

At home Ashok plays the role of Swamiji directing the lives of others, mainly his wife. The younger brother rebels and insists that he would carry on his affair with his mistress, just as the elder brother would continue to support Swamiji. The open space of Lodhi Garden where the family goes for a picnic is shot in bright daylight, which contrasts with the strategy of subversion through dimly lit interiors. In this shadowy world gently the trauma of marital life and its hollowness unfolds. There are mosquito nets around the bed, which could imply a veiling of reality. Perhaps the reality of impotence or some disorder that was clinically diagnosed as "no eggs" by some doctor, as Radha informs Sita. Lines of pain and submission are etched on Radha's face while Sita, the younger daughter-in-law, complains that she responds like a "trained monkey", whenever "somebody presses my button called tradition". It is a deliberate strategy on the part of the diasporic director to take up loaded names like Radha and Sita in the English version of the film, the names were altered in the Hindi version.

Another narrative strategy is the Karva Chauth story recounted by the elder daughter-in-law. It is an interesting scene which is a fantasy for the servant's – Mundu – imagination. It is an amusing mime in which Mundu is the King and Ashok is the Swamiji, the younger brother the dutiful brother, with the incongruous sunglasses.

The story emphasizes the capricious nature of love where in a moment the Queen is denigrated to the status of a maid servant, who in turn, is elevated to the status of a Queen. It reflects faithlessness in a marital life. While the wives are fasting for their husbands' wellbeing on one hand, on the other Ashok is with Swamiji while the younger one is feasting with his mistress's family. The younger daughter-in-law observes that Ashok Bhaiya should have kept a fast for Swamiji.

The diasporic director zeroes her lenses to the world of warmth, companionship and sex that the two lonely women forge for themselves. And then we have a scene where Ashok watches a garish Ram Lila, where an even more crude character portraying young Sita sings hoarsely, "I am pure and fire will prove it," and another character says, "you have triumphed by fire". With the male figures absent - the husbands are lost in their respective world of spiritual and sensual pleasure - the two women play hopscotch on the terrace and in a significant move, go to Nizamuddin Aulia's shrine and tie a thread, seeking understanding and strength from the Sufi saint.

In the well-lit kitchen the two female characters create their space, discussing spices - black pepper for energy and cardamom for fragrance. Jatin warns his wife, "I don't know what the future holds" and chauvinistically feels that a baby would keep her occupied. Sita turns round and calls him a bloody fool, spells it out neat for him and answers his slap with a resounding slap.

Ashok when confronted with his wife's relationship with Sita sits stumped under the posters of "Crush" Soft drinks. What follows is a gratuitous love scene between Radha and Sita imagined through the eyes of the husband and worked through the intention of the director, which is problematic. The crushed husband demands that his wife perform her duty towards him for he has to 'test' his sense of control again. Do we get an echo of Gandhiji's controversial experiment with the truth of his sense of control and vow of celibacy? Ashok does make a reference to Gandhi when he cautions his wife on the morning of the Karva Chauth fast to take things easy for fasting without water had been tough even for Gandhi.

While Sita leaves the house immediately on the discovery of their relationship, Radha feels that she has to talk to her husband before she leaves; severing a long relationship is not easy for her. But the two decide to make a new beginning ironically under the embroidered frame of 'Home Sweet Home', on the wall. The mother-in-law spits at Radha who tells her husband that she needs the "warmth, compassion and the body of Sita". It raises an important issue of sharing and caring as and where it is possible. Radha refuses to play the puppet in her husband's mime of self-control and declares that she wants to live her own life, for without desire there is no life. While her husband screams at her to fall at his feet and seek forgiveness and go to Swamiji for a cure and for cleansing of her sins.

As an actual fire spreads through the kitchen, the husband turns his back on his wife as she is caught in the conflagration and proceeds to rescue his mother. Radha flings aside her enflamed saree and in the act casts aside her fetters and moves towards the only place, which is filled with light in the surrounding darkness, to the shrine of Nizamuddin Aulia and to her companion Sita.

Both the films define feminine space, the intrusions and appropriation of that space, the rigid, unbending patriarchal structures, the hypocrisy and hollowness of family ties. A woman is a Devi and worshipped as long as she follows the patriarchal rules, an act of rebellion or of defiance condemns her to the margins by the same adoring family.

Both the films are open-ended; there is no finality of closures, much like life, which moves on punctuated by both pleasure and pain. They leave the viewer with many questions to think over.

15 Breaking the Silence: Gender, Caste and Transgression in *Phaniyamma* and *Bandh Jharokhe*

Sudha Rai

Prema Karanth's[1] *Phaniyamma*[2] and *Bandh Jharokhe*[3], are adaptations of woman-centred novels which explore gender in the contexts of issues like widowhood and marital rape. Gendering, which commences at girlhood for the protagonists of these novels, is explored within the specificities of Brahmin caste structures and the regional variants of its caste system in Karnataka, themes interrogated in the Kannada new wave cinema from 1970 onwards.[4]

Prema Karanth states that though the two films have not been directed through an overtly feminist perspective, they do represent the survival of individuals amidst the adversities of their oppressed lives. Both novels on which the films are based, however, read as feminist texts, exploring the threads of gender oppression, in the Malnad region of rural Karnataka in *Phaniyamma* and in the urban context of Mumbai in *Bandh Jharokhe*. Karanth's two films are therefore brimming with critiques of the silencing of women's voices, the denial of their right to their own bodies and the thwarting of choices and aspirations.

The cultural frameworks of Brahminism and its normative and repressive principles of 'purity' and 'pollution' constructed from the Vedic period onwards have effectively marginalized women. Originating in the view of the Brahmin as divine, and the essential part played by his wife in rituals and ceremonies, moving on to her stereotyping as a role model, the repression of women within the Brahminical framework is particularly harsh. Karanth's use of image and narrative to represent the action of these repressive forces in the unconscious of the women and the process of breaking the silence of their oppression constitutes the focus of my article. Transgressions of caste and gender boundaries by the female protagonists – Phaniyamma, Dakshayini and Saru, which represent a significant breakthrough in redefining the silenced aspects of their being, are constructed cinematically, as I argue, through spatial metaphors of imprisonment and darkness, banishment and exile.

II

Karanth's *Phaniyamma* based on M.K. Indira's fictionalization of the real-life story of a child widow *Phaniyamma* living in the Malnad district of Karnataka, near Tirthahalli is a realistic rendering of the regional culture of a Brahmin postmaster's joint family. The film commences with a leisurely, guided tour of the family home Anchemane (now empty), and its interior gender-demarcated spaces, where generations have grown up, their horoscopes compared and marriages performed. A symbol of status to the community surrounding it, Anchemane is actually a citadel of Brahminical caste practices and gender confinements. Karanth's film dwells specially on the rituals that the inmates of the house are compelled to perform, day in and day out, in the name of tradition, thereby pleasing the male heads of the household and appeasing the head priest of Sringeri Sri Sri Nrsimhabharathiswamigalavaru, but the punishment of excommunication is visited on them for flouting tradition: "In those times the concept of *madi* was cherished, which gave special place to that which was sacred or 'pure'. Along with *madi* went the upholding of tradition, ritual, and all in all of the attitudes of frogs-in-a-well" (Niranjana 3). The men take all decisions for the women and children. The family jewels too are in the custody of grandfather and are released only on special occasions.

Indira's novel explores the issues of child marriage through the nine year old child-bride Phaniyamma who is married to the 15 year old Nanjunda. When Nanjunda dies of snake-bite, Phani is blamed for the tragedy. She is made to take on the Brahminical strictures of *madi*[5], a traditional practice which involves a self-effacing regimen of fasting, purification, and denial of bodily desires that have been imposed on her widowed state. Phani, because of the orthodox times in which she lives, (1840-1952) and her illiteracy, accepts her stigmatization as a child widow. When she dies at the age of 112, she has become a symbol of the strength of traditional Indian woman, bearing her servitude in silence. Within her own mind however, after steady scrutiny and questioning, Phaniyamma concludes that traditions are meaningless. However, she ends up paying a heavy price for her silent acceptance of the traditional system of *madi*.

Phani's mother assiduously devotes herself to the gendering of her daughter, as preparation for Phani's marriage. With sweet smiles she silences Phani's questions and prevents her from exploring the world outside. Soon, Phani, a gentle child learns total obedience. Her marriage at the age of ten, widowhood a few months later, and assimilation into the Brahminical regimen of *madi* are quickly achieved, and she does not protest.

An important aspect of the novel's structure is Phaniyamma's breaking the silence of her seeming acquiescence with social custom, to her niece Banashankari, (an empathetic and reticent listener), who subsequently narrates it to her daughter Indi, the narrative point of view both in the film and the novel. This section of the narrative contains some important critiques of male-centered myths, and their acceptance and reinforcement through social custom.

In a film in which the codes of customs and belief of rural Karnataka are represented with sensitivity and skill, Karanth exploits two sequences in the novel for their colour contrasts, so as to symbolise the bleak, colourless existence and the unrelieved misery of Phani's widowhood. In the first sequence, Phani who has lovingly purchased a new set of glass bangles (at the fair where her plait, along with its jewelled clasp, has been chopped off by a thief) soon has to face the tragedy of seeing them smashed, when her husband dies within a few months of their marriage. The romanticized rainbow shades of childhood and marriage are drained by the severe impositions of a widow's dress, as young Phani is draped in a drab white sari. She is put away in a dark room. Gentle and reticent by nature, Phani's silence eloquently conveys her helplessness within the regimen of patriarchy, which the women in the family heartily enforce, for fear of offending the patriarchs in the family and the Swami of Sringeri Shankarmath.

A further use of colour symbolism is made by Karanth when the haldi and *kumkum* (auspicious marks of a married woman) on her puja plate (arranged for tulsi puja) are accidentally strewn by Phani.

Fear and hypocrisy being the realities of Brahmin women's lives at that time, when Phani loses her hair and gold jewelled clasp at the neighborhood fair, she is hidden away in the '*katle kone*' (dark room), which becomes symbolic of her imprisonment. The use of force is rubbed in later on when her cherished rainbow coloured bangles are smashed by male hands. Similarly, the shaving of her head is narrated in a string of close-ups which convey the loss of her youth and beauty, emphasizing the act as one of blatant violation of her body. The thick heap of her shorn hair, the camera dwells on, heightens the viewers' repugnance. The focus in this scene is also on Phani's large, protruding eyes and her stony stillness, as victim of the decisions taken by her elders.

As the narrative progresses, the tender rounded body of the young Phani soon converts into the gaunt, wasted frame of the widowed Phani, who denies herself food and burns herself out physically by taking on unflinchingly, the roles of cook, midwife, nurse, and counselor. Though she eventually acquires a legendary and saintly fame in her region, Karanth's camera dwells on the ghostly apparition of Phani, who pops out of the interior spaces more ghost than flesh and blood.

Phani's powerful and definitive transgression of brahminical boundaries (for her time) occurs when she is in her eighties, when, albeit by stealth and in the dark she responds to the distress of the fifteen year old untouchable girl, Sinki, who is in labour. Phani goes across to her home, and delivers her child with her wasted, tiny hands. Unexposed to sex and marriage, Phani is ironically brought into the heart of female suffering and wonders why women accept their role as child bearers. However, Phani has nowhere and no one to escape to. After the transgressive act and a cleansing bath which removes the pollution of child birth and untouchability, she preserves a decorous silence and returns home.

However *Phaniyamma* does not endorse the defeat of women under the clutches of the religious patriarchy as the story of Dakshayini, another widow within the family, (though not a child widow), is narrated. The contrast in the two texts of widowhood is developed through a similar focus on removal of *kumkum*, the breaking of bangles, but stops at that point with Dakshayini's radical transgression of widowhood by regrowing her hair. With taunting abuse, she upbraids the elders in her family, refusing to be tamed. She rejects hypocrisy as a defence mechanism. As she says, "my husband is dead .... not my youth." Phani's sympathies for Dakshayini are evident, as she attempts to intercede with the elders, not wanting her own tortured history of widowhood to be repeated.

In an even more full-blooded transgression Dakshayini flaunts her pregnancy by her brother-in-law, and holds her own ground despite the attempts of her in-laws to evict her. She re-writes her fate by refusing to take on *madi* fasting, or denying herself sexual satisfaction. Karanth focuses repeatedly on Dakshayini's long and lustrous hair, her radiant good health and rebellious, flushing eyes to relish the turn of the wheel for defunct caste and gender practices.

III

> What caste is he?
> I don't know.
> A Brahmin?
> Of course not.
> Then, cruelly... his father keeps a cycle shop.
> Oh, so they are low-caste people, are they?
>
> The word her mother had used, with the disgust, hatred and prejudices of centuries had so enraged her that she had replied ... I hope so. (Deshpande 96)

After a vigil by the bedside of her cousin Madhav, whom she has treated for a high fever, Saru, the female protagonist of Prema Karanth's film *Bandh Jharokhe*, throws open window after window in the rooms of her paternal home, taking delight in another day. Full throated bird-trillings emphasize the moment of rebirth. The later shot of Saru bathing, her expression celebrating a sense of bliss, her body illuminated, physical, rapt in a private moment of total pleasure unmarked by fear, anxiety or pain, underlines the washing away of her fearful and tortured self. The cultural connection between bathing and purification[6] (from 'pollutants') are reified at several points in Karanth's film. "Food is ready... bathe", says Saru's father, for instance.

The close-up of Saru's bathing, is heightened through its duration and can be interpreted as a ritual cleansing. This shot is distinguished in its symbolic connotations from the early shot of Saru, splashing water on a face to refresh herself after the rigours of her journey by bus and by auto, from Mumbai to Dharwad, her parental home, after a gap of fifteen years. In the intervening time between her arrival and this final 'ritual' bath, Saru and her father have engaged in dialogue. The film makes the bonding of father and daughter an essential condition of Saru's breaking two areas of silence which have engulfed her personality. The silence revolving around the death of her brother Dhruva who died in a drowning accident for which her mother particularly, held her to blame. And the second silence relating to Saru's unspeakable trauma over the sadistic sexual behaviour of her husband Manu: "The monstrous invasion of my body" (Deshpande 12). The film depicts the deterioration in the warmth of the early years of their marriage as Saru's steady professional growth as a child specialist erodes Manu's self- esteem.

The most prominent motif used in *Bandh Jharokhe* in its many variations is that of the window frame, which with its bars, suggests the imprisoned self. Occasionally relieved by beams of sunlight which convey an alteration in Saru's depressed, introverted mood opening up a buried dimension of her self, or happy memories, the window frame becomes the backdrop against which Saru's journey into the tunnel of her past is observed. The window in its many patterns, is the spatial nucleus, one of the important frames from which flashbacks and nightmares of the past emanate.

The window is the literal space in whose proximity we find Saru sitting, meditating, or coming closer to her father, for warmth and comfort. Prema Karanth exploits the same barred window, now bathed in a harsh, blue, fluorescent light to symbolize the opening up of Saru's nightmares of guilt over her brother Dhruva's death, (for which she is hardly responsible) and her nightmares of being revisited by the forced sex thrust upon her by her husband. The lurid, garish light, throws up the domain of the negative and abnormal in Saru's unconscious; the twilight world never spoken of, never shared, never confronted even to oneself. Saru's inner journey of self, hitherto drowned out by the spoken and unspoken norms of social convention and the power structures of family, now needs to be confronted, a necessary rite of passage to a balanced and mature personality.

Unresponsive silences gather around Saru's childhood and Karanth's film open up the issues pertaining to the gendering of the girl child within the Brahminical caste structure. Saru's burgeoning intelligence reflected in her curiosity about her environment is rebuffed by her mother's set face and sharp rebuking voice. Her need for warmth goes unheeded. Ponytails are out for Saru, much as she preens over them. Tight, disciplined plaits are her mother's way of telling her she must tread the narrow path of convention in manners and morals.

Saddled with the responsibility of her younger brother from an early age Sarutai detests being addressed as 'tai (sister) because it denies her childhood and individuality. She frets silently at her own neglect, while much ado is made of her brother on his birthday. Her sexual development at puberty becomes a threatening stage to her mother, who, with a frown, stitches in the illogic of further pollution taboos. Her voice is a whip, taunting and alienating Saru. Attaining puberty, yet unable to acknowledge herself at the level of the body – Prema Karanth frames Saru before the mirror, furtively, tentatively feeling her body, taking delight in her new found sexuality, affirming her beauty since her mother has stamped her as ugly. Her mother, to whom she is bound by a woman's body, refuses to mirror Saru's needs for self-worth, casting rather her shadow over Saru, so that Saru cannot see her own self. The mother becomes synonymous with the suppression of Saru's aspirations.

However the irony of such hostile mother-daughter relationships is that, in certain instances, they generate a resultant force where the stronger the repulsion, the greater the strength of the daughter to fight and rebuild her life. The childhood need for security keeps Saru partially silent, so evident in shots of her darkening face, and her silent protest. Her deeper needs are defiantly articulated only on the one occasion when her father supports her desire for medical studies, in Bombay, against her mother's wishes. In many close-ups Saru is pinned against the wall, driven into a no-exit position as it were, vulnerable to attack and unable to retaliate through further speech or action.

Upholding the traditional role model for the Indian mother, as a perfect manager of her home, sacrificing the emergent needs of her being and mind, Saru's mother's harshness is repeatedly emphasized in shots of her unsmiling face and rigid stance, in her confrontations with Saru. Embodying the controlling mother Saru's 'Ai', takes on responsibility for total control of her daughter in the name of total protection. Her limited vision, an internalization of the Brahnimical patriarchy, blinds her to the wisdom that freedom and love – much more than discipline – are the poles around which the personality develops.

Saru's relationship with Manu is the second 'text' of silence in the film narrating the sexual tensions in their marriage. The early rapturous satisfaction of her body's needs convert to the enclosed fury of the sadistic assaults on her body, and the steady failure of communication between them. Saru's nostalgia for an early stage in their relationship when they were closer to one another, or so she thought, until the marriage was tested by Saru's growing professional aspirations, to the prioritizing of her professional time and space, over Manu's sexual needs. Manu's growing anger and discontent at Saru's separation of her body from his, her mind from his controls, is evident in his darkened face, his put-on laughter and gaiety, his "good ... very good" responses whenever he is made to confront her professional status, and the privileges it brings to them in terms of an improved standard of living.

The news of her mother's death triggers her panic-ridden escape from Manu (and the humiliations of forced, brutal sex, endured in silence) to her parental home. The narrative takes on from this point, Saru's entry into the dark tunnel of past traumas of gendering, guilt and blame. She is her mother's scapegoat for all ills in the family. The hated and maligned girl child, required to be self-effacing, passive, accepting a fate designed by her mother. Hostilities between Saru and her mother are narrated through shots of her mother's solid, upright figure trailing Saru whenever Saru finds a quiet corner for herself. She is made her brother's watchdog, and he becomes hers in the process, so that the treasured world of her imagination and private spaces, the transgressive spaces of the mango garden leading to the magical pond, are constantly encroached upon.

Blamed unfairly for her brother Dhruva's death, Saru is cut off from the warmth and support of family relationships. Despite the lingering close-up of Saru's father's broad hand reassuringly closing over her head in protection (affirming his shielding presence as a parent, even as her mother shriekingly accuses Saru of killing Dhruva), her father erases himself from her life, as much as her mother does, until the mother's death through cancer, prompts Saru to return to him. Karanth's film (as Deshpande's novel), privileges her father as parent, exonerating him for the long silence between him and Saru.

Structurally, the third part of *Bandh Jharokhe* projects Saru's attempt to heal her alienation, her loss of self, by re-rooting herself in her childhood milieu and consciously creating anew her significance in her childhood home. Her apparent regression into traditional womanly roles – tender of the tulsi plant, cook, and nodal centre of the many requirements of her father and cousin Madhav in the house – is an attempt to connect to vital, though traditional roles, which can invoke her self into being. She makes a full fledged attempt to bring gladness to her father, to teach Madhav English, and to serve the neighborhood needs as doctor. She has turned her back completely on Manu, her husband, putting away his stacks of letters to her, leaving them unopened in disdain. His crime apparently is so heinous it cannot be revisited. Mechanically living through each day of this stage, enables her to cope with trauma. Tulsi-puja, the churning of butter, (a beautiful rhythmic parallel for the act of recall, which Karanth uses as a trigger for a flashback) the claiming of interior spaces such as the kitchen, puja room, and her mother's room with its wardrobe and mirror-box, lead Saru to recover her self-esteem in the domestic sphere. Home is a place to heal.

At the cognitive level, Saru confronts the bubbling, choking miasmic memories which lie trapped beneath the surface, like her brother Dhruva's body, trapped beneath the marshy bubbling quagmire. Following closely the ideological line of Deshpande's text which privileges Saru's father as a pragmatic-rationalist, Karanth employs him as a sounding board and counselor figure to extricate Saru out of her terror-ridden dark, and show her an exit towards the light of self knowledge. Both her father and Madhav, who is studying for his C.A. and looks up to her as a successful professional from the city, relate to her at the level of family, and thereby bypass oppositional gender conflicts. It is only Manu with whom her gender conflicts are activated at the site of the body and the mind.

Flashbacks of the growing tensions in Saru's marriage and Manu's brutalities are shot in a psychedelic blue light. Gradually, Saru's father frees her from guilt when she is able to talk to him about her innocence over Dhruva's death. Her relapse into hysteria at the news that Manu, whose letters she has not responded to, is arriving, suggests once again the closure of the windows of her self. Saru's closing of doors and windows in the penultimate sequence of the film becomes a spatial metaphor for the withdrawal into her own self in order to confront the realities of a troubled marriage.

At this point Saru as nurturer comes into her own. Treating Madhav for a high fever, she is rewarded by his recovery. The saving of the brother figure Madhav juxtaposed against the guilt of her brother Dhruva's death, injects new energy into Saru. Her work as the 'neighborhood' doctor as distinguished from the different connotations (threatening in its individuation to patriarchal perspective) of a "lady doctor", rebuilds her self-confidence. And the film comes to rest on Saru's determined stance, to break the silence of non-communication between her and Manu. No romantic reunion is hinted at however: Saru's work comes first, but the traumas of her relationship with Manu will be examined, as she promises her father.

Saru's silence which works as a metaphor for the suppression and near extinction of a woman's self, is related to other levels of silence perpetuated by an unnamed patriarchy. Her mother has told Saru at every opportunity not to ask questions. Saru is doomed to guilt because no one asks for an account of Dhruva's death. Layers of silences build up – the silences of girlhood, marriage, silences of unshared losses and unfair blame, the silence of her father and mother unbroken for fifteen years (as if they had made a pact to outcaste Saru).

An early prefiguring of the woman's split self, through patriarchal violation, comes to us in the shape of the middle aged woman, possessed by the Devi, Saru's mother takes her to in childhood. The inarticulate and frenzied mutterings emanating from her mouth, until she falls down in a trance, her inhumanity and abnormal behaviour scare Saru so much that she withdraws from the scene. The warning connotations of 'division' are sounded out. In the novel, Saru reflects: "That a person could be so divided in herself, into two entirely different beings, was something unknown to me then" (Deshpande 103).

Saru's return to her parents' home enables her to appreciate the many burdens of a women's life her mother too had undergone (cooking, for example). Noteworthy however, is her individual stand on issues like fasting perversely eating on Dhruva's birthday (unlike her parents who fast in his memory), refusing to be penalized, again rejecting Brahminical norms.

Karanth's film makes one significant deletion from the literary text (possibly to preserve the tautness of the narrative). In the novel Saru has invented an imaginary friend, the boy Hemant. This fantasy enables her to deal with her loneliness within her own family. Touchingly, Hemant acts as Saru's defense, believing her version of her own innocence over Dhruva's death, at a time when both her parents have withdrawn from her.

IV

The theme of gender oppression and the culture of silence it encourages can be dealt with powerfully through the medium of film. The fearful, tentative attempts of women to combat the regimentation of their desires can be conveyed through their facial expressions and body language more powerfully than through their faltering speech.

Karanth's portrayal of the gendered girl child is sensitive and touching. Saru's legitimate questionings and the denial of information by her elders (women) is a familiar gender situation. The fact that puberty as a developmental stage is insensitively handled by women, compounded with the masculine revulsion against the biology of the female body leads the girl child to be caught within a web of fear, incomprehension, shame and guilt. The "dark room" reserved within Brahmin spaces for menstruating girls and women highlights the rejection of the woman at this level of her body by the male. Gendering is expressed also through a Brahmin woman's hair which she is denied her right to style, grow, or not grow.

In the context of marriage, marriage within caste is a norm. Saru's mother's query about Manu is about his caste: "What's his caste ? Do you know or not ?" A veil of silence is however drawn over any breaches of caste morality by the Brahmin men. For instance the relationship Putta Jois has with Subbi, who has been cast off by her husband's family because she has not conceived. As Phani observes cynically: "men who slept with a hundred women were still as pure as fire."

Karanth's two films clearly exploit the symbols of (i) hair (individuality); (ii) mirrors (hand-held; cupboard mirrors; and box mirrors whose reflected images shift between the girl Saru; Saru the woman; and Saru's mother – the clouded mirror signifying the hidden, and submerged aspects of her self); (iii) water (in its destructive and life-enhancing aspects; (iv) rain (a mounting crisis); (v) the bead curtain in Saru's mother's room (return transition to the past); (vi) colours of dress (especially the rainbow yellow, bright pink and green of Saru's saree to convey her happy and fulfilled self in the final scenes of the film); (vii) windows and doors (open, they signify the hopeful self, closed they symbolise the trapped, tormented self; (viii) music, (flute notes for Saru's past); and the sitar and tabla for her immediate present); (ix) the tulsi plant (symbol of a woman's tradition – bound self); (x) space: (transgressions of interior, confining spaces into open spaces are fraught with risk and tragedy. Saru's sole act of such transgression in childhood – the camera follows her, as she crosses the threshold of the gate of her family house, into the unsanctioned private space of her imagination, is 'punished' with the death of Dhruva); (xi) shadow sequences (the dark larger, shadow self thrown up in profile on the wall projects Saru's fear and anxiety, and the tragic split in her self that occurs when her mother, blaming her for her brother's death, screams at her – "*Tune hi use maara hai!*;") (xii) the train (the clattering rhythm suggests the fear of intrusion by Manu, into Saru's secure childhood space).

To conclude, Phani can carry out her transgression against caste norms only upto a point, when she delivers the untouchable Sinki's child, in the protective guise of darkness. Her actions are still instinctively governed by the internalization of Brahmin practices of purity and pollution, whose victim she remains.

Dakshayini breaches the dogmas of widowhood, questioning the denial of her sexuality and beauty. Her rebellion, we must remind ourselves however, takes place within the threshold of caste and family, when she accepts her brother-in-law as her husband.

For Saru, a lady doctor living in modern Mumbai, the transgressions against caste are flouted in her marriage to Manu. She is punished (in my reading) by being 'banished' from her family. The new dilemmas of role conflict, where being a lady doctor questions her traditional wifely role, are frightening excavations into the darkness of gender oppressions Mothers (like Saru's) desensitized to such oppressions will never mirror the authentic needs of their daughters, fretting to be rid of residual gender bondages. A perpetual cycle of conflicts leading to transgressions (from the patriarchal perspective) appears to be the inescapable reality of the urban, married Indian women who gives her profession and therefore herself, serious worth.

Notes

1. Prema Karanth is Karnataka's first and most renowned woman film director. She came to fame with *Phaniyamma* (Kannada) in 1982. *Band Jharokhe* was produced in 1997. Karanth also has a sterling reputation as a costume designer having designed costumes for six films and 120 plays. She is deeply involved with the children's theatre movement in Karnataka.
2. *Phaniyamma* won three international awards in Paris as well as the best Kannada film award. The widely traveled film has been shown at 13 film festivals including the International Women's Festival in Paris.
3. *Bandh Jharokhe* (Hindi) (1997-1998) was co-produced by NFDC and Doordarshan.
4. See for example, the interrogation of Brahminism in the films *Samskara* (1970) and *Vamsha Vriksha* (1971); untouchability in

Chomana Dudi (1975); and widowhood and patriarchy in *Ghatashraddha* (1977).

5. As a practice, *madi* continues to be observed by male priests and also Brahmin men on culturally 'special' occasions. However, the strictures of *madi* for women, tied as they are to the female body, and to widowhood, are much more binding, taxing and confining.
6. Hindu cultural norms, especially the Brahminical, demand that individuals bathe at the start of the day, before eating one's first meal, before prayer, after visiting the house where there has been a death, before visiting a temple, not during the first two days of menstruation and only on the third. The statement "I haven't bathed" within modern Indian society, continues to carry connotations of the traditionalist Brahmin reconstruction of 'unclean'.

References

Deshpande, Shashi. *The Dark Holds no Terrors* (1980). New Delhi: Penguin, 1990.

Indira, M.K. *Phaniyamma* (1976). Translated Tejaswini Niranjana. New Delhi: Kali for Women, 1989.

16 Journey into the Mind of a Woman: From *Rajni* to *Mashaal*

Tripti Jain

A novel and a film are two totally different mediums, each having its own artistic compulsions, though the purpose is the same – the telling of a story. Since the time film has shifted its focus from animation to story telling, the relationship between fiction and cinema has been close and significant.

The novel is the raw material which the filmmaker is eager to use, and this is the point where the two mediums meet – the point where they are close to each other. This is also the point from where they take off in their own different directions, the film sometimes assuming a different form altogether.

The writer is a creative person, and the fictional world that she has created is populated by characters living a life, which is the product of his imagination. The director is also an artist, and though he takes his raw material from the novel – the characters and the story line – the way he uses the raw material has to be different. The film is ultimately his craft and what he makes of the novel is determined by his own creative impulses and his own perceptions underline the unfolding of the story.

The writer uses words to say many things, and delving deep into the minds and hearts of his characters makes their feeling and ideas explicit. He uses his own imagination and plays upon words to give each character a particular persona. Going beyond words, the director constructs a living world with light and shade, natural and artificial props. He builds up an ambience with the use of sound, music, dialogue and even silence, to convey his meaning. It is this ambience which leaves a lingering and enduring impression on the mind of the audience. The greater this lingering effect, the more the re-run value of the film.

There are bound to be variations between the novel and the manner in which it is interpreted by the filmmaker. These variations can be at all levels – the story, the characterization, and even the end. The novel and the film represent two different genres. When the writer conceives the novel, he sees it in one way, locates it within one cultural milieu and his characters live in a certain framework of time. When the film director visualises it, he looks at it from a different angle, for there is always more than one way of looking at a thing. It is the creativity of another mind which moulds the story and shapes the characters of the film. He is not telling a story in the manner in which the writer has written it. He is narrating his own story and wants to tell it in his own way. He feels free to add to or subtract from the story and tell the story in his own way, for the film is his creation, a vehicle of his creativity.

The relationship between cinema and literature has always been important. This is true not only of Hollywood, where most of the literary bestsellers have been filmed, rated among top quality productions, and consistently supported for Academy awards.[1] It is equally true of Indian cinema where bestselling novels from all languages have been filmed in more than one language. In its early phase, Indian cinema depended very heavily on literary works.

In fact it is widely acknowledged that films become a medium of including the larger society, the masses as it were, within the 'great tradition'. Stephen Bush, as early as 1911, observed that "it is the business of the moving picture to make them known to all" (quoted by Boyum 4). Indian films based on the epics are another dimension of this belief. Literature is "proven property" (Boyum 4) and allows space for reinterpretation not only of the classics but also of human action.

Indian cinema in the 40s and 50s made abundant use of classics, specially Bengali classics and several novels of Bankim Chandra Chattopadhaya and Sarat Chandra Chatterjee were filmed.[2] M. Madhava Prasad in his work *Ideology of the Hindi Film* has observed that the middle class cinema is "marked by an overwhelming dependence on Bengali culture for its narrative and iconographic material as well as film-making talent. This cinema was founded on the twin distinctions of primacy of narrative and the ordinariness and authenticity of the world represented" (Prasad 164). But as both the film and the novel relate to the world-out-there, it becomes necessary to interrogate the changes which the director makes in order to bridge the period between the writing of the novel and the filming of the narrative. How does he transcend immediate social relevance to become relevant in the new present and thus acquire a new contemporariness.

For the purposes of this paper, I have chosen to focus on Bankim Chandra Chattopadhyaya's novel *Rajni* and compare it with the film *Mashaal* which was based on the book. *Rajni* was written sometime in the 1870s and *Mashaal* was made in 1949-50. Produced by Bombay Talkies, it had Ashok Kumar, Sumitra Debi, Ruma Debi and Kanu Roy in the main leads. Directed by Nitin Bose, lyrics were written by Pradeep and the music was by Sachin Deb Burman. I have tried to underline and analyse the differences between the two, and to evaluate the influence of each on its target audience. It is significant that a gap of 70 years separates the two. And today when I write this, another half-a-century has elapsed. What is there in the film which can appeal to the modern audience – character, images, music, or meaning?

The novel revolves round a blind girl Rajni, who is the daughter of a flower seller, and is a frequent visitor to a zamindar's haveli, where she is patronized by the zamindar's second wife, the youthful Lavanglata, an arrogant and clever woman. The zamindar has two sons from his first wife and Rajni is in love with the younger.

Lavanglata was earlier engaged to Amarnath, but the engagement had been broken off due to some old scandal in his family, and she had been married off to the old but rich zamindar. Amarnath had left home, to wander from place to place, and it was during those travels that he had come to know that the zamindari belonging to Lavanglata's family was actually the inheritance of a blind girl Rajni who was untraceable.

Lavanglata had arranged Rajni's marriage to a married man, but Rajni leaves home to escape the marriage, and by a strange twist of events meets Amar, who now sets the legal machinery into motion to claim her estate for her, and also announces his plans to marry her.

As Rajni's claim is established Lavanglata now wants her stepson to marry Rajni and seeks to retain the estate in the family. She seeks the help of the family Guru who through tantra convinces the stepson of the desirability of the match. Lavanglata also decides to meet Amar and threatens to expose him by telling everyone about an event which had taken place after their engagement had been broken off. Amar, in a reckless moment of love, had entered her bedroom at night to remonstrate with her. She had locked him up and with the help of her servants, had branded him 'chor' with a hot iron, to punish him for the unforgivable act. It was this incident which lay behind Amar's wandering during the course of which he had discovered that Rajni was the real heiress. It had seemed like a god-sent opportunity to him to avenge himself on the cruel and arrogant Lavanglata.

The meeting between Amar and Lavanglata is crucial. On one hand Amar discovers that Rajni loves Sachindra, and on the other Lavanglata comes face to face with the truth that love is too strong an emotion and cannot be stifled by branding the person you love for daring to break into your room. Amar also realizes that in most cases, women in this country are often compelled to accept whatever is dealt to them by the cruel hands of fate or family, and can do very little to fight against the oppressive system which is heavily loaded against them.

This is the brief sketch of the novel which ends on a happy note. Amar leaves home again to return to find Rajni and Sachindra married and Rajni's eyesight having been restored by the medication of the family Guru. It is an interesting tale of love, intrigue and revenge, focusing on how women are treated as pawns wherever property is concerned.

The film *Mashaal* follows the same storyline by and large, but some significant changes are there. These changes add to the strength of the story and give a new slant and substance to the characters, interpreting them anew.

The two protagonists Amar and Lavanglata come to occupy the center stage and Rajni and Sachindra become incidental to the story. It is no longer the story of Rajni, but is the story of the pain and anguish of a man who has been unjustly punished and carries the fire of revenge in his heart. The central problem is the flagrant violation of the strict social code by Amar and the punishment meted out to him. In the movie, the branding is done by the heroine's father and she is a mute and helpless witness to the inhuman act, but not a party to it. This scene sets the tone of film by underlining the helplessness of a woman caught in a piquant social situation. It is the story of the oppressive system which holds women in this country in its thrall.

The names of the main characters were also changed in the film. Lavanglata becomes Tarangini and Amar is Samar – a soul in torment, Sachindra becomes Jatin and Rajni becomes Sarla. In the movie, Jatin is shown to be in love with Rajni, But does not express his feeling for he thinks her to be socially beneath him.

Differences between the story of a novel and a film are natural, for the film is a visual medium. Things that can be described at length in the novel are picturized, perhaps very briefly in the film, and in such a manner that they create a distinct ambience in which acts, thoughts and feelings are portrayed in manner which heightens the dramatic quality of the narrative without obtruding on the story.

The essential difference between a novel and the film is that they are both the creation of two different persons with different perceptions and sensibilities. The film director's initial response to the book may have been that of a reader. Taking the book and it characters as an outsider he seeks to interpret their actions in the light of his own understanding of the situation that he is confronted with. He fills in the gap that he feels exists in the narrative or in the characterization.

In *Mashaal* Samar is not the weak and vacillating character overwhelmed by the tragic events, seeking to lose himself in oblivion and anonymity. Overwhelmed he is, but has the strength of character to come out of it and set up a large legal practice in Calcutta. He learns about the property from the munshi of the estate and sets out to discover the legal details and profits and to locate the missing heiress. The depiction of his search heightens the dramatic situation. His dress – the manner in which he muffles up his face so as to avoid identification – all make it mysterious. The dark shades of the deepening twilight, the time he goes out on his search, all add to the piquancy of the situation. His determination to avenge himself on Tarangini comes through. His whole demeanor speaks of his purpose – his harsh and abrasive tone, the set expressions on his face – all indicate the fire of revenge that burns within him like a mashaal.

Even the manner in which he finally meets Sarla is filmed in a way which is highly dramatic. The dark shades of night obscure the fight between him and the boatman who is trying to molest the blind girl. The scene is visually beautiful and the moving light and shade, portrayed by the rippling waters of the river, the swaying branches of the trees, which hide and then reveal what is happening, projecting a conflict between right and wrong, heightening the tension.

Tarangini, as the wife of a man of wealth and social standing, is fully conscious of her own consequence. She knows the duties of a traditional Indian wife even if the marriage has been imposed on her. She is devoted to the family, and there is a touching scene of care and devotion between her and her husband to highlight this fact. She refuses to listen to any gossip or news about Samar from her maidservant and scolds her saying that it does not behove her as a married woman. She has accepted her lot with fortitude, and her feeling are poured in a song.

> *Kitni sach hai yeh baat, koi maane yaan na maane,*
> *Kis ki kismat mein kiya likha,*
> *Duniya mein koi naan jaane.*
> (Whether you accept it or not, the harsh reality is that no one knows what lies in their fate).

When she learns that Sarla is the real owner of property and that Samar is marrying her, she is convinced that he is doing this to humiliate her. Somewhere deep down in her heart is the hurt that he had failed to understand her predicament as a woman trapped in the traditions of the Indian middle class. As has already been said above, Tarangini can feel outraged at Samar's temerity in breaking into her bedroom, but she is not cruel and inhuman. Her character in the movie comes across as one of a sensitive woman who is the victim of social injustice, guilty only of a resigned acceptance.

She has mastered passion and stood steadfast in the face of temptation. She comes for her meeting with Samar, decked in all her jewellery, very much the lady bountiful, proclaiming her social status. She is convinced that he will come out the worst in this battle also. She sneers at him and threatens him with exposure. But Samar is a stronger man now. He tells her that he will himself tell Sarla about the events of that night. When he reveals the dark secret of his soul, Tarangini realizes that the ugly episode is as much her shame as it is his, and the telling of it as humiliating for her as it is for him. It needs to be admitted that Tarangini does in some measure represent the ideal Indian women, specially the Bengali heroine, who is strong yet traditional, in full control of herself, guided by the principle of family honor. But even to do that requires strength and dignity.[3]

The confrontation between the two is set in a room, which is full of jewellery and clothes bought for the wedding and the bride to be is in the next room. It forms a befitting backdrop for the conflict raging between the two protagonists. The room marks the boundaries so to say, the past is on one side and the future behind the door, unseen and unknown, and there can be no running away as they are trapped in the present.

Samar abandons the idea of marrying Sarla when he learns that she loves Jatin though Sarla is still willing to marry him for she feels it to be her duty. It is at this juncture that he comes face to face with the truth that a woman is a prisoner of her fate, and a victim of circumstances. She is a commodity to be used for pleasure, prestige or duty.

Tarangini finally confronts the ultimate truth that love does not die despite the harsh social code imposed on the woman, A woman is capable of loving deeply and forever, even if she is forced into a marriage to another. She tells Samar how women in this society are compelled to live lives of repression and are not even permitted to protest. She also accepts in a veiled manner that she still loves him by telling him that perhaps things may be different in the next birth.

All the rancour and bitterness in his heart is washed away. Leaving all his personal wealth and property for Sarla and Jatin, he leaves for an unknown destination. Confrontation is transformed into reconciliation. The backdrop remains the same but the tones of the two are softer and disarming. A new love that transcends the physical restraints of existence and birth has awakened in their hearts. This liberates them from social constraints and they can now talk openly of love.

Tarangini assumes a greater dignity in her humility. When she tells Samar that Sarla will not desist from marrying him even though she loves Jatin, she brings home to him the tragedy of the Indian woman. The last scene – of Samar's departure – has been filmed in a very simple and stark manner, but the visual impact of the scene is tremendous. With his back to the camera, a stick in his hand, he is shown walking towards a new dawn – a symbol of a more happy scheme of things to come, a soul redeemed.

The lyrics are uniformly good and are employed by the director to highlight the pain and tragedy of his characters very effectively. The lyrics by Pradeep and the music by Sachin Dev Burman draw heavily on Bengali folk music. They support the narrative, they also enrich the atmosphere.

The opening scene was used to underline the theme and set the background of the story. Following the usual style of so-called social movies of that period when the town was closer to the village, the song was sung by a tongawala, in whose tonga Samar is returning to his village. Sung by Manna Dey in his resonant voice, it was a powerful signature tune, both lyrically and musically.

Uper gagan vishal, neeche gehra patal
Beech mein dharti, ae mere malik,
Tune kiya kamaal
Tune racha ik adbhut prani
Jiska naam insaan
Jiski nanhi jaan ke bheeter chupa hua toofan.
Is jug mein insaan ke man ko kaun saka pehchaan
Is mein hi shaitan chhupa hai, is mein hi bhagwan

Bada gazab ka yeh khilona, iski nahin misal
[Between the vast sky and the deep nether world,
lies this earth, my master
you have done wonders
you have created a unique living being
called the human being.
A storm lies hidden in his fragile life
None in this world can guess what he desires.
Both God and the devil are lodged herein
He is a marvellous toy, without any parallel.]

The scene itself is a visual treat with the shadows of the trees and the open brightness of the sky merging into the horizon, emphasising both the vastness of nature and the complexity of the human mind.

Two songs are picturized on Tarangini, and they have also been used to underline the social reality. They depict both her helplessness and her pain. Both the songs have been placed indoors. One is in the manner of a prayer, a cry from her heart to the Almighty. It has been already referred to above. Placing the song indoors indicates her confinement within a harsh social code. Her helplessness comes through as also her awareness of the burden she carries on her shoulder and the conflict between her desires and the socially accepted code of behavior.

Meri mohabbat aaj jalana sambhal ke zara chiraag
Mein kagaaz ke ghar mein baithi lag nan jaye aag
Lag nan jaye daag meri kismat mein
Lag nan jaye aag meri izzat mein
Is desh ki nari ko koi keh na de durbal
[My love, be careful in lighting the lamp
I am sitting in a house of paper – it may catch fire.
My honour be not stained, none should
accuse the women of this country of faltering in the performance of their duty.]

A simple lyric in itself, it at once calls into play the complexity of the forces at work – the traditional code of behaviour which idealizes women and demands sacrifice from them, the division in the human heart between desire and duty and the linking together of a woman's fate with the construction of the nation. This is where the public and the private meet and the institutions of family and marriage have to contend with the idea of individual desire. The two marriages – of Tarangini with the zamindar, and of Rajni with Jatin – rest on two entirely different equations. In the process of the change from one generation to another, greed and revenge both are subdued. Even the idea of woman as property is questioned. It has however to be conceded that despite these subversive tendencies, the sanctity of marriage is upheld even as it is propped by the individual's own ability to live with his conscience.

The film, in contrast to the novel, makes a stronger feminist statement. Tarangini and Sarla are both pawns in a game which is played by men, and where property, personal honor and social status all are at stake. Both refuse to go against what has been decreed for them, and prefer to bear everything in silence, as has been instilled in them by the social code.

Both, however, are depicted as women of strength, though willing to sacrifice themselves in the name of family honour, yet capable of standing up for themselves. In the film Tarangini wants to stop Sarla's wedding, not because she wants the property for her family as in the novel, but become she knows that Rajni and Jatin both love each other. She doesn't want Sarla to be put in the situation that she herself has been placed in. Even Sarla who is blind and dependent on others, has the courage to leave her home, to escape a marriage arranged for her by Tarangini to a married man. She agrees to marry Samar for she thinks it to be her duty, as he has saved both her life and honour. The director has given Tarangini's new character contours and substance. She seeks a new deal for women and is willing to strike a blow for it. Remaining within the confines of the novel's narrative the film manages to deviate significantly to enable the novel to transcend its temporal contexts and acquire a relevance for contemporary society. Tarangini acquires an active role as she is transformed from the role of the zamindar's passive wife into an agency of restoration of compassionate values.

To get back to some of the questions I raised earlier, what is it that can relate to a modern audience. I additionally pose another question – would a male viewer respond differently from a female viewer? Amongst the strengths of the movie are its juxtaposition of the real and the ideal, the actual and the possible. In its review of events it does not follow the Rama-Ravana polarity; it does not foreground woman as body – neither as a sexual object or its maternal aspects. It values restraint and integrity. And the characters themselves move towards self-analysis and transformation. A much-needed antidote to projections of contemporary cinema, its, family dramas and fragmented characters. The play of events is centred on a debate about values and relationships. Tarangini has, by the end of the film, become the controlling figure, the active principle.

Notes

1. Boyum commenting upon film adaptations of classics writes, "to adapt a prestigious work was to do more than borrow its plot, its characters, its themes...it was... to borrow a bit of that work's quality and stature. Certainly, this is one of the reasons that adaptations have always held such a privileged place in the movie industry and why at the Academy Awards, 'its' adaptation more than any other kind of film on which the industry bestows its honours" (4-5).
2. This is not to say that other literatures were not tapped. Indeed we have films based on novels from other Indian languages as well as from European literature like *Man ka Meet* (Hardy's *Tess*),

Bawra (Hardy's *Return of the Native*), *Phir Subha Hogi* (Dostoevsky's *Crime and Punishment*) and several others, films which provide a record of cultural interpretations.

3. There may be, in this, an element of romantic idealism, but it is a kind which appeals to the reader/movie-goer as it contains within it a strong tragic element of unrequited love. Thus while it foregrounds love it underplays sexuality and voyeurism. And while it confines a woman to her social space, it allows her to handle it with dignity. Remember the heroines of *Parineeta*, *Devdas*, *Bandini* and a host of other movies, where social codes prohibit fulfilment. In this there is a critiquing of wrong social values, a critiquing which appeals to the emotions and can bring about an attitudinal change.

References

Boyum, Joy Gould. *Double Exposure: Fiction into Film* (1985). Calcutta: Seagull Books, 1989.

Chattopadhya, Bankim Chandra. *Rajni* (1877). Trans. into Hindi from the original Bengali by Shriram Nath Suman. Delhi: Hind Pocket Books, 1986.

Prasad, M. Madhava. *Ideology of the Hindi Film: A Historical Construction*. Delhi: Oxford University Press, 1998.

17 Maternal Enthrallment in Satyajit Ray's *Aparajito* and *Devi*

Madhuri Chatterjee

Satyajit Ray is one of the greatest luminaries in the world of cinema. His films are a brilliant blend of intellect and emotion. All his works look contemporary and universal, easily transcending the barriers of time and space. The films chosen for study are *Aparajito* (1956) which captures the nuances of mother-son relationship most poignantly and *Devi* (1960) which explores yet another family/power structure. In some ways both are the most explicitly Eastern of Ray's films – manifest in the depiction of Hinduism and the ways in which it penetrates all aspects of Indian life.

Bhibuti Bhushan Bandhopadhya's *Aparajito,* the second film in the Apu trilogy, is a deeply moving document of the many-hued relationship between a mother and son. One can very well feel the distance creeping in between Apu and his mother as he grows from childhood to adolescence. They are slowly but inescapably moving into different worlds. It is a bittersweet relationship unveiling new layers of interpretation every time you see the film. The film won the Golden Lion Award at the Venice film festival. However in Ray's opinion it was less than technically perfect. But then he was a perfectionist. The film strangely was something close to his heart as Ray himself was close to his mother and was brought up by her, his father Sukumar Ray having died when he was a child.

Satyajit Ray was an absolute master. He used to have each and every frame of his movies planned precisely and at times he used to have the frame sketched beforehand – that is why while watching his movies we can only marvel at the spontaneity of the scenes. It never looked structured or pre-meditated to the point of making the scenes perfect but stilted.

There are so many scenes that one is unable to forget. In one scene, Apu (Pinaki Sengupta) comes home learning that his mother is ill. He arrives to find the front door half open. He searches for his mother and then comes out not finding her. Outside he finds the old man Bharbartan standing, looking ancient. He says nothing but turns away from Apu. In a deft and ingenious juxtaposition of shots and remarkable composition, Bharbataran looks almost like Death. Ray had this magic of conveying so much with so little. Not a scene or word out of place. Harihar Ray, the father's (Kanu Bandhopadhya) death continues to haunt the family. After collapsing at the steps of the ghat near the holy river, Harihar who earns his living by reciting religious scriptures gets ill and proceeds to leave the world. Sarbojaya (Karuna Bandhopadhya) tends to her husband when Harihar meekly mumbles "Ganga". Sarbojaya asks Apu to fetch water from the Ganges, walking past many alleys (ambience of Benaras). Apu returns and helps his mother raise his father's head, and pours water into his mouth. Harihar's head then drops back. What we next see is a flock of pigeons taking off into the sky. So many directors have since repeated the last scene but the original remains unmatched. Also the music based on *raag Jog* literally bursts forth upon Harihar's death and helps in elevating the scene.

The beauty of the film lies in its authenticity and the in-depth study of relationship. After Harihar's death, Sarbojaya works as a cook in a prosperous Brahmin household. Apu is seen plucking hair from the head of Mukherjee Moshai (the family head). He gets a coin as a tip and flies off. Shortly afterwards Apu goes into one of the rooms and blows a *chillum*. Sarbojaya says nothing but frowns as she comes down the stairs. Is her son going to grow up as a mere household help? Next we hear the train whistle and mother and son going back to the village. Everything is written in their eyes, looks and expression. No statements, no explanation.

The film has many shades, but the real strength of *Aparajito* lies in the brilliant depiction of the nuances of the mother-son relationship which is the basic nexus and the ultimate paradigm of human social relationship. There are lot of things left unsaid and it is the silence and glances that actually convey more. Apu, as he grows up, is so excited and eager about going out to the world that he at times is not able to understand his mother's emotions. Naturally there develops a void between them and the young boy trapped in his own world cannot do much about it, however hard he tries. On one of his visits home Sarbojaya insists Apu stay for a ceremony. An upright and earnest student, Apu cannot oblige. He must leave the next morning and would not listen to her pleadings. He leaves for the railway station all prepared but cannot bring himself to board the train. The world out there beckons him but the love for his mother holds him back.

In another scene Ray shows how normal conversation can be used to suggest something deeper and profound. Back home from the city, Apu is lying in bed and reading. Sarbojaya comes in, sits on the bed and starts a conversation, asking him what he has seen in Kolkatta. He talks about the Victoria Memorial, Whiteway, Laidlaw and a whole lot of places. Sarbojaya then asks: "The Temple of Kalighat?" Apu replies that he had been to Kalighat and Keoratala. "What is there in Keoratala?" – Sarbojaya asks her son. Apu replies in English – "Burning Ghat". His mother does not understand and Apu clarifies that it is a cremation ground. He then turns away from his mother and settles down to sleep. Here the dialogues are used to embellish a story and carry it forward.

Another powerful human portrait and late masterpiece of Ray – *Devi* is seen as everything from a religious satire to fanaticism to a feminist tragedy. The story captures the subtle terrors of the myth of *Devi* – the great Goddess who as Kakar hints, constitutes the "hegemonic narrative" of Hindu culture. The Hindu religion includes multitudes of Gods and Goddesses, and Kali, portrayed with a necklace of human skulls, is one of the most feared. In the Bengal region, which flowered under the British Raj and became India's intellectual and cultural centre, she was specially revered. The city Kolkatta in fact derives its name from her.

Unlike *Aparajito,* which is an ode to adolescence where we find a natural maternal presence permeates Apu's relationship with Sarbojaya, the maternal feminine image is reversed and reconstructed in *Devi* (story by Prabhat Kumar Mukherjee). It concerns a nineteenth century landowner Kalinker Ray (Chobi Biswas), who has a revelation that his 17 year old daughter-in-law Doyamoyee (Sharmila Tagore) is the incarnation of Goddess Kali, the Hindu Goddess of Destruction. Overwhelmed he weeps, falls to his knees and worships the startled girl. The shy girl is so luminous in her mantle that the widowed man lavishes praise on her, calling her "Mother" and honouring the day she entered his family "Why haven't you told us who you are"? He cries after his dream "Now I know my devotion hasn't been in vain". Ray once again explores the power of family and religion. As a maternal feminine, we see how Doyamoyee accepts the mantle placed on her, the new position of power and influence she holds in their household and starts to believe that she is indeed blessed. Her husband Uma Prasad (Soumitra Chatterjee) studying in the university in Kolkatta is shocked at this conviction of divinity, inspired by his father's dream and fascination for her. He returns to find his wife made a virtual prisoner of his father's obsession. Doyamoyee is decorated as a living Goddess and forced to sit all day in a temple where people come to offer her prayers and pay homage, bringing sick children to be healed and begging for her wisdom and blessing. As we watch in wonder, this girl Doyamoyee moves gradually and enigmatically from sweet teenager to queen of the household to Devi.

There is a terrific scene in *Devi* when Uma walks in and sees Doya, his wife in her new guise. Without dialogue, Ray captures a flood of emotion through his actors' eyes; the shock on Uma's face, the embarrassment, fear and silent pleading on Doya's. A religious progressive, Uma Prasad regards his father's orthodox faith as a folly. When an impoverished man brings his only son to this reluctant Goddess Doyamoyee and the child is cured, everyone believes she has performed a miracle. With an inevitability that becomes increasingly tragic, he feels too weak to defeat his father's conservative ideology. The sister-in-law (Karuna Bandopadhya of *Aparajito*) is equally horrified and helpless. Then Khoka, the nephew falls ill. Uma Prasad tries hard to rescue his wife from his father and their home but Doyamoyee herself weakens and begins to wonder if she is an incarnation of Kali after all.

The film makes explicit the link between culture and psyche and emphasizes the fact that the construction and experience of the self are influenced by culture from the very beginning of life. There is a strong pull in Doyamoyee for surrender and re-immersion in the enveloping maternal fusion in which she is cast. One of the more dominant narratives of this culture is that of Devi, the great Goddess, who especially in her manifold expressions as mother, possesses the inner world of the Hindu son. In India at least, a primary task of psychoanalysis, the science of imagination (in Wallace Stevens's, words) or "the science of illusion" – *Mayalogy* – is to grapple with Mahamaya – the great Illusion (Kakar 293). The concept of *adya shakti*, primal or original power, is entirely feminine in India. It is the male principal in the Godhead, *purusha*, that is reliable but relatively passive, weak, distant and secondary (Nandy 73). Probably in the father-in-law (Kalinker Roy) we see some sublimated desire to be born a woman facilitated by the culture's views on sexual differentiation and permeability of gender boundaries. Thus myths like 'Ma' and 'Devi' constitute a cultural idiom which aids the individual in the construction and integration of his inner world and which are constantly renewed and validated by the nature of subjective experience. The role of mother has a specific cultural configuration and identification with the mother gives immense pleasure to the Indian male. In other words, the ultimate authority in the Indian mind has always been feminine.

The film *Devi* bears all the hallmarks of Ray's best work - gracefulness, exquisite pacing and composition, love for his characters and a deep regard for the power of silence to tell a story. Despite the sensitivity of the subject, there is an absolute lack of melodrama. Every frame and step is measured, designed, intentional and purposeful. The music is used sparingly and at the right moments which further uplifts the film.

The maternal aspect in the female psyche has been captured brilliantly in both the films - with its intricate mosaic of psychological insights and emotional nuances. For the mother, the son is the major medium of self-expression and it is only in this role that she traditionally exercises her authority. In both the films, the wife's role is underemphasized and the dominance and presence of the mother depicted, who despite being marginalized is yet the controlling presence in our society.

References

Kakar, Sudhir, "Culture and Psyche", *The Essential Writings of Sudhir Kakar*. New Delhi: Oxford University Press, 2000.

Nandy, Ashis, "Woman Versus Womanliness in India", *Women in Indian Society: A Reader.* Ed Rehana Ghadially. New Delhi: Sage Publications, 1988.

18 The Mythical Text of Woman's Re-Presentation in Cinema: The Image-Icon Interface in *Devi*

Anu Celly

Popular cinema may be considered as a site of plural signification, in its role as a vibrant and dynamic medium for effectuating social change, a catalyst of public and private manifestations of human conduct, a signpost of cultural values and a receptacle of dominant ideologies. At the same time, it has been used as a reflector of confirmatory and resistant positions, sometimes filtering our prejudices and biases and often acting as a tool of our allegorizing hallucinations on love and hatred, heroism and villainy, riches and poverty, vice and virtue. Movies of all kinds have a conscious and self-referential relationship to questions of ideology, politics, culture, identity, representation and of course, aesthetics, all of which are involved in a tenuous link with technology.

This paper proposes to examine the facets of woman's image in popular cinema which employs "a reductionist aesthetic" (Felski 425), reinforcing repressive ideological concerns in juxtaposition with an essentialistic images of women. Any average and mainstream Hindi movie, in the last fifty years of our cinematic history, has displayed a consistent mode of female caricature much in keeping with the monolithic construct of womanhood supported by a selective incorporation of certain deterministic ideals. The victimization syndrome often formulates an irrevocable component of the women figures' life history, while the normative 'gaze' of the male protagonist almost always curbs her subjectivity and sexuality into the stance of being a mere "object, a conglomerate of attributes to be predicated and controlled" (Alcoff). Sexism enters into a nexus with dynamics of class, wealth, family, marriage, morality and convention to perpetuate the hold of patriarchal ideals, as the woman figure is embedded within certain "mythic structures which have defined the Indian civilization" (Vinay Lal 232).

The fact that cinema is a mediator of social realities and personal dreams, collective concerns and individual aspirations, makes it assume a seminal and polysemic dimension as a humanistic discourse which has the potential to redirect the cultural and material fabric of our everyday lives. To the same extent, one needs to examine and decode the dissonance and discrepancy inherent to the re-presentation of women's position, both in popular and the so-termed alternative cinema. Since the art and craft of representation has a role to play in the perpetuation of and resistance to power relations, the cinematic image of woman as a mere spectacle or an object of dominant cultural discourse needs to be analyzed. Annette Kuhn considers representation of woman image, whether through the cinematic, literary or artistic media, as the site of a gendered narrative:

> Representation sets in play certain relations of power through which, among other things, discourses around sexual difference and subjects in and for those discourses are ongoingly produced. In this sense, representation may be regarded ... as a strategy of normalization. Representation participates in the various relations of power with which we are surrounded and in which we are always in one way or another implicated. Representation can be understood, then, as a form of regulation. (407)

The pace of evolution, through popular Hindi cinema, seems to have taken on a reverse gear and the representation of women's image has become successively typecast, wherewith an entire range of regressive role models, right from the sorry figure of the mother to the submissive though harassed daughter-in-law to the rebellious or conniving sister to the seductive mistress to the Machiavellian vamp are presented on a platter, catering to the tastes of a cross-section of elite and maverick masses. They are supposed to lap up the sumptuous feast of titillation, moral upliftment, ethical outrage and righteous self-glorification, all rolled into one. The identity-politics inherent in the stereotyping of women's image make it mandatory for her to be a perfect combination of certain typical traits and idiosyncrasies used in an oft-repeated pattern of mythical iconography. Quite often, especially in parallel cinema, the 'image' derived from the societal categorization of womanhood frees itself from the 'icon' which has remained encased in a mould of superimposed ideology, to assume shades of defiant though often aborted shades of self-presentation. The inscrutable nuances of self-reflexivity and referentiality are then to be demapped by the spectator, whose gaze and position becomes a vital and relativistic tool of interpretation. De Lauretis takes into account the role of the spectator colluding with the cinematic apparatus and the mode of production as the vital determinant of the narrative of a particular film, when she asserts:

> In the narrative film the spectator's movement or passage is subject to an orientation, a direction – a teleology, we might say, recalling Freud's word – that is the movement of narrative .... The codes whereby cinema articulates or inscribes both the narrative movement and the subject's passage in the film, the codes which constitute the specificity of cinema as a semiotic practice ... may be usefully emphasized: the centrality of the system of the look in cinematic representation. The look of the camera (at the profilmic), the look of the spectator (at the film

> projected on the screen), and the intradiegetic look of each character within the film (at other characters, objects etc.) intersect, join and relay one another in a complex system which structures vision and meaning and defines the 'visible things' of cinema. (86-87)

A semiotic and psychoanalytical approach to the representation in popular cinema reveals that the image of women is not wholly congruent with the reality of women's life and conduct outside the cinema hall; on the contrary, woman functions as a 'sign' within the definitive parameter of myth, custom and ritual. The functional allocation for such a 'sign', as per the view of Roland Barthes is to remain active as the signifier of an ideology which will denude it of all its denotative meaning, in order to invest it with purely connotative dimensions. Claire Johnston makes a succinct analysis of myth as a patina for the exercise of 'the political unconscious' beneath the cinematic production and the circulation of women's image, when she says, "Myth, as a form of speech or discourse, represents the major means in which women have been used in cinema: myth transmits and transforms the ideal of sexism and renders it invisible - when it is made visible it evaporates - and therefore natural" (32).

In this context, one may refer to Satyajit Ray's film *Devi* as a kind of revolutionary and pioneering effort to present the image of its female protagonist as the 'text' of a critique aimed at making startling and revelatory explorations of the use of myth as a normative paradigm for the ideal 'construct' of womanhood. In the adaptation of a short story by Prabhat Chatterjee, Ray displays a characteristic brilliance in captivating the 'essence' as well as the 'construct' of femininity and sexuality against the backdrop of a cultural scenario which is, in a way, both topical and universal, in the context of the predominance of the familial tradition in India.[1]

In the very act of converting cinema into "an arena for political and representational contestation" (Brooks 162), Ray uses the film medium as a powerful intervention in the production and circulation of women's images, as and how these may be guided by the definitive parameters of custom and convention.[2] Even in the opening scene, the overwhelming impact of ritual and religion as the potent shaping force of community life in India, manifests itself in the demonstration of mass adulation accompanying the scenario of the immersion of the idol of the female Goddess. Equally apparent is the designation of women's place in upper-class Bengali families, fraught with the interplay of multivalent associations, ranging from the romanticization of women's role as the quintessential *bahu* to her literal idolization as a benevolent mother figure. As an obedient and self-abnegant daughter-in-law to a smug and self-righteous father-in-law, Doyamayee, literally the Compassion Incarnate, has to enact conformity to a set of inviolable precepts regarding woman's domestic role-fulfillment. Right from the kitchen to the bedroom, she has to cater diligently to the needs and expectations of the entire family, while relegating herself to being a mere object of "dual masculine myopia" (Cooper 108). Elizabeth Cowie makes a semiological analysis of the cinematic image of Woman, when she asserts:

> The image of woman refers not to the referent woman, existing in the real world outside of representation, but to a meaning produced by and for men. Patriarchy controls the image of woman, assigning it a function and value determined by and for men and in the service of the construction of definitions of the male and especially of masculine desire. Patriarchy and the interests of men become a unified field which is able to determine meanings outside of the process of signification (19).

Yet, right from the first scene of her conversation with her husband, it is apparent that beneath the visage of a naïve and demure woman, lurks the spark of self-awareness rooted in the consciousness of a double standard of social convention. It accords the privilege of education, social eminence and financial independence to the men in the family who take the gullible servitude of her secondary position in the household for granted. Doya revels in the well-springs of heart-felt contentment not through the network of adult relationships amidst the joint family, but through the guileless affection of a little boy who is not even her own progeny. On the other hand, the Freudian implications of her father-in-law's exercise of erotic and infantile desire towards her, renders her position as a "fetish" for the male "voyeur" almost implacable. Laura Mulvey takes into account the psycho-sexual dynamics of women's positioning at large, when she asserts:

> Woman thus stands in patriarchal culture as a signifier for the male other, bound by a symbolic order in which man can live out his fantasies and obsessions through linguistic command by imposing them on the silent image of woman still tied to her place as a bearer, not maker of meaning. (59)

The transfiguration of Doya, from the docile though animated agent of domestic chores to the mythicized *tabula rasa* of the Goddess Incarnate occurs through the mediation of a male fantasy. The trance-like state of a dream wherewith the father-in-law envisions her image intermingling with that of the *Devi*, is the actualization of a male pathology which invests the female form with attributes of manifested divinity as a kind of compensation by default. Ray excels in the use of space, sound and motif as the vital tools for the enunciation of his narrative that traces the process of dehumanization progressively inflicted on the woman in the guise of deification. She is placed, physically and figuratively, under the duress of a ubiquitous pattern of archetypal mythic material that has romanticized and denigrated by turns, the symbolic image of womanhood. Right from the radical and fiery self of Medusa and Durga to the benevolent and chaste image of Saraswati and Madonna, women have been placed within "ideologically complicit structures of identification and desire" (Hammett 295).

Doya is banished to a sanctified space that symptomizes an insular sterility, thronged by people who expect therapeutic miracles from the *Devi*. Sharmila Tagore, the actress who plays *Devi*, still in the fledgling phase of her acting prowess, displays exceptional depth in the use of expression as a signifier of experience, wherewith the close glimpse of the camera into her eyes reveals the undulations of protest and despair beneath the prostrate stillness of her body. The director highlights an ironical contrast between her petite physical form versus the colossal and awe-inspiring cut-out of the Mother Goddess which interposes a mutative shift from stark unadorned benignity to an all-devouring ferocity enhanced by the black and red hue of its body and tongue.

The untold sphere of 'silence' so often used by the women writers as the site of muted discourse, acquires in the cinematic medium, a voluble mode of stylistics for the revelation of woman's inner being. Doya's intimate tête-à-tête with the parrot serves to make a symbolic rendition of her unrealized yearnings and the curtailed need for self-affirmation through a soulful communion with another creature, even if it's a bird. In direct proportion to the woman's vulnerable need for emotional support is the divine beneficence of the Goddess who has the miraculous ability to infuse life into a dying child. A subtle critique of the superstition prevalent among people who celebrate the *Devi's* healing touch in having cured a seriously ill child, is a part the sociological documentation of a simplistic faith which often brings succor to a sea of humanity racked by poverty and deprivation. Yet, the toll that it takes on the woman's sensibility is apparent from the progressive erosion of sanity and stamina that reduces Doya to a debilitating weakness.

The potent exercise of power on the part of the 'icon' is ironically juxtaposed with the tangible powerlessness of the 'image' of the woman who yearns to escape from the clutches of constriction ensuing from her idolization as a Goddess. The attitude of Doya's husband who returns from the city in exuding a pragmatic empathy towards her, is countered by a sense of inscrutable betrayal in her response towards him. Nevertheless, she allows him to appease his conscience by facilitating her escape from the temple of her cloistered existence to the vast openness of an arena, captured by the cinematic eye as a space connoting freedom that is unobstructed by acquiescence to worldly strictures. The enactment of the role of *Devi*, however, had been internalized by the woman to such an extent that she finds her escape to be a reprehensible act of cowardice likely to damage her husband's wellbeing. The image of the woman, so gullible and humane in her wifely concern, in a scene shot amidst the wilderness of tall weeds, overtakes the icon, the proscriptive designation of whose all-embracing love for humanity has all but dowsed the spirit of vitality so integral to womanhood.

The scene where Doya gets a chance to embrace her husband's nephew testifies to the insatiable need for filial kinship felt by a woman who feels severed and estranged from such links in the enactment of *Devi's* role. Ironically, it is her failure to save the very same child from a serious illness which perpetuates a kind of metamorphosis in Doya's persona and the pent-up repository of suppressed rage overcomes the sense of a guilt complex which had kept her tied to the post of an icon. The ire of a woman, wronged by a deterministic order of myth and religion comes of age, exhibiting through Sharmila Tagore's potent use of body language and expression, as the ferocious articulation of a discourse which refutes tradition and overthrows the relevance of mindless custom. The 'image' frees itself from its confinement to an existence fettered by the inscription of an ideology that is bent even now on resorting to the designation of pre-ordained attributes for womanhood by branding the *Devi* as a witch. Hector Rodriguez deconstructs the relevance of ideology as an insidious offshoot of a deeply-entrenched pattern of the sub-conscious human motivation, when he asserts, "Ideologies are distinct configurations of moral thoughts, emotions and practices that play a part in a situation of domination" (268). The dialectic of identity politics in connivance with factors of convention and morality now becomes replete with a dichotomy used by the filmmaker as an in-built device to pose questions pertaining to our conformity to myth and ritual.

Doya's desperate stride towards the open fields, boundless and uninhabited by the markers of civilization, captured by the long shots of the cinematographer as floral and misty terrain, signify woman's quest for 'Nature' as a space immune to the man-dominated forms of 'Culture'. The tableau of the Mother Goddess, bare, unadorned and denuded of a definitive paraphernalia, both of benignity and virulence, now flashes the final note as the emblem of a blankness. Similarly, the woman figure now seeks to elude the static stigmata of being a mere object/other and yearns to inscribe the page of its destiny with etchings of self-realization.[3] Yet, ironically, woman's access to liberation comes only through a suicidal extinction of her physical self, which has been converted through the metaphorical mask of the rage of madness as "a sorrowful and frightened spectacle of sacrifice and guilt" (Cooper 110). Perhaps, Doya has bridged the gap between the split subjectivity of the 'image' of a woman and the 'icon' of a *Devi* by redirecting the fear, anger and protest towards none but herself and what echoes in the mind of the spectator is her haunting realization, "I'm afraid, I am a Goddess, I am a Goddess, I am a Goddess!"

Notes

1. Rita Felski considers cinema to be the potent medium of a narrative wherein the aesthetic faculty is more or less subordinate to its use as a political statement on any aspect of the human

condition within a particular context. In her own words, "The relationship between art and ideology is appropriately conceptualized in terms of a continuum in which the aesthetic function may be more or less dominant but always intermeshes with the ideological conditions governing the text's own historical location" (425).

2. Ashish Rajadhyaksha pays tribute to Satyajit Ray's pioneering role in having accorded Indian cinema with a pioneering or almost revolutionary impetus towards realism as an antidote to romanticism, and avant garde stylistics as an answer to the hackneyed and repetitive mode of technique used by other popular filmmakers in India. In his own words, "Ray's own cinema which has conventionally been seen as the point at which Indian Cinema's initiative towards realism and the mastering of story telling idiom were finally realized, has also provided the post-independence focus for debates about divisions between realism and modernism, high art versus low and after the avant garde practice of some new Indian cinema filmmakers, modernism versus avant garde" (154).
3. The French psychoanalytic critique of Woman use as a 'sign' in the Symbolic order of male-ordained language may be counterpointed vis-à-vis Barthes' view that a sign can acquire a new connotative meaning when it becomes the signifier of a new signified and usurps the place of the original denotation., which makes it a signifier of the ideology of the society in which it is used. Barthes further co-relates the idea of myth as the signifier of an ideology with myths which govern the production of cinema, which, in turn are no different from those governing other cultural products, as and how these relate to a standard value system informing all cultural systems in a given society. See Barthes, op.cit., at random.

References

Alcoff, Linda. "Cultural Feminism versus Post Structuralism: The Identity Crisis in Feminist Theory". *Signs* 13 (Spring 1988): 405-36.

Allen, Richard and Murray Smith. eds, *Film Theory and Philosophy*. London: Oxford University Press, 1997.

Barthes, Roland. *Mythologies*. London: Jonathan Cape, 1971.

Brooks, Ann. *Postfeminisms: Feminism, Cultural Theory and Cultural Forms.* London: Routledge, 1997.

Cooper, Darius. *The Cinema of Satyajit Ray: Between Tradition and Modernity.* Cambridge: Cambridge University Press, 2000.

Cowie, Elizabeth. *Representing the Woman: Cinema and* Psychoanalysis. *London: Macmillan Pvt. Ltd., 1997.*

De Lauretis, Teresa. "Oedipus Interruptus". Feminist Film Theory: A Reader. Ed. Sue Thornham, 83-96. Edinburgh: Edinburgh University Press, 1999.

Felski, Rita. "The Dialectic of 'Feminism' and 'Aesthetics'". *Beyond Feminist Aesthetics: Literature and Social Change*, 175-82. London: Hutchinson Radius, 1989.

Hammett, Jennifer. "The Ideological Impediment: Epistemology, Feminism and Film Theory". *Film Theory and Philosophy*. Eds. Richard Allen and Murray Smith, 244-59. London: Oxford University Press, 1997.

Johnston, Claire. "Women's Cinema as Counter Cinema". *Feminist Film Theory: A Reader*. Ed. Sue Thornman, op.cit. 31-40.

Kuhn, Annette. "The Body and Cinema: Some Problems for Feminism". *Grafts: Feminist Cultural Criticism.* Ed. Susan Sheridan, 11-23. London: Verso, 1988.

Lal, Vinay. "The Impossibility of the Outsider in Modern Hindi Film". *The Secret Politics of Our Desires: Innocence, Culpability and Popular Indian Cinema*". Ed. Ashis Nandy, 228-58. Delhi: Oxford University Press, 1998.

Mulvey, Laura. "Visual Pleasure and Narrative Cinema". Sue Thornham, op. cit., 59.

Rajadhyaksha, Ashis. "Indian Cinema". *World Cinema: Critical Approaches*. Eds. John Hills and Pamela C. Gibson et.al., 151-56. London: Oxford University Press, 2000.

Rodriguez, Hector. "Ideology and Film Culture". Allen & Smith, op.cit., 260-281.

Thornham, Sue, ed. *Feminist Film Theory: A Reader*. Edinburgh: Edinburgh University Press, 1999.

19 *Tamanna*: Desiring the Undesired

Santosh Gupta

Film making has largely been a money making concern, and most film-makers aim to reach large audiences so as to reap huge profits. Such films are conservative in their viewpoint and offer escapist, fantasy worlds. If ever an attempt is made to question any existing social practice, the plot structure manages to subvert the initial rebellion, and brings every character back into the fold of the prevailing hegemonic ideology.

In such a situation however there have also been some socially aware and committed film-makers who have dared to tackle issues of gender or class discriminations, or injustice within social life. In India there have been some very fine films dealing with the problems of widows, education for women, caste and class discriminations, which have moved their viewers to reconsider the existing social practices. This sensitivity to the gender, class or caste issues has been present all through the history of Indian cinema. Seen in films like *Achhut Kanya*, *Sujata* and *Dharm-Putra* where some new solutions are offered for the social problems of widows, untouchability and Hindu-Muslim relations. In creating new possibilities and alternatives, the films reflect, interrogate and invert the existing attitudes towards these issues. In talking of spaces in social structure, Foucault regards the "mirror" as a space that is, and is not there, becoming a possible utopian site. The films that problematize a given social situation too can be seen to become the mirror – like "unreal space" that has an important "direct or inverted analogy with the real space of society" ("Of Other Spaces" 24). Such films subvert, invert and reflect upon the sites of relations within the given world, and other new directions of possibilities of relations, often indicating new ideological trends within the society itself. The 'mirror' reflects elements that are unseen by the masses, focussing attention upon the radical ideas.

In the 1970s, the emergence of the women's movement in India drew people's attention to the increasing exploitation and ill-treatment of women in the country. Dowry assumed new dimensions due to increased consumerism, resulting in both bride-burning and female foeticide. Women's right to life itself was threatened in a society that had promised equal opportunity for growth, happiness and fulfilment to all irrespective of caste, creed, or sex. Women's organizations all over the country and in the world tried to increase people's sensitivity to gender, sexual, and biological issues. Films appeared, as did other art products that focussed on women's needs and problems.

Mahesh Bhatt's film *Tamanna* came in the 1990s, after he had made other films dealing with the institutions of marriage and family, like *Arth*, *Daddy* and *Naam*. The film *Tamanna* was the first to be made under the banner of his daughter Pooja Bhatt. Mahesh Bhatt directed the film, while Tanuja Chandra wrote the screenplay and dialogue. The film is the story of a girl who is ordered by her father to be killed soon after she is born, because she is a girl and the father wants only a male issue. This is the third girl to be born to his wife, and like the earlier two, she must also die and thus pay the price of being a female. The film reflects a new sensitivity towards gender formation through the portrayal of two most "unwanteds" of the patriarchal society – the girl child, and the hermaphrodite. Both suffer from phallocentric emphasis on male superiority, and severe forms of discriminations. *Tamanna* treats with sympathy the search for love, acceptance and family roots of both of these social outcasts.

The little child becomes an outcast as the father hands her over to the maid, an elderly woman, who has perhaps served the family for a long period, long enough to be assigned the task of killing the newborn girls. This time she is unable to kill the child as she is spotted leaving/killing the child in a lonely corner of a street by Tinku, a hermaphrodite, who hears the sound of the child crying and comes closer. The woman, and the black car in which she goes away, are observed by this person. He picks up the child, and is happy enough to keep her with him, as he realizes that she had been abandoned.

Tinku is repeatedly told by his friend, Saleem that "*hinjre ke aulad nahin hoti*" [hinjre (hermaphrodites) do not have children]. But Tinku refuses to give up the girl and persists in taking care of her. This process is shown in the film where Tinku gets help from neighbours and friends and he moves away from the group of other hermaphrodites with whom he had earlier kept company in order to earn his livelihood[1].

The love, acceptance and care that the little girl named 'Tamanna' by Tinku gets from her new father/parent, contrasts sharply with the rejection and devaluation she has experienced from her natural father. As the child is sent away to its doom, the film shows that the father goes to the room where the delivery had taken place. He informs his wife that once again she had given birth to a dead girl. He shouts at her, blames her for giving birth to daughters. He emphasizes the "tradition" of his family where till now only male children had been born. Having just seen their treatment of the daughter born to them, the audience can understand how this tradition is achieved by quietly and regularly destroying female children born there. The husband threatens to remarry if the wife fails to deliver a male issue.

In these scenes the suffering and subordination of adult women within the family is presented. The maid is seen behaving in an insane manner, when she experiences an acute sense of guilt at having killed innocent children, the wife cries and expresses a sense of loss whenever she thinks of the dead daughters. But the subsequent birth of a son brings smiles to every one's face in this family, and the women also gradually get over the earlier trauma. Women's role is limited to bearing and rearing, and they are shown to have no choice in the other important matters, even of keeping the child alive. In the middle class respectable family, women's status is very low in the social and gender hierarchy.

Tinku and Tamanna's family however is based on mutual love and acceptance. The little girl is pampered and becomes spoilt. Tinku is advised to send the child away to a boarding school for her education and better upbringing. His initial unwillingness changes as the neighbours and his friend Saleem argue with him about lack of proper environment. Saleem tells Tinku, "*Abbu ban-ne ka shauk hai to Abbu ban-na seekh*" (If you wish to be a father, learn to behave like a father). Tinku endeavours to fulfill all the duties of a parent, and as Tamanna's marriage is fixed up, he begins to look around for adequate money. He contacts a relative and asks for his (own) share in the family's property. The man turns Tinku away, without any support. In all his efforts to look after Tamanna, Tinku shows his love and devotion to her.

The girl child and the hermaphrodite are seen as sharing the same status of deprivation in the patriarchal social system. Unwanted by parents and a society that values only masculinity, women are tolerated for their reproductive role. But most parents would like the daughters to be born to other parents/families; a daughter is not welcome in one's own family. In this scheme of things, the hermaphrodite is not wanted, or welcome at all since (s)he does not have the potential of reproducing. At the discovery of the mixed sexual characteristics that make a hermaphrodite, such children are turned out of the house, disowned and forgotten by the family. Later in life these young persons are usually forgotten completely by their natural families, and live with other hermaphrodites, and are treated either as harmless diversions on festive occasions or a nuisance to be got rid of. In the film *Tamanna* Tinku's mother is taken care of by Tinku, but for earning a living he has to associate with other hermaphrodites.

In a similar way, the child who is left at the roadside is an abandoned, discarded child, left to face life in all the hardship that such a life contains. Neither the abandoned daughter nor the hermaphrodite can hope to be once again owned and accepted by their parents or their families. The film shows how both these discarded persons wish to have their family but are never allowed to return to the families where they were born.

Tamanna's conflict with the social image of family and her perceptions of its inner hollowness takes place after she gets to know the real identity of Tinku, and the whereabouts of her natural parents. She approaches them with the hope of being accepted by them. She is disillusioned, tries to commit suicide, but realizes how much love she has received from the lonely Tinku. For Tinku she is the most cherished person – the center of his whole being, whereas her father offers her money to buy off her claim to his name, and threatens to get her killed. Tamanna turns away from such a father, blaming their interpretation of tradition, because, as she tells him, the tradition itself has not devalued women. Tamanna's rejection of the family in which she was born becomes an important shift towards a freedom from the existing social values.

Tamanna returns to Tinku who is distraught with the fear that he may lose her entirely. His joy at her return, the complete surrender to her will and decisions, gives her a value that fills her with great sense of satisfaction and self-validity.

The film builds up a continuous series of scenes to bring out the contrast of character, temperament and values of the arrogant, chauvinist 'male' father and the humble, unassuming, self sacrificing, effeminate person Tinku, who adopts the girl, but never expresses any feeling of authority or power. The masculinity of one makes him a rigid harsh selfish person, cruel and inhuman in his treatment of wife and children. The mixed characteristics of Tinku are shown in his expressing emotions through tears, devotion and self-sacrifice in a mother's fashion. If he cries like a woman at his mother's death or when Tamanna leaves him and goes for the father, he can scold her when she tries to commit suicide. His range of human feelings emerges as more wide and complex. It would not be very wrong to suggest that Tinku is seen as a more fully developed human person than the father, that his character subverts the value of the "male" father's sense of confidence, authority and power. Every scene in the film where this father appears, there is a lessening of respect and liking for him. On the other hand Tinku grows into a more worthy and likeable person at each successive appearance.

Consistently these two images of parenthood are contrasted in the film – one endowed with power, that chooses to destroy its child, the other without any sense of authority, but full of love, nurturing care and acceptance. This contrast is centred round their treatment of the girl-child, but goes beyond the issue of the acceptance or love for the girl. The film explores the over-emphasis on patriarchal values, on phallocentric system, and the hierarchical location of the different genders. By bringing in the hermaphrodite character as the other parent, Mahesh Bhatt and his team open up the family structure and its treatment of the non-male, non-heterosexual, non-reproductive sexual relations. The issue of the formation of sexual identity and gender consciousness becomes an important theme in the film for there are not one, but two discarded sexes in the film – the female and hermaphrodite.

Actually society has very little scientific information about the psychological and sexual anatomical changes that take place as a young person gains a clear male-female identity. When a person does not gain such an identity, the person is branded as some kind of a failure, having a "lack" of some positive features, and punished for something over which no one has any control. Freud frequently mentioned in his writings that society's assumption that sexual identity as a male or female was a static unified feature, was a mistaken notion. He has emphasized in his discussion that he did not conceive of sexuality as a ready-made thing in itself, but he found "that normal" sexuality itself assumed its form only "as it travelled over a long and tortuous path, may be eventually, and even than only precariously, establishing itself" (Mitchell 17). In his view the course of development of 'normal' sexualities ran through several sources and influences and unified sexuality was in itself a difficult realization, pushed on by social ideas of masculine, feminine gender identities. He analyses, in his *Three Essays on Sexuality* (1905), that sexuality was composed of a number of component elements, rather than be a "monastic" unity. As Mitchell argues, "Freud was caught between the dualism of masculine and feminine sexes. He also repeatedly emphasized the idea of bisexuality, its presence and significance in the shaping of the adolescent's future sexual identity". Freud realized, the complex nature of sexual identity as it takes shape because "he saw that it was mainly an ideational mental character and it existed within the context of human culture" (Mitchell 18). But in Freud also the focus remains on the formation of the male/masculine and female/feminine identity; the problematic mixed identities of the hermaphrodite is not given any attention.

For most feminists and homoerotic movements also the dualism of gender and sexual preferences becomes the central ideological issue. The hermaphrodite's inability to either participate in the politics of pleasure or reproductive role pushes her/him to the margin altogether. The group thereby remains invisible, insignificant to all contestation about sexual roles, rights and freedom.

Lacan has, in recent years, located the notion of sexual identity once again within social interrelation. He has suggested that "a body is not properly a human body, that is, a human subject or individual unless it has an image of itself as a discrete entity, or as a gestalt". 'His "Mirror Stage" article relates the process of relationships with others that creates the orientation of one's body in space or in relation to others' bodies, stimulating images of one's self in terms of the species and the individual sexual identity. He recognizes the overlaying of culture over the anatomical body giving it specific sexual identity and sexuality. Moira Gatens in her essay "Power, Bodies and Difference" argues similarly when she says that the "human body is a signified body and as such cannot be understood as a 'neutral object' upon which science may construct 'true' discourses .... The human body and its history presuppose each other" (132). In treating the construction of sexual identity as a product of social discourse, these thinkers open up the possibilities of considering "hermaphrodite" also as a category that is formed within social reality. The need to view the hermaphrodite's identity formation becomes an important social concern, to examine the mutual interactions between different genders, and recognize the complexities involved in the formation of the identities.

In the existing social systems however the impact of the overriding phallocentric hierarchy leads to victimizing and penalizing all those who happen to/or choose to be different. Lesbians and gays have been struggling for more than a century for gaining some visibility and acceptance from the social world that continues to harass and ridicule, if not punish them. Pushed into the "closet" as a shameful object, the homosexuals are, Cindy Patton says, "merely a trope of the administrative state, the product of a convenient repressive ideology" that produces a "mobile class of bodies that can readily, easily and publicly be humiliated, taunted, beaten, arrested... driven to madness, murdered ..." (129). Lesbian groups are actively asking for the recognition of diversity, plurality in sexual practices, and to get out of the static categories. The effort is to "open up the public realm to a discussion and appreciation of sexual diversity and variation", to challenge the epistemological and political terms as Judith Butler says. She says clearly that "sex will be shown to have been gender all along" (*Gender Trouble* 8) for she argues that as long as the discussion is centered on duality of male-female gender, the framework remains unchanged, referring all ideas back to these assumptions of fixed sexual identities. "On this model, any dissonance in features, acts or desires can be referred back to a gendered core to which they then become merely secondary and 'accidental' " (24). "What remains unchallenged is the very notion of essential gendered identities", Biddy Martin argues, in her essay "Sexual Practice and Changing Lesbian Identities" (102).

The hermaphrodite's extreme negative self-image is an outcome of the reflections of disgust, disapproval and rejection that (s)he faces in the society around her/him. The identity is constructed on the awareness of a "lack" that turns the person also into a nobody, a void and nonentity. In making this nobody into a person, the film *Tamanna* makes important socio-cultural statements. It presents a new model of family where the two "unwanteds" come together as mutually supportive and form the loving relation of parent-child. The young girl turns to Tinku at the end of the film of her own choice, and decides to live with him as her parent. In place of a repressive and destructive family, another family is created on the basis of acceptance and love, reversing social gender hierarchy. Such a family may not yet have political or legal acceptance, may not have right to society's wealth. But increasing awareness of the different family-patterns that is being created by simple unwed parents, could gradually create the ground for new legal concepts.

The film *Tamanna* is a radical rendering of the unwanted groups of the patriarchal society. The desire for love and family that Tinku and Tamanna show is in itself upsetting. As they get together and form a family they subvert, challenge and reverse the social norms. This film creates a "space" other than the actually existing social world. The "space" of the film reflects, reverts and subverts the existing society as a heterotopic space that Foucault has discussed in his essay "Of Other Spaces". In subverting the existing masculine "father" through the effeminate, powerless hermaphrodite father, the film undermines the rigid roles emphasized in a patriarchal society, and also offers new alternate images. These images are not "ideal" or limiting, they rather seek to extend, to open the existing discourse on gender and sexual identities, roles and functions.

Note

1. I have used male gender for Tinku because for most of the time in the film he is dressed in kurta-pajama (loose shirt and trousers) worn by men. Tinku dresses up in saree and gaudy make-up in a few scenes, towards the second half of the film, when he decides to dance as a hinjra to earn money for Tamanna's wedding.

References

Butler, Judith. *Gender Trouble: Feminism and The Subversion of Identity*. New York: Routledge, 1989.

Foucault, M. "Of Other Spaces", *Diacritics*, Spring 1986, pp. 22-27. trans. by Jay Miskowiec.

Gatens, Moira. "Power, Bodies, Differences", *Destabilizing Theory: Contemporating Feminist Debates.* Eds. Michele Barrett and Anne Phillips. Cambridge: Polity Press, 1992.

Martin, Biddy. "Sexual Practice and Changing Lesbian Identities", *Destabilizing Theory: Contemporary Feminist Debates*. Eds. Michelle Barrett and Anne Phillips. Cambridge: Polity Press, 1992.

Mitchell, Juliet. *Psychoanalysis and Feminism*. New York: Pantheon Books, 1974.

Patton, Cindy. *Inventing AIDS*. New York: Routledge, 1990.

20 From Victimhood to Potential Threat: Rape and Patriarchy in *Damini*

Renuka Pamecha

Rajkumar Santoshi's film *Damini* which belongs to the late eighties, is a movie which takes up for its theme the issue of rape and the manner in which a woman's body is first exploited and then her voice silenced by the overpowering presence of patriarchal values. The word itself literally means *bijli*, the lightning which strikes terror. And the narrative moves from a realization of physical vulnerability to a realization of the manner in which all social, psychological and legal structures are loaded against the woman. It is a double narrative of two women, Urmi who is the rape victim and a maid servant and Damini who represents the voice of protest and is the mistress. Thus both gender and class are problemalized.

Rape is a social as well as a personal crime wherein the female body becomes the site of contestation between power and powerlessness, between imposition and freedom, between the system and the individual. The moment there is a protest, all social institutions – marriage, family, law – all ideas of respectability and loyalty conspire to silence the female voice. It is common knowledge that rape is one of the least reported events due to a variety of reasons. One of them is that it results in a longdrawn legal battle, humiliation and public exposure.

And inevitably it also results in character assassination, attacking the moral behavior of the victim. Further the percentage of convicted rapists is rather low.[1]

In recent memory the rape of the sathin[2] Bhanwari Devi[3] is one such case where several women's organizations collectively helped to draw society's attention to it. I was one of those who followed up the court procedure and have first hand knowledge of the manner in which the victim is humiliated and compelled to regret ever having reported the event. *Damini* similarly exposes the social insensitivity to a woman's anguish and draws attention to the sadistic pleasure of the male figure as the sex act is repeatedly described and the victim forced to be conscious of the violation of her body to the extent of arriving at self-aversion. This is over and above the social ostracism she has to face.

The film takes up for its subject not merely rape but the problem of redressal in a court of law. The aim is not to provide a solution but to raise a whole lot of questions regarding a woman's position in a patriarchal society. Almost all social institutions treat the woman as a 'body' forcing her to subordinate her will and judgment to the imposition of the male other. Focusing on the character of Damini, it highlights the choice which is forced upon her. She can either be true to her own voice of conscience and protest against the rape both she and her husband have witnessed or she can be loyal to her husband and his family by killing her impulse and need for justice and by protecting the principal rapist who happens to be her husband's brother. The first relationship, which is proved to be a fragile one, and rests on one-sided total obedience, is marriage. Damini's fight for justice will alienate her from her husband and his family. The second relationship which comes under attack is the one with her parental home. Her father tells her that once married, there is no place for her in her parent's home. It is not only marriage and family which feel threatened by the female voice of protest, but both social morality and the legal system also feel threatened by this exposure.

The very first scene contains within it the last scene, the ending, and raises a host of questions, pointing out that

- Rape is a business for advocates;
- It is story to sell for the media;
- Rape is an instrument of controlling and silencing the protest of women (i.e. their individuality);
- While stone idols are dressed up in colorful tinselled clothes, the covering is ripped off a woman's body;
- Justice is also male as the silence of the judge shows while the cross-examination increasingly goes on becoming vulgar, stooping to the level of ridiculing the victim;
- A public trial is a multiple rape committed on the woman as the act of intercourse is described in all its ugliness and brutality.

The ending is very dramatic and the narrative comes full circle with the husband finally turning up and giving evidence against the rapist. Having witnessed the act, he had been divided between the curse of family honor and the claims of justice. But he is finally won over by the cause of justice, her anger, her sheer determination and courage. Once the husband's support is available to her, the judge also appreciates her stand. While this is a victory for Damini and Urmi, it is also to be realized that it is only through male support that the battle is won. The agency of women is still subordinated.

Damini does not fall within the category of art films. Thus there are melodramatic and rhetorical elements in it. But it is a film with a social message and rape is only one of the issues. There are several others which are wrapped up within it. Damini belongs to a not-so-well-to-do middle class family, with two daughters of marriageable age. Finding suitable husbands for these dowryless girls is another problem.

Shekhar who belongs to a rich family is willing to marry her without a dowry. But this still does not promise her either self-respect or equality. Not only is she subjected to taunts on this count, she is also unable to fall back upon any parental support. With or without dowry, marriage concedes proprietal rights to the man. The economic disadvantage further reduces her to the status of a household help. The liking for the girl servant Urmi is a natural outcome of working together. All these events comment upon the manner in which money, class and work become important factors in a woman's life.

The film uses several clichéd symbols like freeing pigeons to indicate the falling off of chains and framing the rape incident within the celebration of Holi when teasing and flirtation receive some kind of a social approval and 'bhang' and other intoxicants find favor with many people. It is at such a time that Urmi is raped by Damini's brother-in-law and his friends. Damini immediately summons her husband who breaks open the door and is a witness to the happenings. But the rapists place the unconscious Urmi's body in a jeep and get rid of it in a forest. Shekhar beats his brother (thus not abandoning his sense of righteousness all together), but is content to let it rest at that. It is from here onwards that truth is sacrificed to a tale of lies.

Damini is prevented from meeting Urmi and receives no satisfactory answer to her queries. Instead Urmi's character is portrayed in the worse possible light, of that of a loose woman who uses her sex for small favors. This world of lies, imposition and falsehood begins to suffocate Damini's very being and leads to her dialogue with her own self. And it is at this juncture that she beings to draw upon her own strength. She decides to use her own judgment and act accordingly. She goes to meet Urmi at the hospital by herself and Urmi tells her everything and Damini reports the incident to the police. From this point onwards the viewer is exposed to the corruptions of the social and legal mechanisms.

Reporting to the police does not really help. It leads to more exploitation. As Shekhar's family is interested in downplaying the incident they are willing to spend money, but as the other accused wish to blame Shekhar's brother, they too are willing to spend money. The ones to benefit are the police personnel who exercise their power in this manner. No attention is paid to the rape victim and in every possible way obstacles are planted to weaken Urmi's case. The identification parade is deliberately handled in such a way that Urmi is unable to identify the rapist. Like the police, the media also plays a negative role. Their interest does not lie in aiding justice or exposing wrong but instead in sensationalism and scandal-mongering which may arouse the reader's imagination.

And Shekhar himself, even as he wants to help her is unable to do so assailed by personal doubts and claimed by the concept of family honor. As Damini is pushed out of the circle of the family and sent to a mental asylum, Shekhar finds himself increasingly helpless. An attempt is made on Damini's life in order to silence her, handsome sums are offered to the advocate for framing Urmi as a whore and a loose woman, and after the police and the family, it is the turn of the corruption within the legal system to be exposed as hired witnesses are summoned to prove that Damini is mentally ill.

As a woman activist, I feel that the story borrows a great deal from reality. A fight for any kind of redressal for the rape victim begins to affect the supporters at various levels – family, marriage, social acceptance.

And social responses are loaded so heavily in favor of male control that a woman's body becomes a thing to be exploited, discarded and destroyed. All this activity is garbed within the notions of respectability and honor, but in actuality it serves the ends of power, wealth and self-indulgence. The investigative methods are designed to be an obstacle course or a trap. The whole legal machinery looks upon a rape victim as an outcast and pronounces her guilty. This is the only crime where the victim is perceived as guilty and the male mindset whether of a husband, advocate, police man or judge is unable to see the victim as a person.

For patriarchy, rape is no big deal. It is the male right to a female body. Rape can take place within families, related kin, and even within marriage. It is the taking of a woman without her willingness. In a feudalistic structure, the poor have no rights. Male power is supplemented in this aggressive act by money power and while it privileges the male ego, it ignores the woman's right to her body as well as to her conscience. It is a total objectification of a person. And physical rape is not the only form of rape. Even if Damini's body is not violated, her personhood, her sense of self-respect, her emotions – all are violated. By questioning her sanity and pushing her into an asylum, her very being is violated. The film makes a powerful statement not only against the blindness of patriarchy but also for the courage which supporters have to display. It emphasizes the need for social responsibility and women's solidarity.

Notes

1. Rape cases are increasing in Rajasthan. According to police reports there are 3 or 4 cases in a day but conviction rate is only 3%.
2. 'Sathin' is a grassroot worker at the village level in the Women's Development Programme of the Government of Rajasthan.
3. Bhanwari Devi was gangraped in 1992 by higher caste persons because she stopped the marriage of a one-year-old girlchild and informed the police. Subsequently, the act of rape was inflicted upon her as a punishment. She has had to face extremely embarrassing situation both in the cast and the police inquiries. Cross examination has often been based on descriptions of the sex act coded in a vulgar language.

21 *Mirch Masala*: Film with a Purpose

Krishna Rathore

Feminism is a protest against the relegation of women to a secondary status. It questions the myth of male superiority and aims at empowering women to claim a state of equality. The Roman classicist Horace in his *Ars Poetica* writes "mind is less actively stimulated by what it takes in through the ear than by what is presented to it through the trustworthy agency of the eyes – something that the spectator can see for himself" (85). This view makes film a stronger medium than oral narration and can do a lot for the status of women by instilling awareness and liberating women from the shackles of custom. Ketan Mehta's film *Mirch Masala* explores many feminist issues in the seemingly simple story projected through a very powerful narrative.

The film has Son Bai (Smita Patil) as the protagonist who is assertive and knows her mind. The Subedar (Nasiruddin Shah) symbolizes power and occupies a position of authority. He is the revenue inspector so the villagers are shown as trying to please him and even his unreasonable demands are fulfilled. He finds Son Bai different from other women he has been associated with and lusts for her, but she slaps him when he forces himself on her. This becomes a big issue in the small village community where this act of rebellion is seen as subversive in its intention and the village is divided on the basis of gender. Men of the village wish to hand her over to the Subedar lest they incur his wrath. Son Bai who is a worker in the spice factory, the 'karkhana' where women make mirch-masala, runs to take shelter in her work place. Old Abu Baba (Om Puri) is the chowkidar who takes the side of the women and upholding traditional values refuses to open the gate despite the orders from the owner of the karkhana. When finally the gate is broken, Abu Baba fires a shot which misses the mark and the Subedar merely falls from horseback. The Subedar shoots him and enters the factory. But as he forces his entry, the women throw the red ground chillies into his eyes and manage to defeat his purpose. The structure of male supremacy collapses through a very female weapon, flimsy and weak as compared to the guns in male hands. The last scene shows Son Bai standing with a sickle in her hand.

The compact plot structure raises a number of feminist questions. What makes a woman challenge the societal roles? Are women equipped to protect themselves? From where do women derive the strength to do so? Son Bai is a woman whose husband has gone to the city with the intention of taking up a railway job. This in fact was necessary to project Son Bai's character according to feminist perspectives and also happens to be a social reality with male migrants leaving behind their womenfolk in the villages. She refuses to succumb to the unjust demands of the Subedar, who is furious at this unaccustomed resistance. Women had been willingly brought to him in order to curry favour. For practical purposes three narrative frames are used. The first frame has Son Bai and the Subedar interacting as individuals. When the film begins Son Bai and other women of the village are shown filling their metal pots at the lake. Subedar and his men on horseback come across as forces of evil. The women give a warning shout, "Subedar has come!" Son Bai says, "He is just a man not a monster" (*Aadmi hi to hai hauwa nahin*). All women except Son Bai run away throwing their pots and are chased by Subedar's horse riders, the sipahis. The Subedar asks for a drink of water and Son Bai pours water in his scooped palm, which he drinks. In this frame there is no power equation between the two central characters but in the next frame the situation alters: the Subedar stands as a power symbol and Son Bai without her husband as an easy prey. When he misappropriates his power she slaps him to show that she cannot be taken for granted. There is a reversal of roles as we see that the object becomes the subject. The third frame has the subedar screaming in desperation and Son Bai standing with a sickle in her hand. The frame is successful in projecting the idea that when the garb of passivity is discarded, power equations are forced to change. The frame is important as it shows Son Bai picking the sickle and ready to defend her honour. The women in the factory get the message that by self-assertion only would they be able to end the nefarious practice. The should not depend on outside help, this has to come from within. The female bonding surfaces and the women throw chilly powder in the eyes of the Subedar the aggressor. Foucault commenting on the power equations has rightly said: "Power is not an institution; it is not a structure, it is not a certain power with which certain people are endowed, it is the name one gives to a complex strategic situation in a given society".[1] Men are shown as spineless creatures who are ready to offer Son Bai to the Subedar for their selfish interest. They know that if the Subedar remains displeased, they would be severely taxed. A very strong message is conveyed that it is work, which empowers women, chilly-spice not only provides subsistence but also becomes a mode of protection. Simple gender divisions are not possible for while the village men wish to yield to the pressures of power, the old watchman resists this pressure. And over and above the power frames there is the use of the factory space as an enclosure where the women are self-imprisoned. They are the prey which the predator is hunting.

Supplementing the feminist cause is the story of Saraswati, the wife of the village Mukhiya. She is the mother of a daughter and is a neglected wife. She wishes to educate her daughter and for this reason sends her to school. But this does not have her husband's approval. Education is perceived as an empowerment which can threaten patriarchy and her husband exercises his authority by dragging the girl back home. Men unite in the efforts of maintaining patriarchal authority even as they themselves are exploited by the men in power in the social hierarchy. Women are subordinated to male control and desire – a subordination which is seen as necessary for patriarchy to continue. There is the facade of protection. The protection which the men claim to provide is conditional. If a woman deviates from the set code of behaviour, the protection is withdrawn. Men are afraid of women's strength so education is denied to them lest they might question their subordinate status, and refuse to be subjugated. Saraswati puts her foot down at her husband's night-outs. She refuses to open the door for him when he returns in the morning. Commenting on such an attitude of women Edward R. Lee observes that "The woman hero uncovers fractures in the surface of reality, contradictions in its structure, gaps in its social ideology. In so far as she resembles the male hero, she questions the conventional association of gender and behaviour" (4-5). Men in the lives of women have been dispensers and withholders of approval. They have assumed positions of control because the social and familial structures have been in their favour. Moreover the property laws have given them a position of advantage. These attitudes have defined the concepts of love and freedom. Moral norms and public behaviour are also defined by this male supremacy but once a woman becomes aware of her strength she can explode the myth of male superiority.

When Saraswati comes to know about Son Bai's plight she is seen as a pillar of fortitude. She goes from door to door apprising women of the situation and asks them to join her in supporting Son Bai. Some are reluctant while others are supportive. She succeeds in collecting a group of women who are with Son Bai but when men come back after their negotiations with the Subedar all the women including Saraswati are thrown back in their houses by their respective husbands. Space is a very crucial factor. Women are controlled by the space men allow them. The patriarchal structures enclose women in this private space called home and render them inert and useless. Saraswati is locked up in her home and her protests go unheard.

There is also the story of Radha (Supriya Pathak) who loves Mohan (Mohan Gokhale) who is the Mukhiya's brother. The director has taken up the money factor and shows that love is meaningless without money in the propertied class. We see the proposal of marriage between Radha and Mohan is turned down by the Mukhiya and at this point one of his cronies says that Mohan being Mukhiya's brother would be weighed with money.

As already mentioned earlier, the film avoids divisions along gender lines. There are several men who resist the imposition of male desire on female lives. There is the school master who is projected as an agent of change, and he attempts to persuade people to send their daughters to school. He tells Saraswati that one does not have to render an unquestioning obedience to custom. Later he is punished for siding with the women. Barot, like the schoolmaster and Abu Baba, is another of the male dissidents. But rather than stay and be tortured like the master, or die as a martyr to the cause like Abu Baba, he decides to leave the village as a protest against the victimization of Son Bai.

The act of analysis allows the viewer to see "more" in a film as Schillaci has observed in his essay "Film as Environment" (478).

The point is that the narrative not only deals with the story line but also uses motifs, images and symbols to enhance the effect. The title *Mirch Masala* is symbolic. *Mirch Masala* becomes a metaphor for employment, which gives strength and strength in turn gives self-protection. The medium of livelihood is also the shield which protects these rural, uneducated and otherwise powerless women. Again there are actions which are repeated, sounds which are echoed and visual images which evoke memories. The horses, ordinarily a symbol of desire and passion, also express resentment, as they neigh. And again the cacti reflect the barrenness of emotional values, a barrenness which has inhabited the souls of the slave men who yield to the authority of the Subedar. For all this, film becomes a very effective medium as it is able to co-ordinate time and space.

The solution however seems to be not in any miraculous change of heart in the men but in the solidarity of women. This is in keeping with the code reflected in several other films like *Rehaee, Mrityudand* and even *Lajja*. Filmmakers seem to propagate the idea that the division of women along vertical lines through family loyalties and obedience to the husband needs to be balanced by loyalty to the same sex and by responding to one's conscience. Men as they rework patriarchy do so by aligning themselves on the same line. Dissidents amongst men signal hope for gender equality.

Mirch Masala despite its theme of female empowerment and resistance to male terror, was able to evoke a response at the box office primarily because the central issue of sexual exploitation is framed within conventional structures. The issue of modernity is only peripherally reflected through reference to education. Nowhere does it propagate independent women – only strong women capable of upholding their moral self. The right to body is also defined within conventional morality – that of fidelity within marriage. Abu Baba's protection of these woman again falls within the code of conventional chivalry. Yet the film raises several important questions and provokes the viewer to think.

Note

1. *Epigraph* of Susie Tharu's article "Oral History, Narrative Strategy, and the Figures of Autobiography" in *Narrative Forms and Transformations*. Ed. by Sudhakar Marathe and Meenakshi Mukherjee.

References

Horace, "On the Art of Poetry". *Classical Literary Criticism*. Trans. T.S. Dorsch. Harmondsworth: Penguin, 1965.

Lee, Edward R. *Psyche As Hero: Female Heroism and Fictional Form*. Middletown, Connecticut: Wesleyan University Press, 1984.

Marathe, Sudhakar and Meenakshi Mukherjee, eds. *Narrative Forms and Transformations*. Delhi: Chanakya Publications,1986.

Schillaci, Anthony. "Film as Environment", *Twentieth Century Criticism*. Eds. William J. Handy and Max Westbrook, High and Life Publishers: New Delhi, 1976.

22 Spatial Contours in *Zubeida*

Veena Jain

The cinema is the art of today, just as drama was in earlier ages. In recent times, it has come to be looked upon as a serious art form. It is a commingling of the visual, the oral and the philosophical. It is the most powerful medium through which we can express life's shades of light and darkness and transmute them into art.

The history of Indian cinema goes as far back as 1913 when Dada Saheb Phalke, one of the pioneers of the silent feature film in Indian cinema broke ground with *Rajah Harishchandra*. Since then many critical issues have been raised and analysed through films. There have been films dealing with social, political and psychological themes. The Indian cinema also encompasses the lives, aspirations, emotions, problems and struggle of "one half of humanity" – that is the woman. What Shashi Deshpande writes for her book is equally true for the Indian woman in the context of cinema.

> And then I wrote *That Long Silence*, almost entirely a woman's novel, nevertheless, a book about the silencing of one-half of humanity. A lifetime of introspection went into the novel, the

one closest to me personally, the thinking and ideas in this are closest to my own.

(Deshpande 210)

Shashi Deshpande's statement covers the entire canvas of exploitative and repressive categories in the Indian cinema ranging from the stoning of Anarkali to Damini's silencing, from the Bandit Queen's torture to the curbing of Zubeida's spirit. When "one half of humanity" is being silenced, when the space for freedom goes on shrinking, existing social structures become questionable. And when a woman's name is entirely wiped out from history as in *Zubeida*, several challenging questions are thrown at the society vis-à-vis the audience.

In *Zubeida*, towards the end, a much tried and baffled son asks his grandmother a very crucial question – "*Akhir Ammi chahti kya thi*?" (After all what did Ammi want?) Perhaps her son felt that Zubeida had got all that she could ask for. The same kind of response is elicited by most people who feel that she did not get such a raw deal. *Zubeida* is one such movie which does not seem overtly feminist and yet is deeply concerned with women's issues.

I have specially taken up *Zubeida* for my discussion as I feel that the seemingly contented, romantic life of Zubeida was, in fact, a shortlived world of dreams within enclosed parameters. *Zubeida* is not just a beautiful romance, though the word Zubeida strikes a note of romance, beauty, love and loneliness. It is a questioning of the social, feudalistic and patriarchal structures of society with its smug acceptance in relation to both history and the present. If we think of Zubeida only as "*Pariyon ki Shehjadi*" as Zubeida's mother wants her grandson to think, we would miss the point.

The *Oxford Illustrated Dictionary* defines Romantic as fantastic, unpractical, quixotic, dreamy ... preferring grandeur, picturesqueness, passion or irregular beauty to finish and proportion, subordinating whole to parts or form to matter. The *Chambers Twentieth Century Dictionary* explains romantic as a fictitious and wonderful tale which passes beyond limits of ordinary life... a love affair, journalistically, it becomes an affair involving a marriage between different social classes; romantic atmosphere or feeling; a leaning towards the romantic; an imaginative lie... to build castles in the air. The Maharaja is attracted to Zubeida as she is a being out of this ordinary world, a romance for him. The whole story can be seen as a romance. But then the main issue of freedom would be sidetracked.

Before beginning with a discussion of *Zubeida*, I would like to turn to some of the movies where woman's victimization, social exploitation and oppression is more pronounced and blatant in the Indian scenario. *Sahib Bibi aur Gulam* depicts the Indian woman cloistered in the confines of the Rajput family: the male exhibiting his manliness through arrogance, wine and women and the wife desperately attempting to lure her husband from the "kotha", (brothel house) by breaking traditional confines of behaviour. She resorts to drink in order to gain his love and companionship. Similarly, in a later movie *Daman*, the husband is a brute who tortures his wife physically and emotionally. In both the cases women suffer to an extreme degree. In the former, ironically, the wife is murdered. Her unwifely, uncoventional act is seen as a crime against the norms of the Rajput family, in the latter, the wife kills her husband for the sake of her daughter in the guise of Goddess Durga. Her suppressed rage finds an outlet in violence.

Coming to another aspect of sacrificial love as in *Main Tulsi tere Angan Ki*, the male participates in both the worlds. The mistress satisfies his romantic urge and the wife gives him family solidity and respectability. There are innumerable Indian movies where a similar equation can be seen. In all these pictures where the binary opposition of mistress/wife, home/outside world, love/duty and freedom/restriction exists, the mistress has no choice left but to die in the end after giving birth to a child. She has to make place for the wife: the legitimate mate of her husband. Two women are pitted against one another but the husband smugly enjoys both the worlds with nothing to lose.

A more modern version of a similar situation can be seen in *Biwi No. 1* where the seriousness of the issue has been given a lighter touch by making it more of a comedy. Here the male openly lives with his mistress till the wife is successful in luring him back into the family fold by a series of tactics. The title itself becomes misleading as the second woman is never made a *biwi*. For the husband, the affair becomes a mere fling or a weakness easily forgivable by his loving wife.

The above mentioned movies are taken here for discussion to show that Zubeida neither suffers from any kind of physical or emotional torture, nor is she a mistress. And yet the question still lingers – how free is she? There are other questions like – why was her name obliterated from history? What made her life desperate towards the end? In trying to answer these questions, the spatial contours of Zubeida's life have to be defined.

The very fact that the story is based on the real life history of the Maharaja of Jodhpur, Maharaja Hanuwant Singh, brings to light certain glaring realities which exist in our society. History gives the director "an extra-aesthetic authority" as Lionel Trilling says in "The Sense of the Past":

> In the existence of every work of literature of the past, its historicity, its pastness is a factor of great importance. In certain cultures the pastness of a work of art gives it an extra aesthetic authority which is incorporated into its aesthetic power.
>
> (Trilling 260)

The Maharaja of Jodhpur had brought with him a professional singer whose name went into oblivion immediately after the aircrash which killed her and the Maharaja. The life history of Zubeida has been put into the cinematic mould and brought to light by none other than her own son – Khalid Mohammad, the producer of *Zubeida* (and also of *Fiza*). It is an attempt on his part to bring her non-existence back to life and pay homage to her. The medium of cinema gave him an added advantage of giving this true story a universal appeal.

The movie unfolds itself through a multiple narratology – Zubeida seen through the eyes of the music director, the actress Miss Rose, diaries, her mother, the elder Maharani of Fatehpur and its people. He is also able to see the cinematic shots of Zubeida. The son is both the omniscient narrator and the listener concurring with different voices to fill in the gaps in Zubeida's life. It is Zubeida, the dancer, the woman, the daughter, the wife and the *rani* seen in different roles. The flashback technique used by the director Shyam Benegal attempts to put back the broken fragments of Zubeida's life together. One is reminded of Nelly Dean, the controlling voice of Emily Bronte's *Wuthering Heights*.

The last scene is extremely crucial to the movie, where Zubeida's son visits Fatehpur to collect bits and pieces of his mother's life and visualize her as the *rani*. The moment he arrives, he is forbidden from even mentioning her name. He is told that the Maharaja had only one wife, the elder Maharani of Fatehpur. There is no trace of her existence. She is deliberately obliterated, cruelly annihilated. Is it because she is held responsible for the Maharaja's death or is it because she is a Muslim? Whatever the reason, she must have had to put up with a lot of humiliation. For the Maharaja Zubeida was only a romance, a beautiful obsession a distraction which would later become a hindrance in his public and private life. In a perfectly legitimate relationship, Zubeida's second marriage gives her the position only of a mistress whereas bigamy committed on the part of Maharaja is neither questioned nor made uncomfortable for him. It is viewed as a royal prerogative.

Taking a look at Zubeida's life, she is seen as a passionate, beautiful girl, fiery and spirited, filled with a desire to enjoy life and freedom. As a child she is fond of dancing and wants to pursue her career in films when she grows up. But women artists who chose a career of art out of choice or by following the family tradition were branded as social outcasts. It became an oppressive tool for women. Entering such a world meant crossing the threshold or the Lakshman Rekha. Hence her father, who is a film producer, strictly warns her from indulging in any such stupidity. Zubeida makes an abortive attempt. Her only dance in a film, with the song "*Mein Albeli*" sums up her total self – seen in her youth, grace, desire and freedom. The film is never made, nor are her dreams ever fulfilled. Her son is able to procure the reel of this film only towards the end of the movie.

Zubeida's father marries her off to his friend's son in spite of her vehement opposition. She even tries to kill herself while the song "*Mehndi hai rachne wali, Hathon mein hai gehri lali*" ironically plays in the background with the festivities of marriage being carried out. She tries to adjust to her married role and gives birth to a son. But the marriage is annulled when her father-in-law decides to leave the country and go back to Karachi taking his son along with him. Zubeida's father cannot let his daughter leave. A divorce follows. The fathers decide their fate. There is no possibility of either delaying or questioning the decision taken by the fathers. The young lovers are parted, and the child separated from the father. The boundaries of Zubeida's life are defined by her almost dictatorial father who thwarts her at every step.

It is only when she meets the Maharaja through Miss Rose that she decides to carve a niche for herself in a world of limited options. A beautiful world opens out before her for the first time. A world of her dreams, of love, of romance and life. The Maharaja is equally enamoured, almost bewitched by her. Her parents acqueisce to her marriage but set a pre-condition before her. Her son is to stay with them to be brought up as a Muslim. Thus in order to fulfil her own personal desire, she is asked to sacrifice her motherhood.

For a brief period after reaching Fatehpur, she is lost in a world of dreams. The song "*Mehki mehki hai rahein behki behki hai nigahein*" gives a clue to the deep love and happiness surrounding her. Her idyllic world is cut short when she realizes that she has to fall in with the ways of the royal family, which leaves little freedom for women. She is placed in a separate "Mahal" by the Maharaja. Only then does she realize her status in the whole setup. She is only a plaything, a sexual object, to be made love to when the Maharaja is free from his stately affairs and family ties. For there is another woman, the elder Maharani also to be attended to and who performs the customary and traditional duties of the Rajput family. Zubeida cannot and will not take the marginal position of being thrust aside as a sexual object. She rebels as soon as she realizes that she has become an "object" for the male, a "receiver", the "receptacle" as Simone de Beauvoir (65) calls the woman. Hence the desperation seen in her towards the end, when the world seems to be slipping by. She clings to it, pushes aside the elder Maharani and takes her place alongside the Maharaja in the scheduled flight for the election campaign. There is a plane crash and the couple die. Their death is shrouded in mystery, but Zubeida's name is entirely wiped out after her death. Her only remembrance is in the form of an album and the dance reel is presented to her son by the elder Maharani.

The all-imposing patriarchal structure of society does not leave much choice for the elder Maharani as well. The Maharaja is free to satisfy his romantic urge and sexual desire by remarrying. But the elder Maharani is caged within the confines of her home and has to put up with this injustice through restraint and contentment. Actually both the women inhabit worlds that are equally fragile. While Zubeida enjoys her husband's love which borders more on sexual fascination and the Maharani enjoys the privilege of social prestige attached to her title, both women have to bear with partial fulfilment of their married roles. It is the male who satisfies different aspects of himself through these women. For him multiple existence has a social sanction. For the woman it becomes a transgression.

Zubeida is more like a free bird in spirit. The song "*Mein albeli, ghumun akeli, pagli hum mein... Tu rangili, Tu mastili*" throws light on her real personality. She is not passive and hence feels the pinch of the patriarchal hold more strongly. Her father keeps the bird caged from her childhood. He takes all the decisions and controls her life from marriage to divorce to remarriage. It is the Maharaja who gives her love but cannot give her respectability. In her decision of remarrying the Maharaja, she defies her father. As a result, her son is separated from her. She is not forgiven even after her death. If home gives Zubeida a secure foothold, it is also a confining place in her father's authoritarian regime. The outside world is free but is equally precarious in its branding of woman as the social outcast. If she tries to seek more freedom in her husband's house, she meets with disappointment and criticism.

The world "freedom" thus takes two different meanings in society. For the male, freedom would mean realizing of the self: without any curbing of spirit and living with his multiple existences through women. For the female it is conforming to social attitudes, norms, behaviour and code of conduct. She has to fit into the role assigned for her or suffer for overstepping its boundaries. Her area is decided and controlled by male sanction and authority. Zubeida brings out this dichotomy successfully.

References

de Beauvoir, Simone. *The Second Sex*. London: Jonathan Cape, 1960.

Deshpande, Shashi. "The Power Within". *Creating Theory: Writers on Writing*. Ed. Jasbir Jain. Delhi: Pencraft International, 2000.

Trilling, Lionel. "The Sense of the Past". *Literary Criticism: A Reading*. Ed. B. Das and J.N. Mohanty. Calcutta: Oxford University Press, 1985.

23 Battling for Being: Manjrekar's *Astitva*

Ranju Mehta

Pitched as a feminist film, raising questions that rake up the very issues of existence, it is justifiably titled *Astitva*. The film demands space and identity for the fulfillment of the 'being' of women within the institution of marriage. It is an appeal to them to break their silence and consolidate themselves for the final crusade. The film provides a rare glimpse of an enlightened approach. The style and content, in contrast to the run-of-the-mill Hindi films, are simple. The dress, manners, speech and conduct, background and foreground – all blend into a complete harmony. The temptation to shoot on special tourist locations out of context is resisted; rather the locations are selected and thus become special on account of their relevance to the particular trait or character in the story. Also there are no dance sequences for which numerous girls suddenly appear from nowhere to gyrate their pelvises around some central star. The substance of the film is life itself as it does not present an imaginary, synthetic society. A serious theme – yes, but nowhere does the narrative sag and lose the interest of the viewer. The real meaning of a film is contained not in the declaration of its intent but in the total experience which it provides. The plot of *Astitva* forces the protagonist to choose between a life of indignity and humiliation and freedom in the true sense.

Astitva is not merely about existence, as the name may suggest on the face of it. It is the assertion of all that which constitutes a personality with its distinct relationships, anxieties, dependencies, dispositions, impulses and aspirations, prejudices and predilections. *Astitva* exemplifies what the German philosopher, Martin Heidegger, terms existentiality; it refers not to existence in the sense in which stones or sticks exist but to the inner personal being. According to him each is cast into a world not of his own making, referring to it as facticity. From this facticity each has to appropriate, assimilate and transcend the given world.

Astitva is about a woman's struggle to find her identity. It's a poignant exploration of the negation of identity until transcended to an assertion of self-identity. This film can be seen as a counter narrative to the Ram-Sita myth reinforced by most Indian films wherein the woman faces the test of her fidelity and the man reserves the right to pronounce the judgment and sentence on her. It is the woman who suffers the banishment. But in *Astitva* the protagonist shatters this traditional myth of Ram-Sita by (1) establishing that the sexual desire of a woman too is a drive much like any man's, and by (2) challenging the husband's pronouncement to live under the same roof and suffer the humiliation and pain of rejection on the grounds of having committed adultery.

The story revolves around Aditi, the role played remarkably well by Tabu representing what really validates the movement of feminism and what perhaps many women can identify with. Aditi is a beautiful, educated and docile girl married to Srikant Pandit an executive who has toiled his way to floating his own firm. Her husband, though not a brute treats her as a chattel, imposes dos and don'ts on her. But the most refreshing aspect of the film is that he is not a wife-beater and the story does not fall in line with the clichéd, strident feminist tone in treating the subject and yet it is told in the most candid manner.

The film is gripping and the technique used to make the story interesting is the way the viewer is transported in time. At the very outset he encounters not a young but an old character who is feeble and coughing and wants the lawyers to secure someone else's future while the viewer becomes concerned about what may be a short-lived dotage for this man. With this deeply moving emotion the film travels from the more recent times to the living present – a lunch is being organized by Sri and his wife for old friends, Dr. Ravi Bapat and his wife, Meghna. This get-together brings into our view three couples – Aditi and Sri, Ravi and Meghna, Aniket and Revathi; one is the touchstone against the other two.

Sri and Ravi Bapat meet in the garden. The open outdoor location signifies a frank and unhindered exchange between the two friends. Sri comes across to us as ambitious, self-absorbed, pompous. His language is loud, abusive with little or no respect for women – "*Ay Biwi, beaches and bikinis, damn it,*" etc. Through out the party Sri talks pompously as a self-centred man would, whether in appreciating Meghna's youthful looks or disapproving Revathi's pursuit of an independent career. Thus the characteristics in the embodiment of Sri forming the rudiments of what the film has to project and subsequently raze comes out straight, unalloyed and bold. These are what makes Meghna bluntly sum up Sri as "a male chauvinist pig".

Aditi is a woman with fine sensibilities, keen sense of aesthetics, composed and completely dedicated to her family. She has been ever willing to do anything for Sri. In the role of a dutiful housewife she seems quite convincing and raises no suspicion in our minds that she could ever take up cudgels against what later unfolds itself as stifling her.

Dr. Ravi Bapat is a perfect gentleman. He is broadminded and respects women. He has accepted Meghna, his wife, a divorcee with two daughters from her first marriage. From her experience Meghna has come to learn what she wants Aditi also to realize: that society is ridden with patriarchy and male domination. She advises Aditi not to be merely a housewife – "never mortgage your self-esteem, particularly to a man". Meghna herself runs a boutique.

Meghna is emancipated. Aditi is still in the thick of her domestic life. The film reinforces this by locating their conversation in the kitchen. The location has shifted from the open garden to the confines of the house as women come into focus. Aditi is content with household chores and says, "It is a little too late to start now," when Meghna suggests that she too should do something. This casual exchange between the two women prove to be the seeds of an impending change in Aditi's suppressed being.

Revathi is modern, independent and career-oriented, bent upon pursuing her profession at the cost of displeasing her father-in-law who is against women working. However, if at all, she must work Sri, her prospective father-in-law, tenders her a chance to join his firm. But she spurns his offer. In contrast her fiance's personality has not grown to be independent, i.e., Aniket has not flowered under the strongly regimented ways of his father. Revathi's independence reflects the possibility of a future which can come into existence rendering possible a more equal relationship.

The lunch party lands the viewer right in the centre of an informal situation. In such a meeting old chums talk uninhibitedly so they soon unravel themselves. Thus as the viewer gets to know these couples better he feels a sense of participation. And the viewer's coming in sustains his interest.

At the party just when their spirits are soaring high a twist in the story comes about. A registered letter for Aditi arrives. But instead of Aditi Sri snatches it. Meghna protests. But he opens it, declaring with authority, "It's Aditi's letter. Give it to me. She's my wife," sounding as though she were his property. The contents of the letter open up the crucial part of the film.

Malhar Kamath, Aditi's music teacher, has bequeathed all his belongings to Aditi. A windfall from a source Sri could barely recall, throws him into a fit of exaggerated laughter. The same night when he sits down to write his diary a seed of suspicion is sown in Sri's mind. The next day as he flips back through its pages he comes to a shocking conclusion that Aniket is not his son. And he confronts Aditi to get at the truth about Aniket. In the presence of Ravi, Meghna and Aniket Sri compels Aditi to make public how, when and why it all happened without the least consideration for all that Aditi has showered on him for the last twenty-seven years and her gentle protest that the matter be sorted out mutually. He violates her right to privacy and exposes his marital relationship to public view.

Through Aditi's confession about her relationship with Malhar the director takes the audience twenty-five years into the past when Aditi and Sri had begun their married life. Sri keeps extremely busy and has long interludes away from home. Aditi misses him and whenever she suggests taking up a job Sri dismisses the idea. He also rejects the proposal dear to her heart: Aditi's desire to start a family. Aditi is lonely and somewhat choked. At this time planting the visit of a couple, her sister and her husband, sharing an intimate relationship full of romance, love and concern for each other, heightens Aditi's longing for love. But Sri is too engrossed in material gains to be sensitive to his wife's emotional and physical needs. The vacuum and emptiness in her life begins to play on her mind. When Sri in passing suggests to Aditi to resume her music lessons to fill the void in her life Aditi is happy. Driven by prolonged loneliness, yearning for the physical proximity of her husband Aditi gradually gets drawn to Malhar Kamath. His melodious voice, simplicity and informal ways are really different from Sri's matter of fact and calculated behaviour. There is a deliberate play on the word 'Malhar'. The music teacher is Malhar, the *raga* is Malhar and the rainy season is Malhar, a season traditionally associated with the awakening of desire.

The sequence of song, rain and dance offers Aditi a world in direct contrast to the life she leads with Sri within the four walls of the house. This new world is open, vigorous, fluid and the kind which can satisfy her restless craving. In her actions and movements, Malhar's reactions and her ultimate giving away of herself surrendering to her natural impulse her desire does not clash with her thought, a clash that the film did evoke earlier. Remarkable in this short sequence is the way that character, ideas and states of mind of Aditi are projected visually without compromising on the credibility of the situation. It shows us the world as she wishes it to be – a world full of romance, love, life and spontaneity.

The journey from the present into the past is very smooth and knitted beautifully into the motif of the film. The director has strategically used the element of time to unite events which are far apart and dissect those which are continuous. The part of the film where Sri grills Aditi and the part during which Malhar Kamath and Aditi form a relationship are quite distinct and distant in time yet the two parts easily move in and out of each other as if sharing the same moment. Also the scene where Aditi informs Sri about her pregnancy, there is a moment's silence, the camera focuses on Sri's shocked face and then his ecstatic behaviour, has been used twice in the film for different purposes First, when it forms a part of the sequence of events as reported by Aditi. Second, when Aditi during her trial tries to convince Sri that she honestly did want to confess but his overjoyousness and happiness stopped her from doing so.

Using indoor and outdoor situations the director shows the deep contrast in Aditi's life with Sri, as against her life with Malhar Kamath. With Sri the scene remains in the enclosure of the house. She is seen within the four walls and is hardly ever able to assert herself. With Malhar Kamath the camera scans the vista. She is not confined to a closed environment, as for example, the room too faces a spacious verandah, the windows are wide open and the daylight floods in. The world of Aditi seems to have grown and she finds that she is able to express herself freely.

The director is again at his visual best when, not by words, but by Aditi's glance he is able to convey to Malhar Kamath her fear arising from the secret about Baby Aniket. And Malhar, reading her thoughts, promises to keep the secret, a secret.

The film makes a strong statement against gender insensitivity while tracing the subtle levels at which it operates. The revelation of Aniket not being his son was enough for Sri to snap all ties with Aditi. A moment of weakness becomes an unpardonable adultery for Sri, a man who sees nothing wrong with his own 'plunges' just because no babies are born of them. Sri castigates Aditi unreservedly, sounding as if he himself was always above board. The woman has always been singled out for censure and ignominy.. For Aditi nothing could be more agonizing and it is doubly difficult for Aditi to take it because her son, Aniket, too fails to comprehend the isolation, ennui and most all the suffocation she has endured. Aniket goes to the extent of saying, "don't you dare touch me, you...". He shuns her touch as though fearing to be defiled by her. And in the most deplorable manner curses the womb that has given birth to him. He has imbibed the same male attitudes his father nurtures and upholds..

The picture of a happy married life for a man rests on a fundamental assumption of a distinct role allocation and gender bias. The man is the breadwinner of the family, the woman does not work; he is the provider, she is the nurturer. More than once Sri in the course of the film while talking to Aditi emphasises, "Earning is my domain, I don't want my wife's money in my house". Sri can be visualized as a symbol of male chauvinism denying all space and identity to women. He doesn't think it even necessary to treat women with dignity. His planning is final and it is at his mercy that a woman can participate in the decision-making process. In the film he rejects the idea of a family because that did not fit into his planning at that point of time. A child should, he feels, be born in their own house. To this Aditi raises a pertinent question, "Where do I fit in your plans?" But there is no answer, not even a thought that she must have her space too. His total disregard of her desire for procreativity has an underlying assumption that procreativity is a sign of manliness and any decision about it is a male prerogative. During the next twenty-five years after Aniket's birth, no other child is born in the family – clearly indicating that Sri, despite all his display of virility, is impotent. Had Aniket never been conceived, Aditi would have borne the stigma of barrenness in addition to all else. But Aniket's presence in their lives has never led Sri to any self-questioning on that count..

A woman is a man's shadow. This the film brings to the fore as it is so intricately embedded in the socio-cultural fabric that unless a woman is jolted out of it she accepts it unquestioningly and reconciles to it as her lot. Her world, as that of Aditi, is confined to her husband and her household. Meghna was already beginning to dislike and disapprove much of what Sri was doing to his wife, realizes that she can no longer bear the ignominy which is being forced on her. When Aditi decides to leave home, the decision is painful, coming as it does after long years of marriage, loneliness and subordination. But her husband's callousness forces her to realize her own condition of homelessness and worthlessness. It is then that she decides to draw upon her own strength. Similarly when Aniket's attitude towards his mother is revealed, Revathi too finds reason in Aditi's rebellion. The three converge on a common platform. Meghna, Aditi and Revathi come together to pose a challenge to this male-dominated society, working across the divisions created by men.

Aditi's decision is sensitively worked out as she progresses from shock to realization. Sri humiliates her, pronounces on her a sentence of perpetual expiation, and finally when Revathi breaks her engagement with Aniket, he decides to divorce her.

He is the accuser, the jailor, the judge – all on his own. But it is through being shorn of all externals, that Aditi gathers strength. As she lies in agony on the floor of her room struggling with her desperate sense of having been abandoned, a phone call from Revathi shows her the way.

From a docile and submissive woman Aditi emerges a resolute and resilient person. The director creates this forceful impact visually in her descent from a flight of steps. She lands, for the first time onto an open and lighted space where all are gathered. Sri still carries the notion that Aditi is about to plead for forgiveness but no, she has come down to walk out of his life.

As she walks out of his life, she has embarked upon a new course while the husband (Sri) and the son (Aniket) are left with a sense of having been abandoned. Aniket, whose birth is the cause of the collapse of his marriage, is finally apparently seen as part of the house.

The ending leaves the audience with mixed feelings: is the long farewell speech essential, is the visual impact not adequate? Responses may differ, but the two together – the long monologue and the departure, the coming together of the three women, the two men standing together – all these bring out the complexity of the narrative which has gone before. It is not merely a question of female desire or sexuality, or fidelity within marriage but the film attacks through this central event the power relationships as they work in society. It focuses on the idea of personal freedom, on the nature of personal growth, on the enclosures which conventional marriages knit, and on the imposition of rules on individual wills which destroy both men and women.

24 Locating Perception and Paradoxes Within an Image: Manjrekar's *Astitva*

Rakesh Thakur

The contours of human relationship are pregnant with possibilities. From the vortex of "family of procreation" arises the troika of affinal, consanguinal, and fictive, kinship. The range of these three encompasses the major gamut of human relationship. Within the kinship network in general and man-woman relationship in particular the "identity" of the subject is central to the human relationship. This concept of "identity", no doubt is riven by contradictions. Life is like a game of snakes and ladders and is fraught with danger. Ups and downs are inevitable. The predicament that the "human" is caught in appears baffling. Life becomes a mirror image of the chessboard. Every move has certain implications, pros and cons notwithstanding, every move has endless potentialities. To explore a set of moves (issues), various dimensions are traversed. The dimensions are understood at various levels. To comprehend, one has to analyse. The faculty of thinking or reason allows human being to analyse the socioeconomic, political, cultural or any other individual existential situation he/she finds himself in to underscore the immanent contradictions in the ongoing dialectical process. With this analysis inspired by consciousness of his/her being and a desire to resolve the predicament he is caught in, a human being tries to transpose the manifest empirical reality that surrounds her/him into certain specific constitution of the signifiers which lead to a creative dialectics, a dialectics which plays a mediatory role in the cultural continuum, transforming its inherent contradictions into a revolutionary process of culture change.

It is these very contradictions which are being explored in the film *Astitva* directed by Mahesh Manjrekar. The narrative is a point of departure at many levels. There exists a narrative of the sequence (frame by frame) which outlines the story. Aditi is a happily married woman (seemingly), mother of a son, glorified housewife living her life at the dictates of patriarchy. Her husband Mr. Srikant Pandit, has his own firm, his own bungalow with a swimming pool, spends his evening with Scotch and friends, has all the trappings of an upper-class lifestyle. The son Aniket is a handsome replica of the (supposed) father, engaged to a modern and progressive woman, Revathi. To sum it up, the protagonist, Aditi's identity begins as Mrs. Srikant Pandit and ends up as being Aniket's mother. The picture perfect family.

At another level, the technique of flashback throws up another startling narrative. It is a narrative of flashback which truly helps to "locate" the identity of the protagonist, Aditi. Aditi is a "self", a woman, and has an existence and body which transgress the limits of wifehood and motherhood. Aditi sings. Her songs are an extension of her. In her songs she finds a voice of her own. Unbridled and without shackles. She desires, not merely as in marriage, legitimate desire or an act of procreation, as the passive recipient of male touch; but she is a woman awakened by her own self, her own body, and has a deep and primal longing for her own body and its pleasures.

It is a dialectics between the "linear" narrative and flashback narrative, which truly situates the character of Aditi. The linear is a syntactic manifestation whereas the metonymic constitution is actually based on metaphoric and paradigmatic choices.

Whenever, the director feels the need for a correlation to bring out the contours of signification, he takes recourse to the flashbacks. The complete effort stems from the urge to generate signification. Every "claptake-cut" constitutes a "signifier", at times complex and at many simple, partial or loaded, but ultimately, the primary goal is to establish a paradigmatic relation. The narrative is an ensemble of signifiers. The ensemble is characterized by the heterogeneity of the signifier, which throws up questions, for which no apparent answers are available.

Life and happiness are equated for the husband, Mr. Srikant Pandit, when he gets the first contract for his own company, his end of search for a home of his own and the news of his being a father. The troika of fatherhood, ownership of hearth, and a sense of economic well-being bestows upon him the tag of "The Complete Man". A happy home. Indeed, but the unexpected legacy left to his wife leads him to doubt his wife's fidelity. Seeds of doubt and a primal fear of the sexuality of his woman, lead him explore the act of impregnation by which his son was born. The hyperrational calculation of dates, confirms his worst fear. The startling honesty of the wife is a brilliant moment in the film. For the husband it is not adultery for more than betrayal, more than adultery, it is his manhood/fatherhood which he sees as being put on trial. Miseries are manifold. Helpless as a sense of emasculation grips him, his admonishings and accusations go beyond the bedroom. It is a time for a trial. The audience includes the son, and a couple who are family friends. For the husband, the verdict is clear. The wife's shame, and his own helplessness pronounces the wife as guilty.

Aditi is no bra-burning feminist. Her tears ask for forgiveness, she pleads for her last twenty-seven years of life in contrast to a momentary lapse of reason, when one single moment made her weak. The last twenty-seven years have been the epitome of *pativrata*, the definition of womanhood as defined by patriarchy. The attempt of reconciliation is thwarted, the act is unpardonable. The son is equally guilty of harshness. Rejecting his mother's touch he says: "Do not touch me you bloody - don't you dare touch me" This sums it up. The identity of the social and biological father must be one. The question of identity is more important than the question of being born. One is not just born, but one is born in a patrilineage, resides in a patrilocal setting, has a name, the patriarchal structure with its kinship network is there to receive. Women are a mere medium for the patriarchy to propagate itself. The fact that Aniket might have had half brothers and half sisters, too, with his father spreading his seed at random, is accepted as a man's need. For the women to quench her needs, patience is an important virtue. She can wait for her man. For her needs, she can busy herself in the monotony of everyday household chores. It is the phallus perogative to want, to have affairs. The unbridled urge is a metaphor for manhood. The women involved in the act of coitus, are forgotten but if discovered never forgiven. The conjugal/affinal relation with husband stands shattered. The umbilical cord of love between mother and son, the consanguinal, blood-bond has been snapped, Aditi's world is shattered. The sacrosanct husband-wife relationship, the only of its kind mother-child relationship, all crumbles. The chaos is complete. The verdict has been pronounced, the punishment from being repressive, as she is slapped, to restitutive as the intention of divorcing her is made clear.

The bonds of fictive kinship are yet to be explored. It is in the nuances of the character of Revathi (would be daughter-in-law) and Meghna (Ravi's wife, once divorced mother of two daughters from her first husband,) that womanhood emerges. Revathi breaks her engagement, with Aniket. It is in the mother son relationship, that she finds the reflection of her own future. For Meghna and Revathi, Aditi is an epitome of honesty and virtue. What she required, was an awakening of an inner urge, the urge to be herself, to look for her own *Astitva*, as the film ends with the words:

> I was there.......
>
> I am there.......
>
> I will be there.......

The woman's destiny is not man. The contours of human relationship are pregnant with potentialities.

25 En Route to Freedom and Self Discovery: *The Lunchbox* and *Bhaji on the Beach*

S. Asha

Serious cinema/parallel cinema or new wave cinema as it is referred to, has contributed a great deal towards re-defining the woman character. These films raise new questions about the representation of women because of the different accounts of the construction of the female self, agency, identity placed in the cultural contexts of the subject. These non-formula or non-commercial films reflect more nuanced views about the self's complexity. With gradual shift of time the camera's focus has shifted from the women's body to her identity as an individual. This offers more scope for the viewer to construct critical readings. This paper seeks to probe into the negotiation of identity in two films *The Lunchbox* and *Bhaji on the Beach*, located two decades apart and in two very different cultural locations. Both films focus on desire – desire for a full, intense life, for freedom, for romance and communication. While *The Lunchbox* has one female protagonist, *Bhaji on the Beach* takes up the negotiation of multiple identities by a group of women. A prime concern of feminism is the urge to break the silence thereby interrogating forces of gender identity.

The film *The Lunchbox* revolves around something we are familiar with since childhood. That is the literal lunchbox. Director Ritesh Batra creates a refreshingly subtle romantic film around this simple object which is evocative both in terms of the food it contains and the romance it brings about. Located in a middle class home in a limited space, the woman character seeks communication and love in her mundane relationship. The claims of work, the long hours of loneliness, all add up to boredom and frustration. It is out of this a story is woven both of self-awakening and the corresponding loneliness of the male, locked up in his office the whole day long, with only the lunch hour open to diversion. Apart from the characteristic features of Mumbai as a metro with all the rush, restlessness and everyday struggle for existence, a distinct feature of the city lies in its unfailing delivery system of lunchboxes collected from houses and restaurants. Every morning the *dabbawalas* (meal couriers) pick up steaming hot lunches packed into metal tiffin containers from homes and restaurants to deliver them to various destinations. These tiffins are transported from bikes to trains and eventually reach the recipients. The director fascinated by the *dabbawalas* carves out a human tale out of their experience. Harvard Business School commissioned a six-month study into the unfailing delivery system of the *dabbawalas* in 2009 and the findings stated that out of every million lunchboxes that need to be reached from a million homes to their respective destinations in different offices in Mumbai, at the most three could miss reaching the right desk at the right time reference. Batra carved his story out of this study, the rare mistaken delivery of a lunchbox. The entire mechanism of delivery of lunchboxes is captured effectively by the camera-eye. This backdrop highlights the efficacy of the tiffin ferriers and their merry chorus. But the focus of attention is the lunchbox which reaches the wrong destination. It seems to echo the popular refrain 'Sometimes the wrong train can lead you to the right destination' used as a dialogue and caption in the film. As a ferrier of tasty food as well as thoughts, the lunchbox leads two people who have never met, to enter into a unique relationship. Exchange of letters/mails has been the subject of both dramatic and cinematic medium like *A Shop Around the Corner* (1940), *In the Good Old Summertime* (1940) and *You've Got Mail* (1998) in Hollywood and *Sirf Tum* (1999) and *Mitr, My Friend* (2002) in India, but the idea of exchange of letters through the lunchbox is a new exploration of the film medium.

The director weaves his story through the essentially gendered space of the kitchen which triggers this search for freedom and self-discovery. The protagonist Ila prepares a meal and packs it in the lunchbox hoping to get some compliment from her seemingly estranged husband. The lunchbox by mistake gets delivered to Sajan Fernandes, who is still unable to get over his wife's demise and is hardly keen to move on in life. He is surprised to find food different from that of the customary restaurant one. After initial hesitation, he savours the entire food. Ila is surprised to find the lunchbox licked clean. She assumes it is an appreciative gesture by her husband but during a conversation with him finds out that the meal was not consumed by him at all. She prepares yet another meal the following day and sends a note thanking the consumer. This is the first step taken by her towards negotiation of her identity. A series of exchange of notes is thus initiated. Gradually, the unknown recipient acquires an identity and a new series of communications begin. Ila's all efforts at directing the *dabbawala* to reach her tiffin to the right man having failed, her relationship undergoes a transformation; whether it is feedback on the cooked meal or advice on family issues, a negotiation of identities is soon in process. This exchange in turn builds up a unique bond between two unknown strangers. Ila not only finds way out of her loneliness but begins her personal route to freedom and self-discovery. She begins to realize the need to find her true self, to plan out her life and to do what she wants to do. She is unfazed at the knowledge that her husband is having an affair. This is made evident through a recurring image of Ila smelling her husband's clothes while washing them, without any perturbed expression. She contemplates the prospect of moving to Bhutan for a better life and discusses it with her new friend. This can also be seen as a proof of her amassing courage to shift both personal and literal space. On the other hand, Sajan also gradually overcomes his moron image and prepares for a better life and strives to be a cheerful being.

Ila discovers that the mistaken delivery of her intended lunchbox was a blessing. Passing notes to each other through the lunchbox, Ila and Sajan quickly find that the best part of their days passed in reading each other's letters. There is feeling of warmth, tenderness and communication which is reflected through images such as Ila reading the letters while sipping coffee and Sajan stealing moments off from work to read the letter as soon as the lunchbox arrives at his desk. The two characters have deep sources of dissatisfaction in their present state of being. They find it being remedied as the lunchbox becomes a medium of expressing their anguish and desperation. In each other Ila and Sajan find consolation in the midst of the hardships in their lives. The attraction is not of the love at first sight flavour, but is instead a result of their trust, understanding, respect and acknowledgement of each other's hardships. While the audience knows about the significant age difference between Ila and Sajan from the very beginning, the characters themselves do not know to what extent this difference is. Both in very different phases of life, their relationship not only explores themes of love but also of different stages of life. Having many more years of life experience, Sajan not only provides Ila with warm companionship, but also with valuable advice. In one of the notes, Sajan even advises Ila to plan a second child to rid herself of the present state of boredom. Ila provides Sajan with the ability to dream and hope for a better future. Through the notes in the lunchbox Sajan also experiences a renewal in his outlook as his relationship with Ila grows. The transformation of Sajan is furthered by another youth, his newly assigned trainee. With a stubborn and eternally optimistic attitude, the new trainee Shaikh, serves as a foil to Sajan. He helps Sajan to learn to care for someone other than himself. The image of Sajan acting as best man at Shaikh's wedding is adequate proof of it. This understanding between the two men may be attributed to his sharing of the meal from the lunchbox. Shaikh gently pursuades Sajan to open up and realize the need to live an intent life.

At the superficial level, *The Lunchbox* may appear to be about loneliness experienced by its protagonists, Ila, who is being ignored by her husband either because of his work or because he is having an affair. It is also about Sajan, on the verge of retirement from his job, having no friends or family to look up to and forced to spend his evenings smoking and vaguely staring at a family dining together in the neighbouring house, reminding him of the past and the absences in his life. It is also about Shaikh, an adult orphan seeking companionship and care. It is about women (Ila's mother and the woman upstairs) tired of caring for their ailing husbands and unable to move out with their friends. How many substitutes are to be found? Letters, chits, talking through the windows, messages in the basket and interior monologues? But this seemingly negative picture of loneliness is converted into sheer positivity due to the director's craftsmanship.

The limited space of the kitchen offers little scope for reaching the outside. In Indian culture every woman is expected to work within this space to shoulder the responsibility of her household. Ila too seems to be content with her confined space. As a devoted housewife and mother she concentrates on the daily household chores, gets her daughter ready for school, washes clothes and cooks food. The confined space of the kitchen serves as a space for her empowerment. She tries to please her husband at first through the generally prevalent notion that, 'the way to a man's heart is through his stomach'. Towards this end she tries new recipes. Her culinary skills are appreciated by the chance consumer. The director uses a visually absent character, a mysterious auntie's voice-over narration. The delineation of this character is an innovative experiment within the visual medium. "Auntie" guides Ila through her preparation of recipes, advises her and lends her relevant spices by lowering them down her window in a basket. The spices and the music strike positive vibes. This warm relationship with 'auntie' fulfils Ila's desire for companionship to a large extent. There is communication, mutual understanding and tenderness in this relationship. This female bonding is as fulfilling as is the one between the two male characters Sajan and Shaikh.

As the lunchbox leads the protagonists to the right destination, an interesting feature of the film lies in its open ending. Ila and Sajan never get to meet. The bold act of sending the lunchbox without any food after Sajan fails to turn up at the restaurant they decide to meet may be seen as an act of protest. Sajan is forced to confess that he slipped away on noticing "how young and beautiful she was". Will he get over his hesitation? Will Ila decide to move on in life on her own? These questions lead to an open ending. Through a brief visual clipping of bereavement in Ila'a family where her mother confesses her dissatisfaction with her own married life, the route to freedom opens up for Ila. By tracing her way to Sajan's office through the *dabbawala*, Ila takes yet a step further to negotiating herself. A remote possibility of their reunion is revealed through the final image of Sajan fanatically trying to locate Ila's address with the help of the *dabbawalas*. The protagonist finds the route to fulfilment of her desire for life, communication and romance.

Thus the symbolic image of the lunchbox pervades throughout the narrative. The challenge for the filmmaker is to portray the women characters with an individual identity still maintaining cultural values, at the same time staying away from practices that are regressive. As such, the character of Ila comes out more defined, confident and independent. It is interesting to note the male perception of feminine issues, that too through the space of the kitchen, has been taken up by a male director. He succeeds in probing into feminine psyche. The filmmaker is critical in the decisions he makes and can shape the perceptions of a society he reflects and portrays. The director of *The Lunchbox* makes a worthwhile effort in this regard. The nuance of the relationship with all the warmth of love and companionship and delicate handling of the subject make it appreciable.

Bhaji on the Beach (1993) also deals with the subject of self-discovery but the treatment is at the hands of a woman director Gurinder Chadha and the setting is diaspora. The film focuses on a group of nine Asian women spending one day at the seaside, in Blackpool. There is Ginder, who has left her abusive husband and Hashida who has just discovered that she is pregnant with her Black boyfriend. Madhu and Ladhu, teenage sisters who are coming mainly to get away from boredom at Birmingham, and also Simi, the coordinator of Saheli Asian Women's Centre, by whom the trip is organized. Included also are Pushpa, an elderly and extremely judgmental wife of a shop owner Asha, who has been suffering with headaches and visions of the God Rama, Bina, her friend and Rekha, who is visiting from Bombay. The women set out on a journey of discovery not only of the picturesque and 'flashy' Blackpool but their secrets and problems as well. Eventually they are confronted by Ginder's husband who comes to Blackpool to convince his wife to return back with him. Hashida makes up with her boyfriend Oliver who is looking for her in Blackpool in order to discuss the future of their secretive relationship and her pregnancy.

These women, struggle with their conflicts of gender, ethnicity, race and generational differences and the many shifts these require. The group indulges in songs, clapping, comments on the scenery around, individual reverie and confrontation and reconciliations. Each of these women reaches some crossroad en route to the discovery of what she wants and where lies her true identity. One could track the route of the diaspora space in which Chadha's female subjects are caught up. Each of these characters steps out on this trip to get out of gender discrimination both interior and exterior. This diaspora space as pointed by Brah is "the point at which boundaries of inclusion and exclusion, of belonging and otherness, of 'us' and 'them' are contested as a conceptual category is 'inhabited', not only by those who have migrated and their descendants but equally by those who are constructed and represented as indigenous" (208–209). There is questioning of their place as South Asians as well as they (particularly the older women) indulge in discriminating Hashida's friend because he is 'kaala kaluta'. The differences between the older women and the younger generation are taken up by Chadha through the dialogic confrontations. The film does not seek to merely present an authentic picture of South Asian experience. It stresses upon heterogeneity and the 'living' of 'identity through difference' as stated by Hall (57). The characters find themselves struggling to find their place in the English seaside resort while clinging to the ideas of homeland they left behind, caught between conformity with Indian cultural norms and their own integration into British society. The older women have carried loads of entrenched values of Indian culture. The aunties Pushpa, Asha and Bina seem to be nurturing memories of Indian values from oblivion. They try to condition the younger generation in the same values regarding dress and food which seem outdated in the present context. This results in perpetual conflict.

The dream sequences featuring Asha have religious connotations as well as they serve to articulate desire. The one involving Lord Vishnu confronting her with the slogan "Duty, Honour, Sacrifice" symbolizes patriarchy trying to bind her into the domestic fold and subordination. In the rescue and brief escapade with Ambrose, an actor-historian, she escapes into yet another reverie where she indulges in a romantic adventure with the unknown male character. This scene makes Bollywood (where the scene is located) the site for shaping gendered as well as ethnic identities. The reveries provide an opportunity to express thoughts, dissatisfactions and secrets and permitted space to articulate and resist oppressions. Even the younger characters Ginder and Hashida strive for personal freedom, one wants to break loose from a confined patriarchal construct – an abusive husband and in-laws while the other battles to choose between a promising career and an Anglo-African lover.

Food as one of the most important parts of people's lives; like in *The Lunchbox* is also focused on in *Bhaji on the Beach*. The very title is suggestive. "Bhaji" is a mix of vegetables with added spices. There is constant attempt on the part of the characters to add spice to their lives. They are out to rediscover their personal being as well as their Indian identity, and to gather courage to rebel. There are several scenes in the film where eating together represents one of the inseparable parts of Indian family life. There is a section depicting an idyllic moment on the beach where all the women sit down for an Indian style picnic including *samosas, poppadoms* and *bhajis*, which could be viewed as a kind of family reunion, with the beach substituting for the kitchen. Whereas all the food eaten in the film is either traditionally Indian or typically British fast food, there are scenes in the film that seem to serve as an attempt at assimilation of two cultures. In the scene where the two eldest and most judgemental Indian ladies of the group, Pushpa and Bina, buy chips and after having tasted them, realize that the food is not spicy enough for an Indian. That is why they season their chips with some chilli and finally enjoy them. There is a scene where Asha is having another reverie about Ginder as breaking traditional Indian values particularly regarding food. This even causes her mother-in-law a heart attack. Ginder consequently spills all the water on the floor instead of passing it to Ranjit's mother and seems to revel in her unpleasant behaviour which is uncharacteristic in Indian culture. Discussions at the dining table and the kitchen also feature in the context of Ginder and Hashida. The director captures yet another image of Indian food in a fast food shop, with the sound of samosas being fried in oil. The location might be thus perceived as a metaphor for a kitchen, which can make or mar a woman's space; Ginder, the subject of discussion in this case. All these scenes depict food as a basic ingredient in the "recipe" for a contented and "proper" Indian family life which, in fact, represents one of the building blocks of Indian culture. Moreover, food in *Bhaji on the Beach* does not serve only as a way of presenting traditional Indian values but on the contrary, it provides the viewer with an example of the changing attitudes of second generation Indians in Britain. As a representation of these changes, Madhu and Ladhu, the teenage sisters, eat mainly fast food such as fries, burgers as well as sweets, which could be understood as their attempt to escape the traditional perception of Indian culture/cuisine and become a part of white, non-Indian community as opposed to the representatives of the first generation of Indians living in Britain, Bina and Pushpa, who enter a café and start eating their home cooked food. As Chakravarti points out in her article "The children's acculturation and the immigrant parent's fears collide and through the medium of eating the differences become more lucid" (20). The dessert however, presents the idea of a potential union of the two cultures provided both sides are willing to "taste" something new. Through the negotiation of displacement, the film raises pertinent issues relating to the construction of multiple identities of the women concerned.

The two films located in two city scapes, one India (Mumbai) and the other in Birmingham/Blackpool are creations by filmmakers who have tackled issues of gender and class discrimination - one male and another female. Female desire has finally become a speaking subject. These two films treat themes of female desire and personal freedom with sympathy. The women seek personal freedom, not from values and roles but freedom from subordination. They undergo self-examination of their lives. This introspective analysis enables them to emerge not only as strong women but as strong human beings.

References

Brah, Avtar *Cartograpies of Diaspora: Contesting Identities.* London, Routledge 1996.

Chakravarti, Debnita. "Feel Good Reel Food: A Taste of the Cultural Kedgeree in Gurinder Chadha's What's Cooking?" in *Reel Food: Essays on Food and Film.* Ed. Anne L. Bower, London: Routledge 2004.

Hall, Stuart. "Old and New Identities, Old and New Ethnicities" in *Culture, Globalization and the World System: Contemporary Conditions for the Representation of Identity.* Ed Anthony D. King. Basingstoke: Macmillan.1991.

http://blogs.mindtree.com/mumbai-dabbawalas. 10th April 2009. Viewed on 5/11/2014.

Filmography

Bhaji on the Beach. Dir. Gurinder Chadha. Screenplay by Gurinder Chadha and Meera Syal. DVD. Channel Four Television Corporation, 1993.

'In the Good Old Summertime' Dir. Robert Z. Leonard, Buster Keaton, Perf. Judy Garland, Van Johnson 1940.

Mitr, My Friend Dir. Revathi. Perf. Shobhana, Nasir Abdullah, Preeti Vissa. 2002.

Sirf Tum. Dir. Agathian. Perf. Sanjay Kapoor, Sushmita Sen, Priya Gill. 1998

The Lunchbox. Dir. Ritesh Batra. Perf. Nimrat Kaur, Irfaan Khan, Nawazuddin. 2013.

The Shop Around the Corner Dir. Ernst Lubitsch Perf. James Stewart, Margaret Ullavan, and Frank Morgan 1940.

You've Got Mail Dir. Nora Ephron, Perf. Tom Hanks and Meg Ryan. 1998.

26 Strengthening Identity and Choosing Freedom: *Queen* and *Hasee Toh Phasee*

Manasvini Rai

Relevant as it may be across geographical boundaries, divisions of culture, community, social or economic class, and even gender, feminism today fails to gather much favour as a subject in Hindi cinema. Though there have been some films in Bollywood in recent times like *English Vinglish* (2012), *Queen* (2014), *Hasee Toh Phasee* (2014), *Highway* (2014) and *Gulaab Gang* (2014), which touch upon and showcase various dimensions of feminism with varying detail, Hindi films that deal with this widely debated subject seriously, are few and far between.

Primarily, the above mentioned films just show the journey of one female character from a state of being caged or oppressed by society's norms, towards finding freedom and empowerment in a vague sense. It is an individual journey and not a movement of any kind. The problem is made clear. But what appears to be lacking are more films that attempt to find workable solutions that can contribute to the emancipation of all women. *Gulaab Gang* is the exception here as it involves activism and takes up various pertinent issues related to feminism and the well-being of women on a larger scale. In most cases, a film may have nothing to do with feminism directly but becomes the subject of much feminist analysis owing to the fact that it is female-centric. Highlighting the present plight of women in Bollywood, Jyotika Virdi says that: "Women have no access to the means of film production and are still virtually unrepresented as directors, producers, or screen writers. As actors they perform – directed by male fantasies and patriarchal values" (Virdi 2003: 61). Films such as Priyanka Chopra's *Fashion* (2008) and Kareena Kapoor's *Heroine* (2012) are examples of woman-oriented cinema but they fail to avoid clichés and aim only to fit the box office success mantra. This is an understandable and even predictable trend in an industry that is male-dominated, and starved for cinema that responsibly deals with feminist matters, doing so in an impactful manner.

More often than not, owing to the stark reality of the subject matter, a film dealing with feminism acquires solemn shades and loses out on its entertainment value ensuring that the viewership remains restricted to a niche and small audience. In such cases, it becomes difficult for the film even to recover its production cost. If feminism and film is not a profitable combination then what will motivate filmmakers to continue to create such films? And who is even watching? With respect to the movie audience today, Javed Akhtar is of the opinion that: "Whatever is happening on the screen should make him laugh, should make him cry; he should be able to identify with it. He should be able to fantasize and at the same time: if it is too real, then he won't like it. If it has nothing to do with reality, then too he won't like it" (Ganti 2012: 284)! The question remains, must a film that deals with feminism, which is in fact a serious matter, be concerned with catering to the easily bored crowds that are mostly numb to the issue?

Owing to financial and other aspects of filmmaking, trends are slowly changing and a few refreshing films are now being made that speak of feminism, while simultaneously managing to hold the attention and interest of both male and female audiences. Comedy is often added to spice up the mix. Two recent Hindi films that touch upon feminism (if even vaguely) and do so in an entertaining manner, also additionally achieving commercial success are *Queen* and *Hasee Toh Phasee*. Both managed to get a moderate to high degree of approval from film critics. And in the vast ocean of today's Hindi films and item songs which are largely built around sexist and chauvinistic mindsets that are biased against women, these two are films of note, for having portrayed some of their women characters as real and free people with needs, aspirations and capabilities that are waiting to be developed.

In both the films the main female protagonists are daughters of businessmen, but in totality we see all kinds of women. There are the kinds that are happy in their enclosed life of domestic labor and child rearing fulltime, as they know no other type of world. There is the "hippy" type of woman who wears scanty clothes and expresses her sexuality freely and unabashedly. There is the wise grandmother who has seen life in many shades, knows all about adult films, and advises her granddaughter to take risks, travel, keep an open mind and be happy. There are the women who see marriage as the solution to all problems in life and happily take to a life of only reading fashion magazines and attending kitty parties. There is the defiant tomboy drug addict who steals from her own family to fuel her career and passion. There is even a stripper abroad who unknown to her family back home, is in the profession by choice and happy with its financial and other bonuses.

And then there is the interesting mix of men. The opportunist, the sexists and chauvinists, the kind hearted and broad minded patriarchs, the gentle, considerate and helpful men, the businessmen, the artists, the musicians, the quirky travelers, the chefs, the obnoxious uncles who only know how to hit and scold, the respectful professionals one meets across desks and the doting and protective brothers. At most times, the men in these two films are the supporting cast, in keeping with the focus which is centered around a woman. Both *Queen* and *Hasee Toh Phasee* can be given credit for providing to the audience a large variety of male and female characters to consider and form one's own judgment about how far is too far as far as choices and actions are concerned, in any direction – conservative or free.

In order to better understand how the subject of the two films is linked to feminism in varying manner, we must look at them in some detail. Firstly, *Hasee Toh Phasee*, roughly translated as "she's snared if she smiles", is the story of Meeta and Nikhil and how as events unfold they fall in love with each other and come together. The film has a large number of supporting characters who provide obstacles to or aid in the fulfillment of the same. Similar in their failing to live up to their parents' expectations, Nikhil and Meeta are shown to jell together very well. In childhood and as young adults both are shown to be getting into trouble often. Both have contrastingly "perfect" siblings who are impossible to live up to. Nikhil's brother is an achiever and Meeta's sister Karishma is tall, slender, and statuesquely proper – a model and an actor. Meeta on the other hand dresses "like a boy", has short hair, is not the least bit interested in behaving "like a girl", and also knows how cricket, gadgets and cars work. Even though she is a chemical engineer from IIT and a Ph.D., Meeta is often reprimanded for being a tomboy. According to Judith Halberstam in her discussion on tomboys:

> Tomboyism tends to be associated with a "natural" desire for the greater freedoms and mobilities enjoyed by boys. Very often it is read as a sign of independence and self-motivation, and tomboyism may even be encouraged to the extent that it remains comfortably linked to a stable sense of a girl identity. Tomboyism is punished, however, when it appears to be the sign of extreme male identification (taking a boy's name or refusing

> girl clothing of any type) and when it threatens to extend beyond childhood and into adolescence. ... We could say that tomboyism is tolerated as long as the child remains prepubescent; as soon as puberty begins, however, the full force of gender conformity descends on the girl. (Halberstam 2002: 358)

Running away from oppression and home, stealing a huge sum of money, a young Meeta first meets Nikhil by a barbed wire fence that she is attempting to climb across. He helps her off the wall and walks with her carrying her bags as they talk about cricket (amongst other things) until while leaving, she invites him to come along but he refuses. Back at the wedding, Nikhil and long haired Karishma fall in love. There are sexist references to Karishma, who is quite a contrast to Meeta, as "a naked electric wire" and "an item for seven lives". The two get engaged and are all set to get married. However, there are some pending issues.

Nikhil is a struggling businessman and needs to procure money, upon which the wedding hinges. Karishma bosses over Nikhil regarding this and keeps threatening to break-up with him. Next, much to Karishma's disdain, Meeta returns. An important flashback informs us that prior to running away Meeta had asked her father for money to fund her research project, but he had refused owing to her being a girl and her possible involvement with drugs. Additionally, Meeta's uncle had slapped her, making a long speech about her unwomanly attire and how she had been given "too much freedom" by sending her out to study in a hostel. Also that she would in all probability, bring a bride home, not a groom. Distraught, Meeta had escaped with the money she needed. And unknown to anyone, she is back to steal again.

Karishma asks Nikhil to keep Meeta away from her family by putting her away in a seedy hotel but he sympathises with Meeta's plight and invites her to stay at his house. The new Meeta is highly eccentric and has many quirks in her body language and behavior. She pops pills and once even empties many sachets of sugar into her mouth. Not only is she strange and unconventional, she frequently takes some drugs to keep herself from feeling emotion. Nikhil and Meeta end up spending a lot of time together sharing laughter and teaching each other many things, mainly ways to deal with life and handling its many stresses. Meeta falls in love with Nikhil, who has made her quit drugs, resist the urge to steal again and helped her meet her father and apologize to her family. She tells him to leave Karishma and be with her. Nikhil refuses, but the two eventually come together at the end of the film with Nikhil and Karishma breaking their engagement. What brings them together is the fact that Nikhil understands and accepts Meeta and is very kind to her, which is what makes Meeta fall in love with him. Meeta is a girl who is passionate about her career and beliefs. She is headstrong, funny, very intelligent and knowledgeable about many things and Nikhil likes that about her. He is not threatened by her brilliance. He defends and protects her when needed and stops her from doing the wrong thing. He is her friend and she no longer feels like a misfit among conformists.

Hasee Toh Phasee is connected with feminism owing to its main female protagonist who is unconventional and follows her head and heart even if it involves breaking barriers and taking risks. And not afraid to make the first move, she finds love in the process. The thrust is that feminism does not indicate that men and women exist in isolation, always competing. They can provide comfort and support to one another. The man in Meeta's life is not a sexist. He appreciates her uniqueness just as she values his. They support each other. And it is important to note that a character such as Meeta is not dismissed as a freak because of her high intellect and her unusual and footloose nature. She is celebrated for who she is. The film is as much a love story as it is the tale of a spunky woman and how she finds happiness. Meeta of *Hasee Toh Phasee* does not start a movement, neither is she an activist. She is a sensitive, intelligent female, and an individual who fails to give up on her theories and dreams.

Now moving away from this story of a gutsy woman and her love, I proceed to look at a tale of rejection in love and how it positively changes the life of a woman. *Queen* is the story of Rani, a young Punjabi girl in her 20s living in Delhi who is deserted by Vijay, her husband to be, just before their marriage. The narrative traces her recovery from the shock of betrayal to when she embarks alone to their pre-booked honeymoon in Paris and Amsterdam, changing in many ways and finding herself happier in the process. This is a journey of self discovery and healing through travelling alone to a foreign place, learning to fend for oneself, seeing a whole new world, and making a few good friends of diverse cultures and both sexes in the process. It is a story of coming of age and finding courage and answers within oneself. At the beginning of the film, Rani starts out as shy and inhibited, dependent on her parents for everything including permission for all her actions. Additionally, everywhere she goes she is chaperoned by her much younger brother Chintu, even to her first date with Vijay. Rani is docile and content with her prospective life of marriage to a patronizing, controlling, and possessive man who never tires of telling her what to do. Vijay does not want her to dance in public and dishonor him. He even wants her to get his name tattooed on her skin. When she asks him if she should take up work after marriage he responds by telling her not to, as he does not want her to be out till late and the matter is put to rest. He wants her to trust him to provide for her. The question of work is limited to a mere providing for, when it could mean much more to her in terms of becoming an independent adult. Earlier, Rani is shown in college studying Home Science, also helping her father with business decisions and food preparation at his sweet shop.

Rani is excited about her honeymoon as is her friend Sonal, who expresses joy for Rani to finally lose her virginity. The set up is every bit conservative and so it leaves Rani shocked and heartbroken when foreign-returned Vijay informs her that he cannot marry her as he has changed owing to his new life abroad. She no longer fits into his world. The rest of the film is interspersed with flashbacks of her memories of good and bad days with Vijay, as she reels under the trauma of her current circumstances. At this stage, Rani's grandmother tells her to move on and open herself to life's possibilities and so Rani decides to set out for her "honeymoon". The grandmother character is modern and refreshing, while still rooted in Indian culture. Rani begins her voyage of coming to terms with herself and finding meaning within her seemingly shattered life, away from her protective parents and annoyingly sympathetic relatives.

Rani reaches Paris and as she drags her heavy suitcase up the stairs all alone into her room it is driven home to the audience that she is entirely by herself for the first time. At this point, Rani decides to see the city and makes friends with a French/Spanish/Indian woman, Vijaylakshmi, who is almost diametrically opposite in character to Rani. Vijaylakshmi is loud, uninhibited, and promiscuous. She drinks and dresses skimpily. At first meeting, Rani is scandalized but owing to Vijaylakshmi's part-Indian heritage and the fact that Rani knows no one in Paris the two eventually hit it off and bond very well. It is in Paris that Rani opens her eyes to the world but remains dressed in an Indian Kurta and a pair of jeans with neatly braided hair. She starts out unhappy, lonely, and uninterested in the lively city around her, even almost getting mugged once. But when in the mugging scene, Rani wins and the thug leaves, she begins to find grit and strength within herself. She visits a disco pub, gets drunk, tells all to strangers in a drunken rant, and even dances on top of a bar. She unleashes years of repression in her long speech about how she always did everything her parents told her to and yet had to come alone to her honeymoon. Rani talks about how women are not allowed to burp in public in

India and lets out a few burps, uninhibited. It seems as if she has had enough of being a "good girl".

It is at this stage that we ask, must she be drunk and dance atop the bar to prove that she is free? The answer lies in the flashbacks which reveal how Vijay controlled her. Now without him she is free to dance as much as she pleases. It is a vengeful dance of freedom and she begins to feel relieved, enjoying herself. Later on, it is revealed that Vijaylakshmi is a single mother. She has a son, not by her husband but by her boyfriend and is happy with her decision. Rani and Vijaylakshmi go shopping and Rani dislikes the "hippy" type clothes in the women's section of the shop that fail to conceal much skin preferring to shop in the men's section, saying the "hippy" clothes are not her style. She sticks to her individuality.

A selfie in a revealing top, Rani sends by mistake to Vijay instead of Vijaylakshmi, gets Vijay's attention who then starts pursuing Rani in order to get her back. It is interesting to note that Rani also calls Vijaylakshmi by the name Vijay and there comes a time in the film when the female Vijay tells Rani, "So what if you don't have Vijay, don't you have Vijaylakshmi?" This speaks of the immense power of friendship between two women. Speaking of names, the name of the film comes from the English translation for the main protagonist's name – Rani. Also Vijay calls Rani as, "My Queen", in the film and in totality the film is Rani's journey in reaching a place in life where she is not his queen but a queen in her own right.

Rani starts having a great time in Paris, cycling around and laughing at her own jokes. Ignoring the many phone calls by Vijay, she proceeds to Amsterdam all by herself, where she strikes up a friendship with three boys of different nationalities who are also her roommates at a hostel there. Here we see men who are courteous, fun, caring, and far away from the patriarchal male stereotype Rani has been accustomed to, back home. She roams the streets with her new friends day and night, even visiting a sex shop. Rani finds herself at the red-light district where she has gone to hand deliver a package from Vijaylakshmi to Roxette, who is a stripper, described by Vijaylakshmi as a good girl. Roxette tells her story and justifies her prostitution as she is the sole earning member in her family.

In a very important part of the film, Rani meets an Italian chef who notices her pride in Indian food and invites her to put up a stall at his food sale to make some money. Rani's *golgappa* stall is a hit and it is her first foray into employment and entrepreneurship. She loves it, even kissing the Italian chef. On returning to her hostel she finds Vijay waiting for her. Impressed with her transformation, he wants her back, but by now she is hesitant. She puts off meeting him until the two are back in Delhi, and leaves to meet her friends at a rock show, dressed in a western outfit, hair straightened. She is independent. She is peaceful. She does not need Vijay anymore. Rani returns to Delhi and everyone admires her new look. She decisively stops at Vijay's house where he appears, beside himself with joy at seeing the new and "improved" Rani. The tables are turned as Rani returns her engagement ring to him, and this time he begs her to stay. She leaves his house liberated and smiling, with a spring in her step. The film ends with the credits rolling against Rani's Facebook profile where she has uploaded many photographs of her honeymoon – alone!

Queen depicts the journey of a woman, finding herself through the power of time, courage, new experiences, and friendship. It is her journey from belonging to one man, to being responsible for her own life. The film raises several questions and touches upon many issues in the context of women – Indian women in particular. Must an Indian girl wear a western dress and boots, and straighten her curly hair to be liberated? How far is the transformation external? Must a woman be spurned and have her heart broken to realize the power that lies within her? In what other ways could Rani have realized her own capability? Did she need to travel all the way abroad to find out that she could have another kind of life –

whatever kind she wanted? How would she save herself if her parents had refused to permit her to go on this trip?

Many other relevant concerns emerge. Why are the two main female protagonists of *Queen*, Rani and Vijaylakshmi chosen to be thin and stereotypically beautiful? Also, must a girl drink and dance and kiss a strange man to prove she is free? Is this because the filmmakers must cater to the gallery? Rani finally accidentally gets the attention of her Vijay through seducing him by her beauty. It would be refreshing if he could fall in love with her mind and spirit. But that would have to be another Vijay, wouldn't it? Why is it that if Rani chooses a profession, it has to be restricted to cooking and Home Science? Could a sequel to *Queen* have Rani learning French or opening a multi-cuisine restaurant? The film touches upon the matter of love and how far it is alright for a woman to lose herself in it. The message that becomes evident is that falling in love must not result in a loss of identity. The film says a lot about the class of men too. That men can be gentle, thoughtful and funny. That they can be judgmental chauvinists too. That they can ask a woman's permission. That grown and strong men can run screaming, willing to show that they are afraid of lizards. Interestingly enough, none of the nicer men in the film are Indian, with the exception of Rani's father who does respect her wishes.

We know that Rani will now be fine, but what about the emancipation of the other women in the film? Women such as Rani's and Vijay's mothers, and Rani's married friend Sonal whose hands are full with looking after child and home. In some cases, these women are resigned to their plight or by choice may not even want to be emancipated. And what about virginity and the expectation that a women in a conservative society be a compliant "good girl", saving and preparing herself for the man chosen by her father, who will one day marry her and provide for her all through her life, as she accepts the role of a hausfrau and procreating machine with a smile on her face?

What about the woman who does not want to comply with being a housewife? What about career and independence? And what if she wants to be a single mother, capable of supporting herself and her child very well?

Queen also raises feminist questions, regarding women and prostitution and pornography when Rani visits the sex shop and Roxette, the stripper. There are two existing views on this. One is that they involve the exploitation and objectification of a woman and the second, that a woman must be free to choose the ways in which she wishes to express her sexuality. Rani's father and brother do ogle at Vijaylakshmi but it does not bother her. So who must draw the line and where must it be drawn? These are all matters of choice and there is plenty of food for thought.

The two women, Meeta of *Hasee Toh Phasee* and Rani of *Queen* are extremely different and yet very similar in their quest for independence. There is the very important question of femininity and what contributes to making a woman worthy of the label feminine. Meeta may be associated with the tag of "tomboy" while her shapely sister Karishma is perceived as feminine and gorgeous. In fact the first romantic moment between Nikhil and Meeta takes place when she is dressed in traditional Indian attire as opposed to her usual jeans and t-shirt. Rani of *Queen* may be considered to be more feminine than Meeta since she is more virtuous, shy and soft spoken. It is a matter of perception and opinion and there is nothing wrong with a woman being compliant except when it is not a matter of choice but a symptom of repression.

Both the films show diverse examples of the choices women have made, or the lack of them. There is the girl who chooses to "just" be a mother and a housewife, as well as the go-getter who is passionate about her career and even has the courage to propose first, when in love, like Meeta. Though success in one's career plays an indispensable role in acquiring prestige in society and financial as well as total independence, it is important not to trivialize the responsibilities of a mother and a homemaker and her contribution not just to her family but also to society. The problem arises with the attitude where motherhood is considered the indispensable symbol of true womanhood and a woman incomplete unless she becomes a wife and a mother, since this is the job assigned to her by nature. The problem arises when one's understanding and view of gender and gender roles becomes rigid. What must a woman do to be accepted as a "proper" woman by society? How must she talk, think, dress, and act?

Both *Queen* and *Hasee Toh Phasee* succeed in giving to the cinema goer two new kinds of "heroines", splendidly individualistic and independent, while still remaining connected with their friends and families. This is a welcome change in Bollywood. Jyotika Virdi mentions how studies about Hindi films' representations of women "... provide a rich and abundant characterization of its idealized women figures: passive, victimized, sacrificial, submissive, glorified, static, one-dimensional, and resilient" (Virdi 2003: 60).

Clearly there is a dire need for more Hindi films that move away from the hackneyed depiction of women and succeed in not merely touching upon, but tackling holistically, the issue of feminism. There should be not just the telling of a woman's story but also how a feminist problem can be solved. Why are not more films being made that are concerned with educating the girl child who sells flowers at the traffic signal? Of course there remains the challenge of economic viability for the filmmaker, and until the time this problem is solved there will be films like the two just discussed, that sell very well and do make a few good points, but fail to do much by way of bringing change, owing to the necessity that they please the audiences by entertaining them. This is one of the current challenges of feminist Hindi cinema.

References

Ganti, Tejaswini. *Producing Bollywood: Inside the Contemporary Hindi Film Industry*. New Delhi: Orient Blackswan Pvt. Ltd., 2012

Halberstam, Judith. "An Introduction to Female Masculinity: Masculinity without Men". *The Masculinity Studies Reader.* Ed. Rachel Adams and David Savran. Oxford: Blackwell Publishers Ltd., 2002

Virdi, Jyotika. *The Cinematic Imagination: Indian Popular Films as Social History*. Ranikhet: Permanent Black, 2003

Filmography

Hasee Toh Phasee: Director: Vinil Mathew, Cast: Parineeti Chopra, Sidharth Malhotra, Adah Sharma, 2014.

Queen: Director: Vikas Bahl, Cast: Kangana Ranaut, Lisa Haydon, Rajkummar Rao, 2014.

27 *The Road Not Taken*: The Emergence of Women Wanderers in Hindi Cinema

Avinash Jodha

A woman has no business travelling alone.

Anonymous

And you? When will you begin that long journey into yourself?[1]

Rumi

The role of the seeker, the wanderer, the voyager, the wayfarer, the loafer or the tramp has always been men's prerogative in the better known history of the world across cultures, regions and times. Women apparently have not resisted, questioned and less so appropriated the position. Perhaps some of them have been convinced like Penelope (Ulysses's wife) about the necessity of holding on to the bastions of their homes while their men traversed the world in search of action, adventure, wealth, even other women and in some cases truth and salvation. While there are obvious advantages of staying home uncluttered by the perennial presence of a patriarchy-fed domineering husband, it can hardly be fulfilling.

Note: The first part of the title of the paper is from Robert Frost's poem *The Road Not Taken* (1920).

Fictional or cinematic presentations of women taking up journeys of their own calling have been equally scarce. In the dusk of popular Westerns in Hollywood, Road Movies emerged as a powerful phenomenon representing the instinct to escape from the clutches of metropolises and of society into the wilderness on well paved roads. This coincided with the boom in automobile industry marking the beginning of the American infantile infatuation with cars and bikes from which it still has to emerge. However, even in the Road Movies much like the Westerns, women have a secondary role. More often than not, they have been the pillion riders of a man's journey sharing his escape or dream or whim.

Since 1960s, out of the scores of Road Movies just a few like Herbert Ross' *Boys on the Side* (1995), Ridley Scott's *Thelma and Louise* (1991), Joseph Sargent's *Coast to Coast* (1980), and the more recent *Little Miss Sunshine* (2006) have women as protagonists.[2] The picture is grimmer in the context of Indian cinema, more specifically mainstream Hindi cinema. Barring the lovers-on-the-run blockbusters like *Love Story* (1981), *Qayamat Se Qayamat Tak* (1988), and boy-meets-girl-on-a-journey like *Dil Hai Ki Maanta Nahi* (1991) and *Dilwale Dulhania Le Jayenge* (1995), where women are at best co-protagonists, they have rarely featured as protagonists.

The negligible presence of women protagonists in world cinema and the visible absence of women protagonists in the contemporary Road Movies both in the East and the West raises several interesting questions: why even after scaling Mount Everest or playing lead roles in space odysseys women still have the back seat when it comes to fictional or cinematic presentations of journeys, what does it say about the social acceptability of women as seekers or wanderers, how do the notions of man-as-traveller and woman-as-traveller interact and intersect with each other, how does this void relate with the larger questions of women's emancipation? These questions form an interesting relationship with two Hindi movies released in 2014, Vikas Bahl's *Queen* and Imtiaz Ali's *Highway*.

These movies in their own characteristic ways mark a subtle shift in perceptions of women as wanderers and seekers and their great success at the box-office holds subtle clues to the shifting of socio-cultural paradigms in India in envisioning women as travellers, wanderers and seekers. Both Imtiaz Ali and Vikas Bahl belong to the turn of the millennium, new breed of young directors in Hindi cinema. While *Queen* is Vikas Bahl's debut venture as director, Imtiaz Ali in the last decade has produced very successful films like *Jab We Met* (2007), *Love Aaj Kal* (2009), *Rockstar* (2011) and *Cocktail* (2012).

Choice of a woman protagonist at a time when Hindi cinema is immersed in its prolonged affair with hyperbolic action extravaganzas of South Indian cinema and when the music industry is rife with "item numbers," represents a considerable commercial risk. Nevertheless, both the directors took the risk and have been received very well. For Vikas Bahl, it was significant challenge as it was his first film as a sole director but on the other hand Imtiaz Ali over the years has sustained his interest in women protagonists. His films stand out for their powerful women characters and journey is the governing thematic and structural trope in most of his films. In *Jab We Met* Aditya and Geet meet during a train journey on their ways to escape from their families for different reasons but this journey becomes a turning point in their lives. In the same way in *Love Aaj Kal*, the central characters take up journeys that become defining factors in their lives. *Rockstar* presents the journey of a Haryanvi lad Janardan Singh Jakhar turning into a rock star. *Cocktail* again has the journey of its central character Meera from India to London. Journeys in Imtiaz Ali's films are both literal and figurative, the external journey of his characters opens up pathways to their inner selves leading eventually to self-realization and more importantly in most of his films the women characters are at the centre.

Highway and *Queen* have some interesting parallels, both have Delhi in the backdrop and both the films open with the excited preparations for the wedding of their women protagonists. There is slight difference in the social classes of the two protagonists while Veera in *Highway* comes from an upper class powerful political family, Rani in *Queen* is the daughter of a well-to-do Punjabi sweet-shop owner. This slight difference aside the preparations of their marriage bear the similar imprint of lavishness and pomposity of upper and middle class Hindu/Punjabi marriages in Delhi. In fact, the opening of both the films is an interesting departure from marriage-in-the-end formula of Hindi cinema. They are somewhat closer to the opening of *Monsoon Wedding* (2001) that turned out to be a trendsetter in its realistic portrayal of wedding preparations, something entirely different from the superlative, saccharine saturated portrayals of weddings in films like *Hum Aapke Hein Kaun* (1994). Both the films have arranged marriages at their centre and the couples are apparently at ease with the decisions of their families. It is interesting to notice that in both the films *Highway* and *Queen* the bridegrooms hardly show any enthusiasm for their impending marriages. They apparently understand the contractual nature of their marriages. It is with great reluctance that Veera's fiancé Vinay in *Highway* agrees to take her for a small ride to the highway a night or two before their wedding. As Veera sneaks out of her house and joins Vinay waiting outside in his car, they have an interesting conversation:

> Vinay: *Itti kya urgency thi yaar! Zindagi saath bitaani hai hame! Agar bola hai ki kuch din na milo toh ruk jate hein na!*
>
> (What was the urgency? We've to spend our entire lives together! If we've been asked not to meet for a few days, why can't we wait!)
>
> Veera: *Vinay yaar I want to breathe. Ye rasam rivaaz! Aiyeji, namasteji, ghaghra, jhumka, Nathni! Please chalo yaha se. Thodi der is gharse door rehte hein!*
>
> (Vinay I want to breathe. All these customs and traditions....Please let's get away from here. Let's stay away from this house for a little while!)

The conversation is a clear indication of the fact that none of them is excited about their wedding. Vinay has so completely submitted to the will of his family that he does not want to go against any of their instructions. Veera feels claustrophobic amid all the grand preparations of the wedding and yet both of them have agreed to the marriage. This again is closer to the reality of increasing number of young people choosing the convenience of arranged marriages rather than the highly romanticized lovers' escapades in the films of the 80s and 90s where the entire conflict was between the lovers and the walls created by the society. It shows a remarkable shift in the attitude of the young generation today who do not wish to let go off the advantages of arranged marriage (primarily financial), they see any direct conflict with the society or the system as an unnecessary hindrance to their progress.

In *Queen*, Rani looks forward to her marriage with great pleasure as she loves Vijay and it is *a dream come true* for her. They come from similar Punjabi family backgrounds and their fathers are friends. Vijay tries hard to woo Rani and she gives in eventually only when she sees a prospective marriage with Vijay. Here it is important to note that for most of the girls of Rani's social class marriage brings about liberation of its own kind. They are free to move around with their husbands and even alone after marriage. All the dangers are supposedly when they are unmarried and the prime danger is that they might fall in love with a person of different class, caste or (god forbid!) religion. Love aside, Vijay is the safest choice for Rani as she does not have any wish to go against her family.

Rani has always nurtured a dream of visiting Paris for her honeymoon. For Rani, marriage is precondition to fulfil her dream, she has never ever considered the possibility of any other alternative. Thomas Hill's well-known example of the Deferential Wife can serve a very important purpose here:

> She buys the clothes he prefers, invites the guests he wants to entertain, and makes love whenever he is in the mood. She

> willingly moves to a new city in order for him to have a more attractive job, counting her own friendships and geographical preferences insignificant by comparison... She does not simply defer to her husband in certain spheres as a trade-off for his deference in other spheres. On the contrary, she tends not to form her own interests, values, and ideals, and when she does, she counts them as less important than her husband's. (Hill 1991: 5)[3]

Both Rani and Veera fit the bill of deferential daughters and fiancées. But it does not help them much. In fact, Vijay who ensured unquestioning deference from Rani during their courtship makes it the very reason to call off the wedding just a day before it was planned. He blatantly tells Rani that after his stay in London he has changed. It will be tough for Rani to cope up with him. He tries to assure Rani that it is the only practical thing to do and that Rani does not have to lose her heart as she will get any good guy of her "type" in Rajouri. Vijay has already informed his parents about his decision before breaking the news to Rani. His parents are fine with his decision. This brings to surface one of the ugly aspects of the arranged marriages where if the parents, especially the parents of the boy, see the prospects of a better proposal in terms of class and possible dowry, they hardly hesitate to call off an earlier engagement.

The excitement of wedding preparations in both the films dissipates within the first ten minutes. It launches both Veera and Rani into journeys they had never anticipated. Here there is a crucial difference between the journeys of the two. Veera on her small road trip with Vinay is abducted by a gang of highway robbers and Rani still recovering from her broken engagement suddenly decides to go for her honeymoon on her own. Veera is forced to take the journey with her abductors while Rani decides to come out of her misery by taking up the journey she has always dreamt of, alone. For both Veera and Rani the journeys begin as nightmares but not for long.

It is important to understand the points of departure of both Veera and Rani. Whether willing, as in the case of Rani or unwilling in the case of Veera, their journeys are full of uncertainties. None of them is prepared for these journeys. Even for Rani it is not a matter of conscious choice, it is more of a desire to get away from the suffocation induced by the bridal dresses, jewellery, flowers and sweets stuffed in her room, all of them the painful reminders of her shattered dream. The only possibility that remains open for her is the presence of her passport, visa and ticket to Paris on her dressing table and she decides to go for it.

Any journey real or fictional operates at several levels in an individual's psyche and offers multiple challenges. But perhaps the most significant aspect of any journey is the stance of the traveller. Right from Ulysses to Alexander the Great, from Don Quixote to Tamburlaine, from Indiana Jones to James Bond or from Christ to Buddha, the stance of the traveller has remained at the centre. They knew what they sought, they had a world to conquer. Men as seekers or wanderers have always remained in command of their self, projecting more of their visions on the landscapes they traversed rather than receiving from it. Vulnerability has been the least expected trait in man-as-traveller. It is an interesting point of departure in comprehending the social impossibility of envisioning women as wanderers or seekers.

When men cross the thresholds of their homes they supposedly leave their vulnerability at home and women are *the* vulnerability they leave behind. When women leave their homes, it is more of men's vulnerability walking the streets rather than their own. There is always more at stake when a woman walks out of her home. A man's journey is directed by a sense of purpose, the world is his playing field and he has to go out and grab as much as he can from it. There is an interesting scene in *Thelma and Louise* when Thelma tells her husband that she is on a road trip with her friend Louise, her husband gets furious and says, "Have you lost your mind! Is that it! I leave for work and you take complete leave of your senses." Thelma's husband puts it in the simplest way possible, a woman choosing to go on a journey out of her own choice, takes *complete leave of her senses.*

In the Indian context the picture gets even more amusing. In *Queen* Rani's younger brother is a perennial presence beside her wherever she goes. The film brings out the ridiculous nature of the arrangement very well. A twelve year old boy or even less can be entrusted with the task of guarding a fully grown sister. Whether it is a queue or a meeting with the fiancé, the brother has to be there to see to it that nobody misbehaves with his sister. It is taken for granted that she cannot defend herself or speak for herself, it has to be done by her male companion. Similarly, even Veera with her upper class background has to seek the company of her fiancé to go out for a small road trip. Such is the nature of social conditioning that the girls also take it as a natural phenomenon.

Woman as traveller is unpalatable to both Eastern and Western appetites and whatever the difference, it is a difference of degrees not of kind. Women's supposed vulnerability disqualifies them as wanderers or seekers in social imagination and it has been repeatedly manifested in history, fiction, cinema, media and even social blogs. Ulysses can be seen as a classical example of this truncated imagination. He is a hero, adventurer and an achiever. On the other hand Penelope is devoted, responsible and steadfast. From another perspective Ulysses can be seen as selfish, pompous, mean and ungrateful. A hypothetical possibility is worth taking into consideration here. What if Ulysses on his return from years of war and adventure was to find Penelope missing! She taking a cue from her husband's adventurous spirit had gone to seek adventures of her own and to be known for *always roaming with a hungry heart*![4] Jarring as it may sound to many ears and confounding to popular imagination, it is worth a thought. As it takes us into the larger realm of gender stereotypes, role fixations and in implicit patriarchal politics. It opens up the highly volatile zone between what men should do, what women should and what they can really do.

Stepping outside the threshold of the home space is the essential first step in the journey of the wanderer, voyager or seeker. Whether the move is the result of a conscious choice or not, it is certain to put the individual into continuously changing sets of situations, spaces, people and perspectives that challenge the sense of being he or she has always held on to in the familiar space of his/her home. Homi Bhabha speaks of the moment of the "unhomely" in *The Location of Culture*:

> To be unhomed is not to be homeless, nor can the 'unhomely' be easily accommodated in that familiar division of social life into private and public spheres. The unhomely moment creeps up on you stealthily as your own shadow and suddenly you find yourself with Henry James's Isabel Archer in *The Portrait of a Lady*, taking the measure of your dwelling in a state of 'incredulous terror.' And it is at this point that the world first shrinks for Isabel and then expands enormously....In that displacement, the borders between home and world become confused; and, uncannily, the private and the public become part of each other, forcing upon us a vision that is as divided as it is disorienting. (9)[5]

Bhabha recognizes the crucial significance of the "unhomely" for subordinated people and sees it primarily as a "paradigmatic colonial and postcolonial condition" that also has great significance "in fictions that negotiate the powers of cultural difference in a range of transhistorical sites" (9). Incidentally all the examples that he cites are those of women characters. Isabel Archer in Henry James's *The Portrait of a Lady*, Beloved in Toni Morrison's *Beloved*, Bimala in Tagore's *The Home and the World* and Aila in Gordimer's *My Son's Story*. All these characters in different ways experience the moment of the "unhomely" when *the borders between the home and the world become confused* and *the private and the public become part of each other*. Bhabha sees in the figure of a woman the dramatization of the ambivalent structure of the civil state as it draws its rather paradoxical boundary between the private and the public spheres.

Bhabha's arguments open up further avenues of critical inquiry in the context of the significance of moment of the "unhomely" for men in societies subordinated or otherwise and in exploring how this moment can relate with the socio-cultural perceptions of men as travellers vis-à-vis women as travellers, wanderers or seekers. Can men experience the moment of the "unhomely"? Perhaps they can and have but never in the sense Bhabha means it. The revolutionaries like Gandhi or Martin Luther King or Che Guevara or seekers like Christ, Buddha, Mohammad or Mahaveer or fictional characters like Ulysses, Don Quixote or Robinson Crusoe have been "unhomed" too but in their "unhoming" the borders between the home and the world do not get confused, in fact they are reinstated even more powerfully. They are drawn out of their home spaces with a sense of higher purpose. Their "unhoming" is bereft of the complexity and horror of houses like 124 Bluestone Road in Toni Morrison's *Beloved* where "the thoughts of the women of 124, unspeakable thoughts, unspoken" mumble (Bhabha 10). It emphasises the patriarchal, gendered nature of civil society manifested in its division of the private and the public spheres.

There is an essential difference in the motivating forces and the corresponding stances of man as traveller and woman as traveller. For men, the space of home is not a contested territory as it is for women. It is not a site of "ascriptive domestic sphere" (Bhabha 10) for men, in fact they are the agency through which the theoretical distinctions of private and public spheres of civil society are sustained. Therefore, when a man embarks upon a journey he has clearly defined boundaries between the home and the world and the private and the public in his mind. On the contrary a woman's crossing of the threshold of her home is far more complex. More often than not it is the silent creeping in of the moment of the "unhomely" into her psyche and the subsequent shrinking and expansion of the world that propels her moving out of the home space.

The journeys of Veera and Rani are induced by the claustrophobia they feel in their home spaces. Veera as mentioned earlier feels suffocated amid all the grand preparations of her wedding and the pleasantness of the wedding preparations turns sour for Rani when Vijay calls off the wedding. Rani feels caged in her room and the ticket to Paris appears to be the only window open for her. Both of them are vulnerable, Veera in the hands of her kidnappers and Rani alone on her way to Paris. It is important to note here that in most of the Hollywood Road movies like *Thelma and Louise*, *Boys on the Side* or *Death Proof* (2007), the women protagonists challenge the very notion of vulnerability associated with them. Louise shoots a man trying to rape Thelma (albeit in the heat of the moment) but later they blow up an oil tanker because the driver made lewd gestures and did not apologise to them and in the end they dare an entire posse of policemen by not surrendering to them. In *Boys on the Side* Jane, Holly and Robin hit Holly's boyfriend in the head and tie him to a chair. In *Death Proof* three girls go after a psycho killer on the road and kill him brutally.

In *Highway* and *Queen* the women protagonists do not perform any of the heroics of the Hollywood movies mentioned above. In fact, Vikas Bahl and Imtiaz Ali keep the vulnerability of Rani and Veera at the centre of their films. In the beginning both Veera and Rani appear helpless but as they move farther into their journeys, they grow in confidence. As their journeys unfold, they realize the blessing in disguise. Away from their homes on unknown paths and unknown destinations they encounter strangers, together they force them to come to terms with the world outside the protected zones of their homes. Being alone they have to reconstruct their entity, something that they had always taken for granted within the known spaces of their homes, something that had been structured and guarded by their family and society.

Rani and Veera during the course of their journeys get into unlikely relationships and these relationships have no ties with their families. In *Queen*, Rani reaches her dream destination Paris but she is still gloomy and lost in her thoughts of Vijay. Here, she has a chance encounter with a hotel attendant, Vijaylakshmi who is half Indian and half Spanish. Vijaylakshmi is everything Rani has been taught not to be. She drinks, smokes, has many male friends and has a child with her boyfriend and has no intention of getting married. Initially, Rani looks at her with disbelief but she is intrigued by her free-ways. Later Vijaylakshmi helps Rani out in a little matter with the police and they become friends.

Veera in *Highway* gradually establishes some bonhomie with one of her three kidnappers who looks at her with great reverence, the kind reverence a simple poor man might feel for a beautiful upper class girl. However, not all her kidnappers share the same reverence, the boss Mahabir hates her for his own reasons and yet another member of the gang tries to molest her. But Mahabir protects Veera from the man and she realizes that beneath all his rudeness Mahabir was kind and had respect for women. It helps her to come to terms with the situation. In fact to the surprise of her kidnappers and her own she starts to enjoy the journey.

There is a crucial point in both the films when Veera and Rani have an opportunity to get out of their ordeals. Rani decides to cancel her trip to Amsterdam and return to India. On the way back from the travel agent's office she is attacked by a mugger but surprisingly Rani finds enough courage to hold on to her handbag and the mugger has to flee. At this point it appears that she would put an end to her journey and return to India. But later she gets accidently drunk and pours her entire grief to Vijaylakshmi. Speaking with her, she reflects on her life of submissiveness with a tinge of pride:

> *Aapne Mummy Daddy ki har baat maani hai meine, teachers ki har baat mani hai meine. Meine kabhi exam mein cheating nahi ki, kabhi joot nahi bola. Sab...Vijay ki har baat mani hai meine...tum jiska naam lo uski har baat mani hai meine.*

> (I've always obeyed my Mom and Dad, I've always obeyed my teachers, I've never cheated in exams, never lied. I've always obeyed Vijay...you name anyone and I've obeyed everyone.)

Even as she says it she realizes that it has all been in vain. They hear a Hindi song playing in the party and suddenly Rani decides to dance. She gets on to a counter and starts dancing with other girls. She dances her heart out. The expressions on her face suggest that she has had enough of misery and she is no longer going to be sad or even the person she has always been.

She might be drunk but this is the point when the moment of the "unhomely" gets into her consciousness. She starts loving Vijaylakshmi's company, sharing with her all the things girls are not allowed to do back in Delhi. She gradually learns to appreciate the personal freedom Vijaylakshmi enjoys. As she laughs, drinks and burps with Vijaylakhsmi she remembers the constraints that were imposed on her back in Delhi. How Vijay would scold her even if she danced in a marriage. She realizes how Vijaylakshmi was a much better companion than Vijay. She did not impose anything on her but encouraged her to enjoy her life.

In *Highway* when the kidnappers' truck enters into Punjab they are stopped by the police at a check post. The police inspector insists to check the back of the truck and Mahabir gets prepared to face the worst as he knows the police will discover Veera in the truck. He hides his gun in his jeans and waits but to his and his companion's surprise police does not find Veera in the truck. She hides herself in an upper bunk of the truck. As they go past the check post they stop the truck and they find Veera sitting there. Mahabir in utter disbelief asks her that she had such a great opportunity to escape by being discovered by the police and yet she hid. Veera herself is surprised by her act and she does not understand why she did not grab the opportunity to be free from her kidnappers.

What appears to be a foolish move by Veera turns out to have a deeper reason. As she reflects, she tells Mahabir about her childhood and the way she was abused by an uncle who was also a close friend of her father. She tells him how her uncle would molest her in the bathroom and how he would muffle her cries of pain. Later when she told her mother about it, she too asked her to keep mum. Her molestation stopped but that uncle would visit them frequently and would bring imported chocolates for her and would ask her to sit in his lap and this had continued till the point she was about to get married. This is a very significant point in the film, the point when the moment of the "unhomely" *creeps stealthily like a shadow* into Veera's consciousness. It reveals the burden Veera has always carried in her heart, the reason why she felt chocked in her big home and with her powerful family and the reason she hid in the truck rather than disclosing her presence to the police. She tells Mahabir:

> *Tum mujhe jahan se leke aaye ho mein wapas wahan jana nahi chahti, tum mujhe jahan lekey ja rahe ho wahan mein paunchna nahi chahti, par ye raast aacchaa hai! Mein ye chahti hun ye raasta kabhi khatm na ho.*
>
> (The place you've brought me from, I don't want to return, the place you're taking me to, I don't want to reach but this path is good! I don't want this path to end.)

Both Imtiaz Ali and Vikas Bahl establish a remarkable balance between the journeys of their women protagonists and the subtle changes the experience brings about in their perceptions, attitudes and sense of being. The pace of journeys in both the films is regulated with finesse to keep the focus on the gradual evolvement of the protagonists. Rani decides not to cancel her trip to Amsterdam and Vijaylakshmi asks her to travel as a European girl would. They exchange their dresses and Rani puts her stuff in a backpack. At the railway station as Vijaylakshmi bids farewell to Rani, she shouts: "Vijay nahi hai to kya hua Vijaylakshmi to hai" (So what if you don't have Vijay! You have Vijaylakshmi!). Rani knows the worth of this relationship, how much it means to her. She feels immense freedom in this friendship and reflects upon the choking relationship she had with Vijay. On the train when Vijay calls her she hangs the phone saying "Mar gayi Rani" (Rani is dead!). It might look like a small thing but it is a big step for Rani towards attaining her freedom. Like Veera, Rani too is still uncertain of what she would do in the longer run but like her she knows what she does not want.

Veera does not want to return to the hypocrisy and the claustrophobia of her home and Rani finds the thought of putting up with Vijay unbearable. It is the point when they encounter the horror of their shrunken worlds. But as Bhabha points out it is an essential phase in the process that the moment of the "unhomely" initiates. The shrinking of the world and the subsequent enormous expansion comes as a shock or surprise and is disorienting and disconcerting in the beginning because of the sheer nature of its magnitude and implications for the individual. While the revelation completely dismantles previously held notions and the entire sense of being, it does not offer any easy alternatives. It is not a switching over from one state of being to another. It is a process that involves enormous struggle, simultaneous annihilation of the self and reconstruction. The remnants from the former state of being repeatedly claim their stakes and demand a retreat and the realization of the "unhomely" propels the individual forward.

Mahabir in *Highway* undergoes a realization of his own. He carries a deep rooted hatred for the rich in his heart. His hatred of the rich comes from his childhood memories where he had seen the wives of the poor forced to sleep with the rich. Their husbands would take them to the *Sahabs* (rich and powerful men) and would later take out their frustration by beating their wives on return. Mahabir feels, by capturing Veera, he has a chance of settling the score with the rich he has always despised. But later as he learns of Veera's own victimization, his hatred for her dissipates. When he realizes that both he and Veera are the products of broken childhoods, he sees some hope in his otherwise hopeless life by accompanying Veera in her journey without destination.

It is important to understand the reasons behind Mahabir's seemingly impractical decision. He is certain that they will be caught as police is continuously on their trail. From the very beginning when he decided to keep Veera as a captive, he knew about his fate. He had already committed three murders and after this abduction he knew he will be shot down by the police. Veera too finds an unlikely companion in Mahabir. Her love for him generates from the memories of ruined childhoods. At one point in the film Veera's affection gets too much for Mahabir and he breaks down. He weeps as Veera embraces him, he calls out his mother's name and his grief, the pain of his mother sent to sleep with rich men, flows out through his tears. His journey with Veera frees him of the burden he had always carried like a curse in his heart. Next morning they are discovered by the police and Mahabir is shot dead. Death at the hands of police was always certain for Mahabir but he had never dreamt of purging himself of the burden he carried just before death.

In *Queen* when Rani moves to Amsterdam she finds herself in yet another strange company. Her sharing of a room with the three guys; a black Frenchman, a Russian and a Japanese opens Rani further, she learns even strangers can turn into friends and how everyone has his/her struggle to go through. The Russian, Alexander is a painter, he paints to give an outlet to the anger he feels against war for oil. The black Frenchman is a guitarist, he performs in streets and the Japanese had lost his parents in a storm. When she tells Alexander that she too wants things to do on her own. Alexander asks her emphatically, "Who's stopping you?" His words echo in Rani's mind and she recalls an entirely opposite response from Vijay when she sought his permission to take up a job. Vijay categorically asked her not to take up a job because he was in a position to provide food to Rani. For Rani, the contrast between the relationship she had with Vijay and one she has with her new friends is too stark to be ignored. They encourage her, try to understand and empathize with her even with all the barriers of languages. There is a scene where Rani and Taka speak with each other in their respective languages and seeing them speak Alexander smiles. He senses the intimacy of the conversation where none of the two understood a single word the other spoke.

Vijay's character in the film hardly has any redeeming feature. He is downright selfish and mean. He abandoned Rani as he thought Rani lacked the class that he had acquired through his stay in London. Just one picture of Rani in a western outfit is enough to send him lolling after her all over again. The film attacks yet another element of middle class male psyche in India. Most of them like Vijay desire just the perfect combination of dumbness and wit, simplicity and style, docility and effervescence, homeliness and gregariousness in their wives. This concoction of opposites is apparently their idea of a perfect wife.

Queen quashes the idiocy of the notion very effectively. As promised, Rani meets Vijay the next day but soon realizes, she had made a mistake. Vijay's arguments and his pleading fill Rani with repulsion and she leaves the restaurant saying she had to be with her friends for a rock concert. Before leaving she puts the payment of her ice-tea beneath the glass. An exact reversal of the scene when Vijay called Rani in restaurant to inform her that he is calling off their engagement. Now Rani tells him that she will see him in Delhi, for now she had to be with her friends. It is a very significant point in the growth of Rani's character. Her initial tentativeness gives way to greater confidence and faith in the self. All the gloom and uncertainty that surrounded Rani in the beginning of her journey dissipates and she realizes for the first time that she had really something to look forward to and that is her own self.

The journeys of Veera and Rani change them forever. Their journeys are more internal than external. What they encounter outside their homes opens pathways into their own being. Veera and Rani return to their homes but they are no longer the same girls as they were when they left their homes. Both the films build up their climaxes in a very subtle manner. Rani's visit to Vijay's home after her return to Delhi is the final step in Rani's emancipation. She patiently listens to the promise of a great future offered by Vijay's mother and to all the pleadings of Vijay. She is no longer angry or bitter or morose. She is at ease with herself as she returns Vijay's engagement ring. She hugs Vijay twice before leaving with a smile of content on her face. A very beautiful moment in the film as Rani finally walks out of Vijay's shadow and of everything else. She grows in stature in the final moments of the film, her gesture of hugging Vijay is her expression of gratitude to him even though he was extremely mean to her. She knows it was precisely this meanness that put her on the path to self discovery and she does not feel the need to carry any malice in her heart for him.

In the same way Veera walks out of the shadows that have always pursued her in the final moments of *Highway*. The death of Mahabir leaves Veera shattered, she is sedated and forced to move back to her home. While her family rejoices her return they hardly realize it is no longer the same Veera. Her journey has changed her forever. Her family expects that soon everything will be "normal" again. But Veera gives them a shock when she confronts the uncle who abused her when she was a child. She challenges the hypocrisy of her family and speaks her heart out. She voices out the screams of pain and anguish that were forced into silence by her family. She leaves her home, goes back on the journey she had taken with Mahabir in a taxi and finally settles down in the mountains as she always wanted to, establishing a small business of her own.

Highway and *Queen* are exceptional achievements as meaningful and entertaining cinema. Imtiaz Ali and Vikas Bahl have shown rare sensitivity in their projection of women protagonists on their paths to self-discovery. Both the films challenge the stereotypical treatment of women in Hindi cinema and the perception of women in society at large. The journeys of Veera and Rani are distinctive as they are journeys of women as wanderers and seekers. Their journeys are not propelled by a desire to own the world or to save it or to leave a mark but their journeys are to be, to find their self lost in the quagmire of prejudices, forced silences and deeply embedded patterns of gender discriminations. Through Veera and Rani, Imtiaz Ali and Vikas Bahl have traversed a road, "the one less traveled by, and that has made all the difference."[6]

Notes

1. See http: //www.goodreads.com/quotes/49864-and-you-when-will-you-begin-that-long-journey-into
2. See http: //www.filmsite.org/roadfilms.html
3. See http: //plato.stanford.edu/entries/feminism-autonomy/
4. Alfred Lord Tennyson: *Ulysses.*
5. Bhabha, Homi. *The Location of Culture.* London: Routledge, 1994.
6. Robert Frost: *The Road Not Taken* (1920).

Filmography

Highway, Dir. Imtiaz Ali, Perf. Randeep Hooda and Alia Bhatt, Producer Sajid Nadiadwala, 2014.

Queen, Dir. Vikas Bahl, Perf. Kangana Ranaut, Lisa Haydon, Rajkummar Rao. Producer Viacom 18 Motion Pictures and Phantom Films, 2014.

Thelma & Louise, Dir. Ridley Scott, Producer Mimi Polk Perf. Geena Davis, Susan Sarandon Gitlin, Ridley Scott, 1991.

Boys on the Side, Herbert Ross, Producer Herbert Ross, Arnon Milchan and Steven Reuther Perf. Whoopi Goldberg, Drew Barrymore and Mary-Louise Parker, 1995.

28 Female Picaro and the Fairytale Structure: *The Dirty Picture* and *Kahaani*

Vijaya Singh

In the last five years a number of films from Bombay cinema have been hailed for their focus on strong women characters and narratives that look at issues of women's sexuality, autonomy of the self and an assertion of equality in the larger male world. Some of these popular films in the last five years have been *Ishqiya* (2010), *No One Killed Jessica* (2011), *The Dirty Picture* (2011), *Kahaani* (2012), *English Vinglish* (2012), *Queen* (2014), *Hasee Toh Phasee* (2014), *Highway* (2014), *Dedh Ishqiya* (2014), *Bobby Jassos* (2014) and others. These films were celebrated in the media as the coming of age of the Indian heroine who now held her own in films that challenged female stereotypes. Vidya Balan featuring in a great number of these films managed to create a niche for herself through her critically acclaimed heroine centered roles: roles that required her to showcase her acting talent and to not be a mere fashion icon. Other actresses as Kangana Ranaut, Parineeti Chopra, Huma Qureshi, too came to be seen as part of a growing circle of powerful female actors, who were not afraid of being seen as they were and in performing roles that were considered offbeat.

The box-office success of *Ishqiya, No One Killed Jessica*, *The Dirty Picture* and *Kahaani* in quick succession created for Balan the enviable position from which to demand roles that focused on her acting prowess, and to mount a criticism of fashion police's regulatory role in determining sartorial and other choices for women in the film world. Before the success of *The Dirty Picture* and *Kahaani* Balan was struggling with criticism regarding her weight and "fashion sense". But the success of *The Dirty Picture* proved to be a game changer for her and she turned issues of weight and "lack of fashion sense" into an act of performance itself. So that the focus now was more on her skills as an actor and less on what she wore etc. The success of Balan's films, acclaimed for her acting and her not inconsequential personal triumph in matters of body image and sartorial autonomy come together to create a phenomenon in which her persona and her performance came to be seen as one. A phenomenon not too uncommon in the star system of popular cinema, however the fact that she could do this as a female actor in the largely male dominated Bombay cinema is worthy of critical attention. It is not without irony however that Balan who played Silk in *The Dirty Picture,* facing the same recalcitrant and brutal gaze of the media and the film world even if for opposite reasons, succeeds where Silk fails. She brought into play both glamour and everydayness of the female body in the film and in fact, used her performance as a critique of the pressures on women in the film world regarding body image.

Having said this, one must not take attention away from the films themselves and examine them for their alleged feminist stance. For this paper thus I look at two of Balan's films, *The Dirty Picture* directed by Milan Luthria and *Kahaani* directed by Sujoy Ghosh. Both these films, I argue, sit uncomfortably in the twilight zone of claims for autonomy of the self, and the inability to do so. At the same time these films offer a not too straightforward articulation of feminist concerns and causes. This tension between the desire for an articulation of what is politically correct and the politically intransigent makes these texts theoretically interesting. Both films use the fictional device of the picaresque and the anti-hero to bring to life two heroines who tantalize us with glimpses of the wild feminine but fail to live up to the task they set out to do. The reasons as to why this happens are not difficult to guess and are not really the more exciting aspects of this discussion. What is interesting is how narrative strategies that promise to deliver women who have integrated shadow and self, feminine and masculine, self-worth and self-care, turn upon themselves and instead are coopted in the rhetorical claims of family, nation and patriarchy. The end result in both these films is a total annihilation of the self in one case and a loss of the nurturing feminine in the other.

The Picaresque and the Fairy Tale

These two devices of the fairy tale and the picaresque provide a useful framework from which to examine both the films *The Dirty Picture* and *Kahaani* for how they deal with issues of female empowerment and representation. The picaresque as we know is a Spanish term and comes from the term "picaro" meaning a rogue character from the lower strata of society, on a quest to finding herself. She creates disruption in her surroundings by challenging the status quo and provides a "counterweight to ostentatious virtue."[1] Traditionally the term has been used in European fiction from fifteenth century onwards to describe the work of Spanish author as Fernand de Rojas (1476–1541)[2] and to highlight the peculiar predicament of one who is "skeptical of traditional dogma and morality."[3] The picaro thus is a fairly complex character as she uses survival strategies that create instability in her own life leading to unpredictable outcomes. Scholars as Jasbir Jain have traced the concept of the female picaro in Bengali novels (Bankim Chandra Chatterjee's *Kapala Kundala*, 1866 and *Debi Chaudhrani*, 1884) of the nineteenth century and argue that:

> These women who whether by choice or circumstances moved out of family constructs are shifted from roles to character, and from family to a larger sense of community. They learn to question conventions and find a way of rebellion. The picaresque novel moves away from domestic confines and, even from romance and history.[4]

She uses the concept of picaro in the Indian context to highlight how the female traveler through fortuitous circumstances often ended up as an outcast. Her journey as an outcast and her struggle to regain respectability in the family and society brought into conflict wifely attributes of "obedience, devotion, chastity and fidelity"[5] and threatened the "structure and unity of a joint family."[6] By challenging traditional moral values associated with feminine behavior, which is also what social reformers of the time are demanding, these women protagonists in the course of their journey, and in its outcome acquire new roles and identities. Eventually, these women are rehabilitated in family and community and though they have to discard their new found freedom, they gain an inner freedom that changes the equations of the household.

This accommodation of that which is not permitted in the structure of the family may be read as an opening up of the domestic space to accommodate unconventional experiences and behavior of women protagonists. The drama for female emancipation outside of domesticity was often dealt with in fiction from the same era in the lives of courtesans as *Umrao Jan Ada* (1888) by Mirza Mohammed Hadi Ruswa, or women fighting for the national cause as in *Anand Math* (1882) by Bankim Chandra. The Indian feminist history of women characters and women writers themselves dealing with these issues is fairly rich and complex and not within the scope of this paper. But it is important to acknowledge the filtering of a lot of these issues into the discourse of popular cinema. Cinematic equivalents of women running away from home and returning wiser and stronger, to women who never make it back and get lost in the interstices of rebellion and their inability to learn lessons that will ensure their survival in the larger world of male predators and a coercive patriarchy have existed in Hindi cinema from 1930s onwards.

To that extent both *The Dirty Picture* and *Kahaani* make use of existing female stereotypes of the courtesan/actor/dancer and the righteous wife seeking revenge for the death of her husband and injustices inflicted upon the nation.

Dance as the Realm of Feeling

The Dirty Picture, released in 2011, is allegedly based on the life of South Indian actor Silk Smitha. Born Vijaylakshmi Vadlapati, the South Indian star, who came to be known as "Silk" was famous for her sensual and erotic dance performances in South Indian cinema of the 1980s. She was known mostly for her dance numbers but had also received critical appreciation for performances in films as *Alaigal Oviathillai* (1981) and *Moondram Pirai* (1982) later remade in Hindi as *Sadma.* She performed in more than 400 films and nurtured ambitions of becoming a character actor in the footsteps of South Indian actors as Savithri, Sujata and Saritha.[7] Her suicide in 1996, it is speculated, was due to huge financial losses, disillusionment in love and alcohol addiction. In her death, as in the case of other famous film personalities as Marylyn Monroe, she left behind a mystique that has since haunted people for its sheer audacity, innocence and tragedy. A character that rises against all odds to dizzying heights of material success and falls as a result of making wrong choices is really the ingredient of fairytales and classics. The life of Vijaylakshmi Vadlapati too has a certain universal appeal with parallels in fairytales (for example, the fairy tale of Red Shoes) and lends itself to a picaresque rendering in the form of the film *The Dirty Picture.*

Milan Luthria makes use of this universal appeal of a tragic heroine at the level of the story and erotic appeal gleaned from the life of Vijaylakshmi for a visual titillation of the audience.

Thus he combines two different appeals to set forth the stage for a narrative that invokes the pathos of a life of struggle, of choices gone awry, and the spectacle of a female body willingly embracing her sexuality.

Reshma, or Silk in the film is shown as a woman in control of her destiny and sexuality until she loses the plot by becoming a thinking person as the critic Nyla in the film cautions her not to do. If *cogito ergo sum*, or *I think therefore I am* is the rational logic of the modern man then *I do not think therefore I am* by a reverse logic in the film becomes the underlying reason that pushes Silk to leading an unexamined but exciting life. The heady cocktail of sex, money, alcohol and fame pushes her closer and closer to the abyss until she finds there is no turning back. Her battered psyche pushes her towards total self-annihilation, and she takes an overdose of sleeping pills and alcohol to slip into death. This spectacle of what happens to a woman who plays up her unbridled sexuality is termed as the cause of entertainment in the film, and is put forth as the only possible means of entertainment for a repressed audience comprising mostly of men. The other example of serious/art cinema is dismissed as a failed model. Only that entertainment which titillates the spectator and harvests cash for the producer at the box office is held up as a legitimate model.

This binary of thinking/unthinking self, where the unthinking self is privileged as the source of power and pleasure and thinking-self as undermining this exhilaration is not a new one, especially when it comes to representing women protagonists in popular cinema. The film distributes the binary of thinking/unthinking into two women characters, Silk and Nyla; where Nyla only thinks and critiques, Silk only feels and acts. So where Nyla, hard as a nail, takes on the persona of a punishing critic sparing no one, her own life seems unexciting and dry; Silk on the other hand is shown as being driven by feelings alone. Her desire to earn a decent livelihood through her considerable talent for dance is an extension of her feeling side. Nyla and Silk thus form a whole, one complementing the other. Male characters of course do not suffer any such double-bind and have no anxiety about privileging either thinking or feeling; they inhabit both the realms most confidently.

All the male characters except Ibrahim are shown as rooted in families whereas women characters are shown as independent entities cut off from family and community ties. Nyla herself is unmarried and lives alone. Silk has run away from her home in the village to come to Madras in the hope of getting a foothold in the film industry. In the city she lives alone and mostly goes empty stomach surviving on a mouthful of sugar until she lands her first dance in a film. It is interesting to note the isolation the film thrusts upon its female characters, so where Nyla admires Silk, she refuses to allow her entry into her house and never offers to befriend her. She does however offer Silk the patronizing advice to remain as she is and not bother too much with thinking. In distancing herself from Silk, Nyla's critical voice belongs to the same male establishment that declares Silk a "dirty" woman. At the same time, one cannot ignore the class element that informs such a discrimination, for Silk is really a village belle with little education and social etiquettes. She has little social skills, or even an understanding of how the entertainment industry functions.

To that extent Silk is a picaro, a social orphan who must use her wit to survive in the city of Madras even if this means using her sexuality and behaving provocatively to gain entry into the film world. Her first expedition itself as a self-flagellating, whip wielding dancer is an indication of where this stint might take her. That she is vulnerable but feisty has been established for us right at the start of the film. We also see how miserable her existence is and how limited her choices are.

Before she lands the role of the dancer in the film that makes her famous, two incidents take place that highlight not just her vulnerability as a young beautiful woman on the verge of starvation, but also her spunk and zest for life. The five rupee note she gets in response to her complaint about going hungry for the last three days, she uses not to feed her empty stomach but to satisfy her passion for movies. In the movie hall she faces an awkward situation where she is offered a twenty rupee note for sexual favours by a middle-aged man. The association she makes between her desirability and money gives her the confidence to try her luck again at the audition. As luck would have it, the assistant director has an extraordinary requirement of the female dancer, a demand that only someone desperate and reckless enough would comply with.

But Silk is also moved by her passion for the movies. This becomes evident in her refusal to pay attention to her hunger and instead use the five rupee note for seeing a film of her favourite actor. This split in her psyche, where pressing demands of the body/self are brutally ignored to satisfy an imaginary liaison with a favourite hero is indicative of her greater need for romance than food. In underscoring her greater need for a romantic connection with an all-powerful hero, a projection of her own desire to succeed as an actor/dancer in the film world, the film sets her up as one who cannot mark boundaries between the two realms of fantasy and reality; her destitution and sexuality thus become the twin sites that direct narrative action in the film.

All through the film we see a repetition of these basic choices, where she is asked to choose between heeding to the claims of self-respect/self-worth, or success in material terms. Again and again we see she cannot distinguish between the two and chooses that which provides her temporary relief but not autonomy over her own life. Of course the film itself frames these choices as being the only choices available to a woman in an unforgiving male world. When Surya refuses to dance with Silk on one pretext or another, Silk is expected to take it upon herself to appease Surya's lust and soothe his ego. She expects him to promote her for sexual favours; for her to love Surya and to expect him to support her are the same thing. Though she realizes that it is her dance number that drew the crowd to the movie hall she cannot make the transition to asking for work based on her performance but seeks Surya's continued patronage. For her too, "sex" though a thing of the body must be couched in moral terms of love. She refuses to see her own stratagem in using her body as a "boarding pass" as she puts it during her speech and expects men who do so to rescue her.

The Girl Who Could not Stop Dancing

From her first assignment as a dancer to the first big break she gets with Suryakant, and thereafter, Silk takes on the persona of one whose erotic dance numbers, sexy clothes and sexual peccadillos become her identity. Having accepted the terms on which to engage with the world of entertainment her life itself becomes entertainment. Her screen persona and her real life become fused and it becomes more and more difficult for her to separate one from another. Her moment of reckoning arrives when she is brutally pushed into the bathroom by her lover, who then coolly proceeds to make love with his wife. That she is no more than an object of lust for the man she loves is a shattering wake-up call for Silk, and from that moment onwards her dance of self-destruction intensifies.

So far she had breezed through her performances and dismissals by serious filmmakers, film critics and protests of women's groups. But her humiliation at Suryakant's hands sets her on the path of protesting against the double standards of men and society at large, as she points out in her speech during an award function. The irony of the success of her films, where films featuring her are successful but dismissed publically, as she says, is a refusal to acknowledge the truth that films on sex are hugely in demand. She threatens to go on doing what she is accused of, i.e. of continuing featuring in dirty pictures. The speech delivered with so much gusto and clarity is really only an act of bravado, she only half believes her own words. From now on her only desire is to prove that she understands what entertainment is, and that she is not dependent on Suryakant's patronage for her success. But as long as she was happy to do the bidding of the men in her life, Suryakant, Ramakant, Silva Ganesan and other male mentors she was successful for she was an unthinking tool in their hands. It is when she makes the transition to a producer and takes on the mantle of a thinking/business woman that she flops. So much so that she loses all her money even as her dependence on alcohol increases to become an addiction. Just like the young woman in the fairy tale Red Shoes, who cannot stop dancing once she has fastened the red shoes on to her feet:

> And so out the door she danced, and then down the steps, first in a gavotte, then *csa´rda´s*, and then in big daring waltz turns in rapid succession. The girl was in glory and did not realize she was in trouble until she wanted to dance to the left and the shoes insisted on dancing straight ahead. And as the shoes danced the girl, rather than the other way round, they danced her right down the road, through the muddy fields and out into the dark and gloomy forest.[8]

Silk too cannot let go off her persona of a dancer of sexy item songs. Her identification with her persona is so strong that she feels threatened when she finds that a younger woman by the name of Shakeela is the new star on the horizon. In fact, she feels so threatened by the arrival of Shakeela on the scene that she even challenges her to a dance duel in front of a large gathering of film personalities, ex-lover, current boyfriend, his family and other guests.

Ramakant, her boyfriend seems supportive of her as long as she is his muse, but dumps her right in the middle of the road late in the night and calls her names, when he realizes she is not at all under his control. He wants to marry her and rescue her from a life of degradation, but as Silk points out, she cannot pretend to be what she is not and that he should accept her for what she is. But Ramakant cannot do that, for he wants to rescue her not for her sake but his own, to spice up his own dull existence. Left alone, Silk's isolation and addiction worsen, so much so that she cannot even perform during film shoots. Thinking she can still pull off a hit she invests all her money in a film venture only to lose every penny she earned. In her hour of loss Ibrahim who has hated her all along falls in love with her and attempts her final rescue. He begins visiting her, learns about her childhood, her family in the village and shares her loneliness. He brings Silk's mother from the village in an attempt to reunite mother and daughter, but this salve of help is too late in arriving. Silk, like the girl in the story Red Shoes, has danced a terrible dance and exhausted herself unto death.

It is not without irony that Silk who was seen wearing skimpy clothes all through the film and in defiance of marriage itself is seen decked up as a bride in a red Kanjiwaram sari on her journey to the beyond. The symbolism of her sartorial preference in her death outdoes the film's purported discourse of a celebration of sexuality and the female body. Silk, who is shown as most unabashed in her choice of clothing, covers up her body in the last act of her life. Is this an act of hiding the body from the prying gaze of all her male mentors, lovers, audience, or is it simply a hidden desire to garner some respectability by dressing up as a "good" woman is a question the film leaves for the spectators to decide.

Her suicide and the film's handling of her suicide confirm what the film has all along been resisting: portraying Silk as a victim. But victim she is, unable to rescue her life she succumbs to the internalization of the shadow aspect of a culture, where women should not be seen as sexual beings except as prostitutes, courtesans and actors, where such women though required for entertaining and satisfying male appetites cannot be accorded respect.

The film attempts to garner sympathy for the character of Silk by playing up the usual narrative of a woman seeking love, but finding exploitation instead and her inability to maneuver through such difficult straits. The film exploits this vulnerability of the character of Silk not only at the level of the narrative but also at the level of the visuals. Thus the thematic function of the film becomes the formative principle characterizing the use of space in the film. So that the close-ups, mid-shots and long shots, indeed the entire range of film aesthetics, is utilized to showcase the protagonist as an object of lust. Right from the time Silk offers to perform the dance number requiring her to flagellate herself, to Silva Ganesan discovering her, to her first dance with Suryakant and other dance items, the camera's focus remains on her gyrating hips, her heaving bosom, her lips, her hands roving over her own body, or her body writhing on a bed in sexy underwear. The entire range of camera's shots is utilized to put on display a female body in its amatory performance. It is interesting that the spectators frequenting Silks' films in the film too are shown as made up mostly of men. This interplay of a "bold" Silk sizzling on the screen for a male crowd that throws coins on the screen in appreciation is the essential metaphor of the film and one that the makers of the film want us to believe is an act of liberating the female from her sexual inhibitions and a celebration of woman as a sexual being. The film is a terrifying moral tale of what happens to women who dare to express their sexuality in a largely repressive society.

The Heart is a Lonely Hunter

In Sujoy Ghosh's *Kahaani*, released in 2012, the spectacle of a heavily pregnant Vidya Bagchi doing the rounds of police stations, staying in uncomfortable guest houses, walking in crowded streets, climbing stairs to reach offices inhabiting obdurate bureaucrats, desperately looking for clues to the disappearance of her husband is a tale that immediately captures attention for a number of reasons: it is a murder/ terror mystery intricately woven with the narratives of nation, love and motherhood. If *The Dirty Picture* was about sexuality then *Kahaani*'s focus on a married, pregnant woman drew attention to the righteous anger of a wife and a mother. If in *The Dirty Picture* the camera roved over the body parts of Silk, then in *Kahaani*, it is the swollen abdomen of Vidya Bagchi that is at the centre of a visual display in the film.

Vidya Bagchi, a pregnant picaro sets out on the trail to discovering who is behind the terror attack on Calcutta Metro. She too like Silk, is not rooted in family, her husband and her child are dead, and we get no hint of a parental home. Colonel Vajpai, her husband's boss is all she has in the name of a family. It is at his behest that she takes up the onerous task of bringing the guilty to justice. Her righteous anger is not just over the death of her husband and child but over the loss of innocent lives. She has so to speak wedded the nation and like Durga the Goddess, takes it upon herself to punish the culprits of so wanton an act of terror. Indeed, as the voiceover in the concluding scene of the film informs us, "when gods fail, goddess Durga is invoked to avenge wrong and to restore order."

Just like a picaro, Vidya enters an unfamiliar city to unsettle hierarchies in smug establishments of power, as also to quietly carry out her task of investigation, and in the end to prove to everyone especially the arrogant and brash Khan, a senior officer of the IB that she is far smarter and competent than him and all of them put together. Khan, for all his talk of collateral damage and his undying love for the country is really only a loud mouth, with little investigative insight into confounding matters. All the insights that lead to unravelling the case come from Vidya and her sleuthing ways. Her journey from the airport to the police station, to the morgue, to the office of the National Data Centre, to the metro station, to literally every corner of the city becomes the optical lens through which the city and its intricate by-lanes become visible and play out the intricacies of the complicated case. And precisely for this reason an outsider with a fresh perspective, in this case a woman least likely to arouse suspicion or even threat is called upon to solve the case. That a pregnant woman searching for her missing husband is particularly believable and vulnerable is the narrative strategy of the film. A strategy that is immensely successful for it confounds the spectator as well as the perpetrators of the act of terror.

Vidya, the protagonist is smart, intelligent, fearless and tenacious and comes across as a woman who is not a victim by any means. She is always in control of the situation and manipulates the system to work for her and eventually succeeds in doing what she had set out to do so. But it is here that this too good to believe story cracks up to reveal the familiar patterns of representing women in popular cinema. All of this smartness, intelligence, courage and tenacity, literally the attributes of Goddess Durga herself, are called into action to save the nation from demons wreaking havoc on it. As also to highlight that she is a wife seeking justice for her husband and her unborn child. To that extent she is not portrayed as a "sexual being" available for amorous display and games. The visual and narrative focus on her swollen abdomen never fails to highlight her status as an expecting mother.

Men who help her are moved by her plight and do far in excess of what they would for a woman who is not heavy with motherhood. Of course, the most intriguing but also the most believable part of the story, her pregnancy seems a bit of a suspect from the indifference she displays towards the well-being of her child. We never see her visit a gynecologist for a check-up, or even talking to one, or taking vitamins and other pills as pregnant women are wont to do, or being careful of her diet, or while walking the by-lanes of Calcutta, or even visiting dark chambers of the Bureau of Information in the middle of the night. Because everyone thinks her so harmless, no one bothers with the truth of her pregnancy. In any case, a heavily pregnant woman may hardly even draw amorous male attention. Satyuki, the young Police Inspector, however is drawn to her but the boundaries between them are clearly drawn. She is Arjun on a mission, as she points out right in the beginning when she meets him and he becomes Krishna, the charioteer, who wisely steers Arjun's chariot during the battle of the Mahabharata.

But she is both Arjun and Krishna, the clever strategist, for no one suspects her story which is so full of loopholes, to be false. It does not occur to anyone to question her antecedents or her story. She employs her ready wit to wheedle out of tricky situations that call for a close examination of her story, for example when she lands at the guesthouse and refuses to sign on the dilapidated register, or when she visits the school where Arnab Bagchi was a student.

Vidya, herself uses her pregnancy as a smokescreen to deflect attention away from her story and instead draws attention to her swollen belly. It turns out Khan, from the Information Bureau himself, too thinks in a similar vein and wants to use her to get to Milan, no matter that she might lose her life. Khan's coldness of purpose is only matched by Vidya's own cool logic in wearing a prosthetic to fake a pregnancy to get to her husband killers. To that extent, she uses her femininity as a weapon to get even with a cold and calculating killer. But it turns out even Milan, so cruel and cold can be stunned by a fake belly and must be spared no explanations as to why she is killing him. In her righteous rage she is colder than even death, for she is above it.

Triangular Park, where the final showdown takes place between Vidya and Milan, is appropriately enough the site of the final day of Durga Puja: the day when the goddess having defeated the demon Mahishasur is submerged in water until next year when she must be resurrected. Vidya elevated to the status of Durga, seeks out Milan Damjee through a crowd of similarly attired women, and stuns him and the audience by flinging the fake belly at him. Having stunned him, she first pierces his foot with a sharp, needle like object that she wears to hold her hair in place, then she uses the same object to pierce his neck and then proceeds to shoot him dead with his own pistol. That she leaves no fingerprints behind and no information about who she could be, and disappears in the crowd that is on its way to submerge Durga, is as close an allegory as is possible, indeed as the voiceover also claims, of her being not a human but a divine being with extraordinary attributes.

It is in this moment of reckoning when all the missing links in the puzzle of Vidya Bagchi and her husband's disappearance become clear that the broken but fierce woman behind the persona of Vidya Bagchi is revealed to us. In flinging her fake belly the face of her husband's killer she puts aside the weak and inept body of a pregnant woman and transforms into a most agile and alert woman capable of defending herself, killing her enemy and eventually safeguarding the interests of the nation at large. A close look at her narrative, in being the one who persuades her husband to leave for Kolkata for an assignment to enquire into dangers lurking over the nation state; her miscarriage on finding out about Arup's death, her guilt over it, her taking on the persona of Vidya Bagchi at the behest of Colonel Vajpai, to the thrilling denouement, all of these establish her as the prime mover of the story, and its moral agent in always keeping the claims of the nation above her personal needs. She does not want her husband to stick around home looking after her – a feminine thing to do – instead he should be out there defending the frontiers of the nation state.

A close reading of the first and the last link in Vidya Bagchi's story leads to a most brutal interpretation of the miscarriages that take place in the film; the first miscarriage is a consequence of Arup's death; the second – a symbolic one – her flinging her fake belly in Milan Damjee's face, is a willful one. Between both these two miscarriages, she emerges as the asexual, revengeful, goddess of wrath, out of touch with the demands of her body.

The film in creating a female character who is self-reliant, smart and sharp does so at the risk of rendering her un-reproductive, and mournful, incapable of coming to terms with her loss and accepting her suffering as a penance, thus a suitable heir to the innumerable Indian myths of a chaste and pure wife, who is beyond the corruption of flesh and spirit. What is more she is the embodiment of goddess Durga, she is Mother India, who thinks nothing of her own loss in the face of the loss of nation. When the film ends she is still mourning the death of her husband and child, has taken no cognizance of Satyuki's affection for her, and is perhaps ready to take on further assignments to avenge the wrong doers of nation. Indeed, there is speculation that a sequel to *Kahaani* is in the making.

Conclusion

From the sultry siren Silk in *The Dirty Picture* to a vulnerable and heartbroken wife of *Kahaani*, these are still the two poles between which representations of "bold", "powerful" women are played out in Hindi cinema. Of course this is not to say that all the films mentioned earlier too play out this logic but to highlight the continuation of stereotypes even if not in a straightforward way.

The use of the picaresque itself is a complex strategy of narration that refuses to lend itself to any one kind of a reading. To that extent these films complicate any straightforward reading of the narrative. In fact, there are moments of self-reflexivity in both the films, when there is genuine confusion over how to engage with the protagonist, for example in *The Dirty Picture,* Nyla is concerned about categorizing Silk, she cannot decide whether to call her a vamp or a victim; or for that matter, Silk's own critique of the system as an exploitative one and yet her inability to break free of that system. In *Kahaani*, Vidya manipulates the system by employing the stereotype of a helpless pregnant woman and shows that there are different ways in which a female body may perform itself, and that it need not be only that of a glamorous star.

Yet, by no means do these films offer us female characters who have an easy relationship with either their sexuality, or body, or even the world they inhabit. They fail to live up to the ideals of the wild women archetypes, for they inhabit only one dimension of it and are nowhere close to integrating the conscious and the unconscious, nor do they offer us insights into how women may come to terms with loss without themselves turning into either killers or addicts. In the case of *The Dirty Picture*, the protagonist deals with her humiliations, her losses and her pain by annihilating the self, in the other the main lead refuses to come to terms with her loss and cuts herself off from the life of community. An impossible condensation of the vulnerable and the cunning in the figures of Silk and Vidya makes them inadequate role models for women seeking insights into sexuality and relationships, self-worth and self-care. In fact, self-worth and self-care are often the twin casualties in narratives seeking to create "powerful" larger than life women characters.

Neither the films nor the characters themselves offer any critique of the entertainment industry in which women continue to play second fiddle, or of the nation state itself, which in itself is a bundle of contradictions and prefers a forceful suppression of identities and conflicts of land and resources. Yet, at the same time, there is a silent counter-discourse, in the use of the female body in both the pictures, especially in *Kahaani*, where the body subjected so often to subjugation and exploitation, is used to extract help and to camouflage the real investigation. In this case, the woman uses her body to get the better of the system which seeks to suppress facts. But in no case is the female mind undermined. *The Dirty Picture* also goes beyond the exploitation of the female body to expose the tragedy and helplessness of the victim. It holds up a mirror image to the industry allowing it to see its own sleazy side and the ugliness of it all.

Notes

1. Frederick Monteser, *The Picaresque Element in Western Literature.* (Alabama: The University of Alabama Press, 1975) vi.
2. Jasbir Jain, *Feminizing Political Discourse: Women and Novel in India.* (Jaipur: Rawat Publications, 1997) 68.
3. Ibid., 69.
4. Ibid., 66-67.
5. Ibid., 65.
6. Ibid.
7. Filmfare interview, December 1984. http: //www.filmfare.com/features/silk-smithas-bold-interview-4813-1.html#descArticle
8. Clarissa Pinkola Este's, *Women Who Run with the Wolves: Myths and Stories of the Wild Woman Archetype.* (New York: Ballantine Books, 1992) 234.

Filmography

Kahaani. Dir. Sujoy Ghosh, Pro. Kushal Guha, Sujoy Ghosh. Perf. Vidya Balan, Parambrata Chatterjee, Nawazudin Siddiqui, Saswata Chatterjee, Indraneil Sengupta. 2012.

The Dirty Picture. Dir. Milan Luthria, Pro. Dr Luke, Benny Bianco Frrazer T. Smith. Perf. Vidya Balan, Emraan Hashmi, Tusshar Kapoor, Naseerudin Shah, Anju Mahendru. 2011.

Contributors

Somdatta Mandal teaches English at Visva-Bharati University, Santiniketan, West Bengal. Awardee of several prestigious fellowships, she has published extensively. Her works include a three volume *The Diasporic Imagination: Asian American Writing* (2000) and two edited books on travelogues.

Gita Viswanath teaches English at Tolani Arts and Science College, Adipur, Kutch and is at present working for her Ph.D. on war films and military literature at M.S. University, Baroda.

Bindu Nair, graduate of the Film and Television Institute of India (FTII), Pune is an active film maker. One of her short films won recognition and was awarded the National Award for Direction in the category of short films.

Malati Mathur is on the faculty of English, IGNOU, Delhi. She has researched on Australian literature and writes regularly for the newspapers. She has twice been awarded the Katha award for translation from Tamil into English.

Vrinda Mathur teaches in Government College, Chimanpura (Rajasthan). She has worked on American drama and is interested in gender studies.

Meenu Bhambhani worked for her doctorate on John Osborne. She has worked extensively on disability and is engaged in policy formation.

Supriya Agarwal is at the Central University of Rajasthan, Bandar Sindri, Dist. Ajmer and has specialized in nineteenth century writing.

Veena Singh, former Professor of English at the University of Rajasthan, has worked on nineteenth century studies and the novels of the Empire.

Anshoo Sharma worked on the "Narrative Strategies in Jane Austen's Novels" for her doctoral thesis. Dr. Sharma teaches English at the Rajasthan School of Arts, Jaipur.

Jasbir Jain, formerly of the University of Rajasthan, Jaipur has written on a wide range of areas. She has been working on films for more than two decades. Amongst her latest works are *Theorizing Resistance* and *The Diaspora Writes Home*.

Dipendu Chakrabarti, a well-known scholar, is the Sir Gooroodas Professor of English at the University of Calcutta.

Jyoti Bhatia is a lecturer in English at Government College, Kishangarh, Rajasthan. She is working on her doctoral thesis on *The Female Comic Tradition: From Burney to Eliot.*

Bandana Chakrabarty is Pricipal, Rajasthan School of Arts, Jaipur. She has worked on Alice Munro and is co-editor of several books on contemporary drama.

Mini Nanda is Associate Professor at the Department of English, University of Rajasthan. She has worked on "Spatial Metaphors in Graham Greene".

Sudha Rai, former Professor, Department of English, University of Rajasthan. She is currently on a Senior Research Fellowship awarded by the Indian Council of Social Science Research, New Delhi.

Tripti Jain, a political scientist and a freelance translator. She has several works to her credit and is the awardee of the Katha Award for translation from Panjabi into English.

Madhuri Chatterjee teaches English at Government College, Chimanpura (Rajasthan). Her doctoral work was on John Updike. Currently she is working on Indian women's autobiographies and has worked on travelogues.

Anu Celly is in the States. She has worked on Edith Wharton and has a strong interest in feminist writing. She has also worked on Indian language literatures.

Santosh Gupta, former Professor of English, University of Rajasthan. Dr. Gupta has specialized in modernist and postmodernist studies. Her early work was on Iris Murdoch. She is presently engaged in a project on North East writing.

Renuka Pamecha is a well-known woman activist who has been in the mainstream of the women's movement in Rajasthan and has worked closely with women affected by violence. She teaches Political Science at Kanoria PG College, Jaipur.

Krishna Rathore, formerly Principal of Dungar College, Bikaner, has worked on nineteenth century women writers and her thesis was on "Male Mentors in Women's Fiction". Her interest is in feminist theory and Indian Writing in English.

Veena Jain teaches English at Government College, Alwar. Her doctoral work was on Jean Rhys. Since then she has gone on to work on contemporary fiction and criticism.

Ranju Mehta teaches Philosophy at the Kanoria Postgraduate College, Jaipur. She has interest in dramatics and women's studies and is a freelance translator.

Rakesh Thakur teaches Sociology at Amravati University, Amravati. Thakur's research work is related to the Gandhi-Ambedkar interface. He is interested in literary studies and in translation.

S. Asha is posted at Government College, Tonk. With twenty-five years of service behind her, she has papers on drama, language and fiction. Currently she is engaged in research on myths and Indian writing.

Manasvini Rai, a freelance writer based in Jaipur, is a Mathematics (Hons.) graduate and has a Masters degree in Journalism and Mass Communication. She writes a regular blog at http: //ofallwriting-andtalkingmovingpictures.wordpress.com/.

Avinash Jodha, Associate Professor at Dungar College, Bikaner is a writer and a critic. He has made two documentaries and published several critical papers in reputed journals. Dr Jodha's interests are cinema, postcolonial studies and diaspora poetics.

Vijaya Singh teaches English at the Regional Institute of English in Chandigarh. A former Fulbright Fellow at New York University, and a Fellow at the Institute of Advanced Study, Shimla, Vijaya is interested in films, drama and literaures. She has published abook of poems *First Instinct* (Sahitya Akademi) and is writing a novel.

Index

Aa Ab Laut Chale 45
Aandhi 11, 165
Aastha 106, 109ff, 115, 120ff, 125, 128, 135
Abhinay 30
Acchut Kanya 225
Agar Tum na Hote 64
Agashe, Mohan 103, 133
Ahluwalia, Preet Mohan S. 164
Akhtar, Javed 283
Alaigal Ovithillai 320
Alcoff, Linda 215
  "Cultural Feminism Versus Poststructuralism" 215
Ali, Imtiaz 297, 398, 306, 309, 314
Amar Prem 94
Anand Math 319
Angoor 148
Ankhiyon Ke Jharoke Se 94
Ansal, Kusum 122
  Uski Panchvati 122
Anurag 79ff
Aparajito 208, 210ff
Ars Poetica 242
Arth 106, 109, 114, 166ff, 173, 226
Arzoo 77
Asookh 23ff, 30, 33
Astitva 120, 128, 257ff, 267ff
Autumn Sonata 19
Avatar 94
Awakening, The 26
Awara 3
Azmi, Shabana 18, 38, 133

Bachchan, Amitabh 38, 41, 78, 82
Bachchan, Jaya 38
Bahl, Vikas 297, 298, 306, 309, 314
Balan, Vidya 11, 15, 316, 317
Bandh Jharokhe 13, 179, 184ff, 188
Bandhopadhya, Bhibuti Bhushan 208
  see *Aparajito* and Ray
Bandhopadhya, Kanu 209

Bandhopadhya, Karuna 209, 211
Bandini 165
Bariwali 27, 29ff, 35
Barsaat Ki Ek Raat 81
Barthes, Roland 56ff, 217
Batra, Pooja 61
Batra, Ritesh 272
Bazaar 87
Bedi, Rakesh 152
Behl, Mohnish 83
Beloved 304, 305
Berger, John 52, 89
  Ways of Seeing 52, 89
Bergman, Ingmar 19
  Autumn Sonata 19
Bergson, Henri 150
Beyond Feminist Aesthetics 214
Bhabha, Homi 304, 305, 310
Bhaji on the Beach 24, 271, 277, 279, 280
Bhatt, Mahesh 120, 226, 230
  Daddy 226
  Naam 226
  Tamanna 226ff, 229
Bhatt, Pooja 226
Bhattacharya, Basu 120ff
Bhattacharya, Suchitra 20
Biswas, Chobi 211
Biswas, Seema 83
Biwi No.1 164, 252
Bobby Jassos 316
Bobby 94
Bombay 90
Bordo, Susan 120
Bose, Nitin 197
  Mashaal 197, 199ff
Boys on the Side 297, 306
Boyum, Joy Gould 197
  Double Exposure: Fiction into Film 197
Brah, Avtar 278
Bronte, Emily 253
  Wuthering Heights 253
Brooks, Ann 217
  Postfeminisms: Feminism, Cultural Theory and Cultural Forms 217
Burman, Sachin Deb 197
Bush, Stephen 196
Butler, Judith 233
  Gender Trouble 233

Cahill, Madeline and Martin Norden 76
Carson, Diane et. al 9
Cazamian, Louis 147ff
Celebration 26
Chadha, Gurinder 277
Chakrabarty, Mithun 33
Chakrabarty, Sudeepta 30
Chakravarti, Debnita 280
Chalti Ka Naam Gaadi 148
Chandra, Tanuja 226
Chandran, Sudha 81
Charney, Maurice 153, 155, 158
Charulata 26ff
Chashme Baddoor 152, 157ff
Chatterjee, Ananya 20ff
Chatterjee, Bankim Chandra 318, 319
Chatterjee, Madhuri 112
Chatterjee, Mausami 79
Chatterjee, Partha 42
Chatterjee, Prabhat 217
Chatterjee, Sabitri 38
Chatterjee, Sarat Chandra 165, 197
Chatterjee, Soumitra 23ff, 211
Chattopadhyaya, Bankim Chandra 197
  Rajni 6, 197

Chawla, Juhi 53
Chokher Bali 28, 34
Chopin, Kate 26
  The Awakening 26
Chopra, B.R., 91
Chopra, Parineeti 316
Chopra, Priyanka 283
Chotto amar meye 25
Chugtai, Ismat 131
  "The Quilt" 131
Chupke Chupke 148
Cinema of Satyajit Ray, The 218, 222
Coast to Coast 297
Cocktail 298
comedy 284
"Communalising Gender Engendering Community" 48
Cooper, Darius 218, 222
Cowie, Elizabeth 218
  Representing the Woman 218
Crime and Punishment 142
"Cultural Feminism versus Poststructuralism" 215

Dabbawalas 272, 273, 276
Daddy 226
Dahan 19ff, 22ff, 30
Damaad 148
Daman 251
Damini 5, 122, 236ff
Dark Holds No Terrors, The 184ff, 189
Das, Kamala 115
  My Story 115
Das, Nandita 34
de Beauvoir, Simone 92
  Memoirs of a Dutiful Daughter 112
  The Second Sex 92, 168, 255
De Lauretis, Teresa 216
  Feminist Film Theory 216
De Rojas, Fernand 318
Death Proof 306
Debi Chaudhrani 318
Debi, Ruma 197
Debi, Sumitra 197
Dedh Ishqiya 316
Deshpande, Shashi 184, 249
  That Long Silence 249
  The Dark Holds No Terrors 184ff, 189
Devi 5, 170ff, 208, 211ff, 217ff
Devi, Bhanwari 237
Devi, Mahashweta 165
Dey, Manna 203
Dharamputra 94, 225
Dharmendra 59
Dhool Ka Phool 94
Differential Wife 300
Dil Hai Ki Maanta Nahi 297
Dilwale Dulhaniya Le Jayenge 12, 297
Dirty Picture, The 15, 316, 317, 318, 320, 328, 332, 333
Do Aankhein Barah Haath 94
Dostoevsky 142
  Crime and Punishment 142
Double Exposure: Fiction into Film 197
Dushman 83
Dutt, Guru 56
  Pyaasa 56
  Sahib Bibi aur Gulam 251
Dutt, Sanjay 60

Ek Duje Ke Liye 94
Ekdin Pratidin 37, 140, 144ff
Elizabeth 49
English Vinglish 282, 316

Fashion 283
Felski, Rita 214
  Beyond Feminist Aesthetics 214
female desire 280
Feminist Film Theory 217
"Film as Environment" 246
Film Theory and Philosophy 219
Fire 6, 69, 121, 129ff, 175
Fiza 90, 252
food 279
Foucault, M 226, 234, 244
  Diacritics 226
Freud, Sigmund 55ff, 231
Frost, Robert 296

Ganesh, Kamala 66ff
Ganguly, Roopa 30, 33
Ganti, Tejaswini 283
Gatens, Moira 232
  "Power, Bodies, Difference" 232
Gender Trouble 233
Ghatak, Ritwik 17, 37
  Meghe Dhaka Tara 37, 140ff, 144
Ghosh, Rituparno 17–38, 120
  Abhinay 30
  Asookh 23ff, 30, 33
  Bariwali 27, 29ff, 35
  Dahan 19ff, 22ff, 30
  Hirer Angti 18
  Titli 30ff, 37
  Unishe April 18, 23ff, 26, 30, 35
  Utsab 26
Ghosh, Sujoy 317
Gilman, Charlotte Perkins 67, 69
Glendhill, Christine 87
  Recent Developments in Feminist Criticism 87
Gokhale, Mohan 246
Golmaal 148
good girl 290, 292
Gordimer, Nadine 304
Govinda 59, 63
Grafts: Feminist Cultural Criticism 215
Grewal, Simi 101
Guide 69
Gulaab Gang 13, 282
Gulzar 120, 165
Gupta, Chidananda Das 135
  The Painted Face 135

Hadi Ruswa, Mirza Mohammed 319
Halberstam, Judith 285, 286
Half-Ticket 148
Hall, Stuart 278
Hamnett, Jennifer 219
  Film Theory and Philosophy 219
Hariye Jawa 25
Harvard Business School 272
Hasee Toh Phasee 14, 282, 284, 285, 287, 293, 294, 316
Hasina Maan Jayegi 61
Heidegger, Martin 258
Heroine 283
Hesse, Mary Chinery 73
  Women and Disability 73
Highway 282, 297, 298, 299, 306, 307, 308, 310, 313, 314, 316
Hill, Thomas 300, 301
hippy 284, 290
Hirer Angti 18
Home and The World, The 304
Horace 242
  Ars Poetica 242
Hum Aapke Hain Kaun 41, 164, 299
Hum Dil De Chuke Sanam 44
Hum Dono 77
Hum Saath Saath Hain 83

identity through difference 278
"Ideology and Film Culture" 221
Ideology of the Hindi Film 197
In Search of Our Mothers' Gardens 82
In the Good Old Summertime 273
Indira, M.K. 180ff
Ishqiya 316, 317

Jaane Bhi Do Yaaron 148
Jab We Met 298
Jaffrelot, Christophe 40
Jaffrey, Saeed 152
Jahanara 94
Jai Santoshi Maa 94
Jain, Jasbir 106, 109, 115ff, 318
Jain, Madhu 47
Jalal, Farida 78
James, Henry 304
Jha, Prakash 120, 121
Jodi No.1 59
Johnston, Claire 217
Jones, Ann Rosalind 112
Juergensmeyer 48
Julie 94

Kabhi Kabhi 95, 97, 99ff
Kahani 15, 316, 317, 318, 320, 327, 328, 332, 333
Kaif, Katrina 11
Kakar, Sudhir 109, 111, 123, 211ff
Kal, Aaj aur Kal 94
Kannan, Laxmi 109
Kapala Kundala 318
Kapoor, Raj 41
  Awara 3
Kapoor, Ratna and Brenda Cosman 48
  "Communalising Gender Engendering Community" 48
Kapoor, Shekhar 49
  Elizabeth 49
Karanth, Prema 179–193
  Bandh Jharokhe 13, 179, 184ff, 188
  Phaniyamma 179ff, 183
Katha 149ff, 153ff
Kati Patang 94
Kazmi, Fareed 88
  "Muslim Social and the Female Protagonist" 88
Kent, Deborah 80, 84
  Women and Disability 80
Khamoshi 77, 83
Khan, Aamir 84
Khan, Saif Ali 105
Khandahar 29
Khanna, Vinod 79, 80, 103, 104
Kher, Kiron 27
Khushboo 165, 168
Kinara 79
Koirala, Manisha 83ff
Koshish 77, 80
Kuch Khatti Kuch Meethi 61
Kuch Kuch Hota Hai 43
Kuhn, Annette 215
  Grafts: Feminist Cultural Criticism 215
Kumar, Ashok 197
Kumar, Rajendra 59, 77
Kya Kehna 68, 105, 121, 129ff

Lacan 232
Lajja 121, 129ff, 247
Lal, Vinay 215
  The Secret Politics of Our Desires 215
Lee, Edward R. 245
Little Miss Sunshine 297
Location of Culture, The 304

Lonely Passion of Judith Hearn 28
Love Aaj Kal 298
Love Story 297
low budget films 10
Lunchbox, The 14, 271, 272, 275, 277, 279
Luthria, Milan 317, 320

Mahabharata 74
Mahanagar 26, 37, 140ff
Main Chup Rahungi 165
Main Tulsi Tere Angan Ki 251
Majboor 78
Malini, Hema 60, 79, 103
Manasha-Mangal 37
Manjrekar, Mahesh 128, 257
  Astitva 120, 128, 257ff, 267ff
Mann 83
Manusmriti 48
Mardaani 12
Martin, Biddy 233
  "Sexual Practice and Changing Lesbian Identities" 233
Mary Kom 12
Mashaal 197, 199ff
Masoom 94, 95, 97
Meghe Dhaka Tara 37, 140ff, 144
Mehboob 120
  Mother India 120, 165
Mehta, Deepa 69, 121, 175
  Fire 14, 69, 121, 129ff, 175
Mehta, Ketan 242
  Mirch Masala 5, 120, 242, 247
Memoirs of a Dutiful Daughter 112
Meredith, George 161
Minturn, Leigh 123
Mirch Masala 5, 120, 242, 247
Mishra, Leela 152
Mitchell, Julie 231
Mitr, My Friend 273
Mitra, Jyoti 84
Mohammed, Khalid 252
Monroe, Marylyn 320
Monsoon Wedding 299
Moondram Pirai 320
Morrison, Toni 304, 305
Mother India 120, 165
Mrityudand 106, 109ff, 113ff, 129ff, 135, 165, 247
Mughal-e-Azam 94
Mukherjee, Madhabi 26
Mukherjee, Prabhat Kumar 211
Mukherjee, Rani 11
Mukhopadhyay, Shirshendu 38
Multiple Voices in Feminist Film Criticism 9, 13
Mulvey, Laura 52, 54ff, 136, 169, 219
  "Visual Pleasure and Narrative Cinema" 54, 91
  "Women Writing and Writing about Women" 169
"Muslim Social and the Female Protagonist" 88
My Son's Story 304
My Story 115
Mythologies 217

Naache Mayuri 81
Naam 226
Naaz 78
Nandy, Ashis 50
Nawal, Deepti 151ff
Nead, Lynda 44
Nikaah 87
Niranjana, Tejasvini 181
Nishchal, Navin 125
No One Killed Jessica 11, 12, 316, 317
Nutan 99

Oberoi, Suresh 123

Padatik 144
Padosan 148
Page 3 12
Painted Face, The 135
Pakeezah 87
Panchvati 121ff, 125ff, 135
Paranjpe, Sai 148, 151ff, 156, 159
  Chashme Baddoor 152, 157ff
  Katha 149ff, 153ff
Parash Pathar 37
Pardes 47ff
Pardesi Babu 63
Paroma 16, 19, 35, 106ff, 111ff, 120, 140, 170ff
Paromitar ek din 35
Patekar, Nana 83
Pathak, Supriya 95, 246
Pattons, Cindy 232
Phalke, Dada Saheb 249
  Rajah Harischandra 249
Phaniyamma 179ff, 183
picaro 319, 328
Portrait of a Lady, The 304
Postfeminism: Feminism, Cultural Theory and Cultural Forms 217
"Power, Bodies, Difference" 232
Pradeep 197
Prasad M. Madhava 197
  Ideology of the Hindi Film 197
Pratighat 122, 136, 165
Puri, Om 243
Pyaasa 56

Qayamat Se Qayamat Tak 297
Queen 12, 14, 282, 284, 285, 288, 291, 292, 293, 297, 298, 299, 300, 303, 306, 307, 311, 312, 314, 316
Qureshi, Huma 316

Rai, Aishwarya 53, 60
Rajah Harischandra 249
Rajneeti 11
Rajni 6, 197
Rakhi 81
Ramayana 37
Ranaut, Kangana 316
Rani Roopmati 94
Ray, Satyajit 17, 36, 120, 140, 146, 170, 208ff, 213
  Aparajito 208, 210ff
  Charulata 26ff
  Devi 5, 170ff, 208, 211ff, 217ff
  Mahanagar 26, 37, 140ff
  Parash Pathar 37
Recent Developments in Feminist Criticism 87
Rehaee 95, 102, 104, 120, 247
Rehman, Waheeda 38, 99
Rekha 64
"Religious Nationalism, Hindus and Muslims in India" 90
Representing the Woman 218
Road Movies 297, 298, 306
Rockstar 298
Rodriguez, Hector 221
Rodway, Allan 148, 151
Room of One's Own, A 106
Ross, Herbert 297
Roy, Debashree 19, 23
Roy, Kalinker 212
Roy, Kanu 197
Roy, Kumkum 48
  "Where women are worshipped, there the Gods rejoice" 48

Saajan ki Saheli 95, 99ff
Saajan 83

Saccha Jhoota 78
Sadma 320
Sagar, Sarhadi 90
  Bazaar 87
Sahabs 311
Sahib Bibi Aur Gulam 251
Sahni, Parikshat 101
Sangam 94
Sanlaap 20
Sansar 94
Santoshi, Raj Kumar 121, 236
  Damini 236ff
  Lajja 121, 129ff, 247
Sargent, Joseph 297
Saritha 320
Savithri 320
Schillaci, Anthony 246
  "Film as Environment" 246
Scott, Ridley 297
Second Sex, The 92, 168, 255
Sen, Aparna 19, 33ff, 108, 120, 171ff
  Paroma 6, 19, 35, 140, 170ff
  Paromitar ek din 35
  36 Chowringhee Lane 35
Sen, Mrinal 17, 29, 140, 144ff
  Ekdin Pratidin 37, 140, 144ff
  Khandahar 29
  Padatik 144
Sen, Sushmita 53
Sengupta, Ratnottama 160
Sengupta, Pinaki 209
"Sexual Practice and Changing Lesbian Identities" 233
Shagird 148
Shah, Naseeruddin 95, 103, 150, 242
Shahane, Renuka 164
Sharma, Konkona Sen 33
Sheikh, Farooq 151ff
Shetty, Shilpa 57
Sholay 65
Shop Around the Corner, A 273
Shubhkaamnaein 94
Singh, Chandrachud 105
Singh, Neetu 100
Sirf Tum 273
six-ab fantsy 10
Smitha, Silk 25, 320
social agenda 13
Sparsh 81
Stevens, Wallace 212
Sujata 320
Sujata 94, 225

Tabu 38, 258
Tagore 25ff
  Chokher Bali 28, 34
  Chottor Amar Meye 25
  Hariye Jawa 25
Tagore, Rabindranath 304
Tagore, Sharmila 211, 220
Taj Mahal 94
Tamanna 120, 226ff, 229
technology and films 10
Thakur, Dinesh 125
That Long Silence 249
"The Quilt" 131
Thelma and Louise 297, 302, 306
36 Chowringhee Lane 35
Titli 30ff, 37
tomboys 285
Trilling, Lionel 252

Ulysses 296, 302, 303, 305
Umrao Jaan 87
Umrao Jan Ada 319
Unishe April 18, 23ff, 26, 30, 35
Uski Panchvati 122
Utsab 26

Vandlapati, Vijayalakshmi 320
Vaswani, Ravi 152
Veer, Peter van der 90
  Religious Nationalism, Hindus and Muslims in India 90
Virdi, Jyotika 283, 294
"Visual Pleasure and Narrative Cinema" 54, 191
visually absent character 275
vulnerability 302

Wake Up Sid 12, 13
Walker, Alice 82
  In Search of Our Mothers' Gardens 82
Ways of Seeing 52, 89
"Where Women are Worshipped there the Gods rejoice" 48
Women and Disability 73, 80
"Women Writing and Writing about Women" 169
Woolf, Virginia 106, 115
  A Room of One's Own 106
Wuthering Heights 253

You've Got Mail 273

Zakhm 90, 122
Zauderer, Naomi B. 69
Zinta, Preity 105
Zubeida 65, 122, 249ff